ON THE
MONEY TRAIL

ON THE
MONEY TRAIL

*Investigating How Government Decisions
Are Made*

WRITTEN BY
TIM CHORNEY WITH JAY INNES

EDITED BY
CRISS HAJEK AND ELIZABETH LEREVEREND

BREAKOUT EDUCATIONAL NETWORK
IN ASSOCIATION WITH
DUNDURN PRESS
TORONTO · OXFORD

Publisher: Inta D. Erwin
Copy-editor: Amanda Stewart, First Folio Resource Group
Designer: Bruna Brunelli, Brunelli Designs
Printer: Webcom

National Library of Canada Cataloguing in Publication Data

    On the money trail: investigating how government decisions are made
by Tim Chorney with Jay Innes/edited by Criss Hajek and Elizabeth LeReverend.

One of the 16 vols. and 14 hours of video which make up the
    underground royal commission report
Includes bibliographical references and index.
ISBN 1-55002-424-8

    1. Canada—Appropriations and expenditures. I. Hajek, Criss
II. LeReverend, Elizabeth III. Title: underground royal commission report.

HC120.C3O64 2003   336.71   C2003-902304-1

1 2 3 4 5   07 06 05 04 03

Printed and bound in Canada.
Printed on recycled paper. ♻
www.dundurn.com

Exclusive Canadian broadcast rights for the *underground royal commission* report

intelligent television

Check your cable or satellite listings for telecast times

Visit the *urc* Web site link at:
www.ichanneltv.com

About the *underground royal commission* Report

Since September 11, 2001, there has been an uneasy dialogue among Canadians as we ponder our position in the world, especially vis à vis the United States. Critically and painfully, we are re-examining ourselves and our government. We are even questioning our nation's ability to retain its sovereignty.

The questions we are asking ourselves are not new. Over the last 30 years, and especially in the dreadful period of the early 1990s, leading up to the Quebec referendum of 1995, inquiries and Royal commissions, one after another, studied the state of the country. What *is* new is that eight years ago, a group of citizens looked at this parade of inquiries and commissions and said, "These don't deal with the real issues." They wondered how it was possible for a nation that was so promising and prosperous in the early 60s to end up so confused, divided, and troubled. And they decided that what was needed was a different kind of investigation — driven from the grassroots 'bottom,' and not from the top. Almost as a provocation, this group of people, most of whom were affiliated with the award winning documentary-maker, Stornoway Productions, decided to do it themselves — and so was born the *underground royal commission*!

What began as a television documentary soon evolved into much more. Seven young, novice researchers, hired right out of university, along with a television crew and producer, conducted interviews with people in government, business, the military and in all walks of life, across the country. What they discovered went beyond anything they had expected. The more they learned, the larger the implications grew. The project continued to evolve and has expanded to include a total of 23 researchers over the last several years. The results are the 14 hours of video and 16 books that make up the first interim report of the *underground royal commission*.

So what *are* the issues? The report of the *underground royal commission* clearly shows us that regardless of region, level of government, or political party, we are operating under a wasteful system ubiquitously lacking in accountability. An ever-weakening connection between the electors and the elected means that we are slowly and irrevocably losing our right to know our government. The researchers' experiences demonstrate that it is almost impossible for a member of the public, or in most cases, even for a member of Parliament, to actually trace how our tax dollars are spent. Most disturbing is the fact that our young people have been stuck with a crippling IOU that has effectively hamstrung their future. No wonder, then, that Canada is not poised for reaching its potential in the 21st century.

The *underground royal commission* report, prepared in large part by and for the youth of Canada, provides the hard evidence of the problems you and I may long have suspected. Some of that evidence makes it clear that, as ordinary Canadians, we are every bit as culpable as our politicians — for our failure to demand accountability, for our easy acceptance of government subsidies and services established without proper funding in place, and for the disservice we have done to our young people through the debt we have so blithely passed on to them. But the real purpose of the *underground royal commission* is to ensure that we better understand how government processes work and what role we play in them. Public policy issues must be understandable and accessible to the public if they are ever to be truly addressed and resolved. The *underground royal commission* intends to continue pointing the way for bringing about constructive change in Canada.

— Stornoway Productions

Books in the *underground royal commission* Report

"Just Trust Us"

The Chatter Box
The Chance of War
Talking Heads Talking Arms: (3 volumes)
No Life Jackets
Whistling Past the Graveyard
Playing the Ostrich

Days of Reckoning
Taking or Making Wealth
Guardians on Trial
Goodbye Canada?
Down the Road Never Travelled
Secrets in High Places
On the Money Trail

Does Your Vote Count?
A Call to Account
Reflections on Canadian Character

14 hours of videos also available with the *underground royal commission* report.
Visit Stornoway Productions at www.stornoway.com for a list of titles.

TABLE OF CONTENTS

INTRODUCTION

It is impossible to overstate the role that government plays in the lives of all Canadians. It touches our lives virtually from the day we are born to the day we die. The advancement of our modern welfare state means that its role is more profound now than it has ever been. Yet despite the ubiquitous nature of government, few people have a firm idea of how it works.

Money disappears from your paycheque and a government service occurs seemingly by magic: you pay your property taxes like every other homeowner, and your garbage gets picked up each week. You tack on the provincial sales tax to the cost of a new car, and your family doctor gets paid. Employment insurance premiums come off your paycheque, and your laid-off neighbour can take a government-sponsored retraining course.

But is the job really getting done properly? Do you get value for your money, or do your taxes get spent to bolster political support on the other side of town, or the other side of the country? It is very hard to say. Government is just so complicated. Ironically, we are so used to the presence of government that we barely notice how profoundly it affects us. Some people live out their entire lives and never give it another thought. But others are determined to make ordinary Canadians more aware of how their government is supposed to work and what the reality of governance is; through awareness can come change.

Stornoway Productions, a Toronto-based production company, was looking for ideas for television documentaries on Canadian governance. Jay Innes, a television researcher, had long wanted to do a documentary that would follow a dollar right from the time it left the taxpayer's cheque to the time it ended up as a government service. It would be complicated, but a documented journey of this kind would reveal a lot about the way Canada is governed.

Jay's project, the television documentary *Secrets in High Places,* was shot in 1998 and early 1999. It is among the documents that comprise the *underground royal commission (urc)* — a citizens' report that offers a critical perspective on wide-ranging issues facing our nation. The documentary is a motivating force, providing the impetus to get ordinary citizens more involved in the inner workings and possible rejuvenation of their system of government.

This book represents the empirical evidence upon which our conclusions in the documentary and the *urc* are drawn. The voices that comprise each story are drawn from dozens of videotaped interviews conducted across Canada, as a team of young researchers tried to get answers about how tax dollars are spent. The book incorporates material that had to be trimmed due to the time constraints of television, and is in essence a series of essays.

We give voice to both those involved in the story out in the regions and to experts who put everything into a more national context. We interviewed academics, bureaucrats and politicians from all levels. Over the years spent digging into government spending decisions, many of the people we talked to changed jobs. Some retired, left politics, were voted out of office, accepted transfers, came in and out of public life. The Reform Party changed its name to the Canadian Alliance Party of Canada. Unemployment insurance (UI) became employment insurance (EI). Some of the issues our interview subjects raised over the course of the money-trail journey have begun to be addressed — including giving municipalities more powers. Other matters remain unresolved, such as accountability and transparency in government spending decisions.

A "follow the dollar" piece required an investigation into one of Canada's spending programs. But which one? We settled on the Canada Infrastructure Works Program (CIWP) because we thought it would be straightforward. What could be more simple than a program designed to fix roads and sewers? As it turned out, a lot of things.

The Infrastructure Works Program was well worth examining. It was an expensive program at a time when most jurisdictions in Canada were trying to cope with ballooning deficits and mountains of accumulated debt. It was structured in such a way that the money could go out fast, with as little red tape as possible.

Here's how the program was supposed to work. The CIWP was a three-way cost-sharing program paid for equally by the federal, provincial and municipal governments. The idea was that each level of government would contribute one-third of the money toward the construction or repair of specific infrastructure projects. The program was split into two distinct phases. By the time the second or "top-up" phase of the program concluded in 1999, more than 17,000 projects were completed at a total cost of $8.3 billion. Each province signed a separate but similar agreement with the federal government. The First Nations dealt directly with the federal government.

The CIWP was introduced by the Liberals in 1994, fresh on the heels of their election victory in 1993. The Liberals were following through on a campaign promise duly noted in their *Red Book*, which detailed what they would and wouldn't do if Canadians entrusted them with the reins of power for the first time in nine years.

Although it figured prominently in the Liberal election campaign, the infrastructure program idea was hardly new. For nearly a decade the Federation of Canadian Municipalities (FCM) had lobbied hard for government co-operation to upgrade the country's dilapidated infrastructure system. Its leaders argued that Canada's roads, bridges and water systems were falling apart, and that waiting any longer to make the repairs would have catastrophic economic implications.

Supporters of a national infrastructure program also argued that there would be another huge potential benefit for the country. Canada had been feeling the pain resulting from chronically high unemployment since the recession in 1982. It was thought that the influx of CIWP money would alleviate the unemployment problem, in the same way that national "make-work projects" had been introduced during the Depression era. Such programs follow a spending philosophy called Keynesian economics, after John Maynard Keynes. The idea is that in tough economic times governments must spend money to keep citizens employed and the economy stimulated until the next boom cycle comes around.

Job creation was a constant theme of the Canada Infrastructure Works Program. With the nation's unemployment rate hovering at about 10 percent, the desire to be seen as responsive to the unemployment crisis was clearly on the mind of Chrétien's Liberals, as it had been for their predecessors, the Progressive Conservative government of Brian Mulroney. But each Cabinet had a different plan to fulfill the cry for "jobs, jobs, jobs" that coloured the early 1990s.

The infrastructure program was a big symbol of the Chrétien government's effort to create jobs. But how successful was it? Our research team had a difficult time wading through the conflicting answers to this question. We weren't alone. The validity of the job numbers was one criticism levelled at the CIWP by none other than the auditor general of Canada at the time, Denis Desautels. In his annual report Desautels questioned the government's job-creation numbers and criticized many of the projects that were undertaken.

Finding clear-cut answers about job creation wasn't the only area of frustration for the Stornoway team. The scope and application of the Canada Infrastructure Works Program proved to be an elusive quarry. Fast-tracked and flexible, the program became a fixer of roads and sewers in some parts of the country, a job-creation program in others. How was the term "infrastructure" defined? It seems that various recipients had their own ideas about what kind of projects could reasonably be included. In some towns the money was used to build recreational facilities, while in others the fund built roads. One municipality spent infrastructure funds to renovate a movie theatre; another built a trade centre.

It varied from province to province, but the federal government and many of the provinces permitted a percentage of the funds to be used for what they referred to as "soft" infrastructure projects. These could be anything from a theatre to a community centre to a bocce court. Somebody was responsible for these decisions. The question was, who? Even some municipal leaders whose communities got the benefit of infrastructure funds had difficulty explaining how certain projects came to be included in the CIWP.

Were people satisfied that the program functioned the way it was supposed to? Many of those we interviewed supported the CIWP. Their reasons were as varied as the regions from which they came. To some the program's biggest benefit was that it forced three levels of government to co-operate with each other. Others pointed to intangible benefits such as the good feeling that comes from a hard day's work, the architectural splendour of a world-class facility or the sense of community that a new ball diamond may lend to a rural Maritime town. A few spoke candidly of the political payoffs of ribbon-cutting ceremonies. Some were frank in their support for a program that rewarded behind-the-scenes political manoeuvring.

Still many others criticized the CIWP. Several were angered by what they perceived as political interference in a program that was supposed to fix roads and sewers, but on occasion ended up backing privately owned facilities. You will read about cases where municipal priorities were played off against provincial political interests. In others the municipalities themselves juggled projects for maximum public interest. The interviews revealed tugs-of-war among the three levels of government, each proclaiming itself responsible for a high-profile project. The program was frequently criticized for its lack of a transparent structure. Some complained the program funds were not traceable and that there was insufficient accountability, despite their questions about how the public money was used.

For nearly two years we jumped over hurdles and climbed fences, looking for answers about how the money was spent. We tried to get lists of projects, criteria checklists, names of decision makers and hard data about concrete results from the projects that shared in the multibillion-dollar program.

We expected to find the usual types of problems that one might associate with a large-scale government-run capital works program. We found those, to be sure, but we also found surprises in our search. It was one thing to discover that money may have been misspent. But to have people who were directly involved in the CIWP say they had no idea what was going on, or suggest that it was none of our business — that was very hard to take. In the rush to proceed with the CIWP, were two of the major tenets of parliamentary democracy — accountability and transparency — brushed aside by a culture of secrecy in both Ottawa and the provinces?

Infrastructure program spending decisions were made by management committees composed of federal and provincial officials. Generally the municipalities made up priority lists of projects they thought should receive funding, and the federal-provincial officials on the management committees chose and announced which projects would get funding. Even with repeated requests under the Access to Information Act, though, our researchers had difficulty determining the reasoning behind some of the decisions made. These experiences led us to the question, does the Access to Information Act succeed in making the decisions of our government more transparent, or does it actually exacerbate the problem of secrecy? Interviews with experts in Access matters shed some light on how that system, which was supposed to make government more open and responsive, has instead created a climate of official secrecy and suspicion.

Delving into this one federal spending program eventually called for seven researchers. This team of young and talented, yet inexperienced, Canadians examined the government "from the ground up," with co-ordination from Jay. Two of the personal journeys are compiled in companion books to *On the Money Trail* — Brigitte Pellerin's *Down the Road Never Travelled* and Jay Innes's account, *Secrets in High Places*.

The essays from each province in this book tell a story about how the Infrastructure Works Program functioned in that province; viewed together, they offer a complete portrait of how Canada is governed. It's up to the reader to judge whether the portrait is flattering.

Tim Chorney
Summer 2002

CHAPTER 1

ALBERTA

The public was not the primary consideration.

We found that in Alberta, as in the other provinces, the lines were blurred between public funds and private benefit and between traditional infrastructure definitions and a more flexible program scope. We asked questions about how the province set its spending priorities, determined job-creation numbers and estimated the long-term benefits from its portion of infrastructure program money.

One thing became quite clear: it is impossible to discuss the Canada Infrastructure Works Program in Alberta without talking about sports. The city councils of both Calgary and Edmonton took a large part of the program money that was allotted to them and used it to update hockey arenas and baseball stadiums where professional teams played. In Calgary $12 million in CIWP funds went to renovate the Saddledome, to the benefit of a private company, namely, the Calgary Flames. The Foothills Stadium in Calgary and John Ducey Park in Edmonton also got CIWP funds. Two professional baseball teams, the Calgary Cannons and the Edmonton Trappers, played at the stadiums. These funding choices drew an angry reaction from some observers, including Jim

Silye, former Calgary MP. Although he had been a professional Canadian Football League player himself, and held season's tickets for the Calgary Flames hockey games, when Silye was interviewed for the *Secrets in High Places* documentary, he said that infrastructure money could have been better spent.

Supporters of the Saddledome funding maintained that the CIWP money went to renovate the "public" areas of the arena, and thus was a benefit to everyone in the city. In response to this claim Silye noted that at the same time the public areas were improved, a number of expensive "luxury boxes" for the high rollers of Alberta's business community were constructed. The luxury boxes are now a key revenue producer for the Flames.

Our research uncovered some curious details: the original proposal for the Saddledome upgrades mentioned creating luxury boxes. That original proposal was rejected. When the proposal was re-submitted to the management committee, there was no mention of luxury boxes; the funds were to be spent on renovating the "public" areas of the arena. That proposal was approved, the renovations went ahead and the luxury boxes were "coincidentally" built at the same time. To a cynical observer it might seem that those involved in approving the decision to fund the Saddledome renovation may have used a few little tricks to make the money look as if it were going somewhere it wasn't.

In their interviews the renovation supporters' arguments gave new meaning to the phrase "splitting hairs." Calgary's manager of transportation services, Tully Clifford, provided us with some candid insights into the project selection process and related matters. Rick Smith, who was an alderman at the time the funding decision was made, insisted that the luxury boxes that were installed along with other upgrades at the stadium were paid for with money that wasn't really part of the infrastructure fund.

Former Federation of Canadian Municipalities president Ron Hayter also weighed in on the issue of sports funding in Alberta, and provided background on the evolution of the infrastructure program since its early days as a plan to revive the nation's roads, bridges and sewers. Hayter's interview was especially interesting because he appeared to change his mind quite dramatically on the issue of CIWP money going to sports facilities. At first he opposed the funding of the Edmonton Coliseum in the press, but changed his position a few months later.

Lydia Miljan, a Ph.D. candidate from Calgary, was our researcher for Alberta. Lydia found it difficult to get information from the aldermen responsible for spending decisions because most of them were no longer in office. However, "the federal government was quite accessible and good about giving me the information that they wanted to give me," Lydia said. "The provincial government also was good at returning calls. Once I started asking questions there were a lot of people who wanted to provide answers and appease me. So for the most part the official channels were quite good — it was just a matter of trying to get the people who actually made the decisions to give me the rationale for those decisions. That was where it became more difficult."

A big challenge for Lydia was finding out how Calgary's Saddledome project became a priority, when such proposals as water treatment facility upgrades were on the initial CIWP list submitted by the municipality. She asked the federal and the provincial offices how spending decisions were made, and by whom. "Both said the decisions were made at the municipal level. So I went back to the municipalities and they said, 'No, no, we didn't make all the decisions. We were just playing the game because if we didn't we wouldn't get this money from the federal and provincial governments, and we would be losing out on this free money.'"

Lydia concluded: "The city essentially decided that they did not have to pay for their one-third share if they got the Saddledome Foundation to do it, so they knocked three water treatment facilities off their list and paid for them with another budget. The city helped the Saddledome Foundation out and made themselves look like the good guys in keeping their own budgets down. Everyone benefited, and no one really ended up being accountable because spending decisions were made at a totally different level of government than the offices that actually collect the taxes."

TULLY CLIFFORD

CIWP Manager, Calgary

Tully Clifford is a civil engineer with more than 20 years' experience in both the public and private sectors. While he worked with the City of Calgary he managed Calgary's infrastructure program, setting priorities and making project recommendations to city council.

As the manager of the national infrastructure program for Calgary, I am the municipal contact for all the Calgary and area projects. I initially brought together all the funding requests from across the city, from public and private enterprises. I then had to compile those requests, cost them out and take recommendations for municipal projects to the city council for them to consider and debate. I included in that list projects that would probably be rejected by the province and the federal government. I think the City of Calgary was very fortunate in its project approval. We didn't have any projects overturned by the province or the federal government.

After we went to council I would automatically send a list of project applications for consideration for early reviewing. For the most part they were very timely in getting back to us and saying, "Your project is approved." If they had questions, they asked the questions, so we were able to incorporate that into the applications. I think we cut out a whole series of steps that probably would have shut down a bunch of projects.

Because of the size of our city — about 800,000 people — we were treated differently than some of the smaller centres, but not the same as some of the smaller provinces. We did get treated well. We did all the projects that we wanted, but not necessarily the projects that we needed.

In preparing the list of projects for the infrastructure program, we looked first at the guidelines and basic criteria of the program. Was it infrastructure-related? Was it providing a benefit to the public? Was there funding in place not from a related government program? For example, the provincial government has a community-financing program that gives to organizations such as the Centre for the Performing Arts. They could not use those funds as their one-third share. If something was within the three-year capital budget and was already funded and approved by council, we could not use that as a CIWP project.

All the projects that we included in the infrastructure program that were City of Calgary responsibilities would have been done by the City of Calgary. There were no projects dropped that had been approved by council in order to accommodate the Saddledome project. Instead council determined that the priority was higher for the Saddledome than for other projects that had previously been submitted. There was a series of recommendations taken to council. The Saddledome did not appear on the first go-round, but did appear subsequently.

A cost-benefit analysis was not explicitly done for each and every project. We looked more at the public need. For example, if we look at an interchange project, that is a transportation need. It's very difficult to assign a cost/benefit which would be equivalent to a cost-benefit analysis of a performing arts centre.

City council looked at, for example, what was in our five- to 10-year capital-funding envelope, to determine what could be accomplished through the national infrastructure program project allocation. When they looked at the Bonnybrook Wastewater Treatment Plant, they determined that what was being done was not sufficient and that more comprehensive funding was required. Because of the projects they'd already approved, council couldn't allocate enough money to the Bonnybrook program and felt it would be better to do that through the capital budgeting program instead. What happened was that another waste-water treatment plant received upgrade funding.

The council minutes don't capture all the discussion when council is considering the infrastructure program projects. All they capture is the bottom-line decision to take out Bonnybrook and to put in the Saddledome. In fact there was discussion and it was referred back to the administration for capital budget discussions. There was more involved that unfortunately the public doesn't see by reading the minutes. Nowhere will you find a record of how the decisions were made, why they were made and the subsequent actions that were taken by the city administration. In reality the only people who know are the board of commissioners and myself, as the manager of the program.

I think the downside of the national infrastructure program is that it came in bits and pieces. It forced us to move some items forward to fit the funding formula. It affected the timing; it didn't allow us to work through priorities the way we wanted to. If the City of Calgary had been told at the outset, "You have $190 million," we very clearly could have allocated projects on a priority basis. We could have met the requirements of job creation and public benefit. Unfortunately we weren't able to do that.

We weren't told all at one time, "Here are the exact dollars that are available." We had to determine how the proposals fit in a priority for funding. Quite frankly, sometimes we determined the priority based on the dollars that were left. So if we had $3 million left in the program, we then had to look at our priorities based on a $3-million project.

The Saddledome and similar projects were actually submitted by the public, the Saddledome Foundation or the Calgary Exhibition and Stampede Board. They submitted their project outline and said, "Here's what we feel is the public benefit, here's how the costing could work and here's why we think the city should accommodate the project." There are other projects that are from private areas.

City council looked at the basic good to the public when they considered the Saddledome project. They looked at things such as the concourse areas, the restaurant areas and areas that are accessible to the public. The initial application from the foundation said, "We would like to do private boxes, we would like to do a bunch of enhancements." What city council looked at were the benefits from encouraging more events to come into the city and the spinoff economic benefits that these events generate.

We have to look at the intent of the program as well when we consider the Saddledome approval. In the proposal there was also a key component in the national infrastructure program: job creation. Council felt that increasing the size of the food kiosk and the number of people that could circulate there would confer an ongoing employment benefit.

I'm not entirely certain how many jobs were created, but there are two components to job creation. If you consider the short-term construction jobs, how many jobs were created and was it staff from the foundations, or were they actually people that were hired to do it? The second component is how many people would be required to operate the facility on an ongoing basis.

Typically, when we were calculating the employment creation for any project, the requesting organization — be it the city or a private organization — submitted the initial numbers. We then reviewed them, asked questions and asked for amendments as required. The construction man-hour estimates from any project come from the contractors: how many people are required for the job and how long will the job take? And then those are converted into years. The operating component is based on the operations. For example, in the Saddledome, if they added 10 extra kiosks, how many people would be required to staff the kiosks, how many events per year, and how long would they expect that facility to remain in that configuration?

Most of the contracts that were let in the national infrastructure program were through a bid process. The contractors step forward and say, "Here's how we are bidding on the job." If they're cheating on their labour, so to speak, that normally meant they wouldn't get the bid because they would not be in line with other bidders. There was difficulty in some projects, and the primary reason is that Calgary's economy is booming, so construction costs are escalating, which led to some difficulties in calculating the labour component.

For the City of Calgary the national infrastructure program was definitely a positive. We were able to do a lot of projects sooner than we would have. In some cases the growth of the city has changed. That has been a tremendous benefit. If we look at some of the public projects that have been undertaken, there's a very clear, direct benefit that the public can grasp and see.

The city could clearly benefit from another infrastructure program. Working with the three levels of government was very frustrating. You always hear all the jokes about government bureaucracy, well, you get that three times over. Was it a good way to provide funding? Yes, I think it was beneficial. What we've done all through this program, mind you, is to send word back to the province and the federal government about how we think it can be done better, relating to time frame and to the project approval processes, including public involvement.

There has to be less focus on the timelines of the program. Your hands are really tied when you're told you have to be done by such and such a date, or this approval has to be by this date. The national infrastructure program was not set up to intentionally exclude the public. Because of the timelines and the approval process with council — to the province and then on to the federal government — there wasn't time there to include the public, even in a cursory way.

The only public involvement then was through the media. When the media was at council and said, "How can we accept something such as the Saddledome?" or "Why wasn't this other project considered?" that was in reality the only access the public had. So in other words, no access. The media involvement was a matter of too little, too late. The media had the reports two or three days prior to the council meeting, the same as any member of the public. But they didn't have the ability to do any background research, to talk to members of the administration, to talk to people at the different project levels. There was also no opportunity for public opinion to influence councillors' voting.

As members of the public and organizations submitted ideas for projects, they were not afforded the opportunity to address council. So I was the only one who compiled the list to the board of commissioners, which then went to council. There was no public hearing on it. The only way people could express any dissatisfaction would be by writing a letter to their alderman or to the mayor or to council. In other words, they could not get any resolution of their concerns at this stage. All that would happen would be, "Thank you for your concerns."

It should have been turned into a public-hearing process. Members of the public would then have had the opportunity to step forward, for example, with the Saddledome, and say to council directly, "I do not see the benefit to me as a citizen. I see the benefit to the Calgary Flames and the people using it, but I don't see the benefit to me."

It would have been far better if they'd said at the beginning, "You have six years, you have $190 million, and here are the requirements of the program." The City of Calgary could have then participated in a far better manner. We would have also had greater public participation. We could have gone back to the public and said, "Here are a series of projects that are being considered. What do you think?" We had to guess. We had to hope that we were correct.

Was it the best use of funds? I don't think so. Was it a good use of funds? Yes. If we could have changed the parameters of the program, we would have gotten the best use out of the funds, from the point of view of all three levels of government. For example, if we'd looked at our transportation infrastructure, if they wanted to tie the three levels of government together, we could have done improvements to Highway 1, which goes right through the middle of town. That would have benefited the province, with the free trade border to the south, and it would have benefited the federal government because the Trans-Canada Highway's the national link.

In Calgary when you ask who is accountable, what I can say is, "I'm the manager of the program, the projects were approved by council." Is that accountability? I'm not entirely convinced that it is. There's nobody who's clearly identified as the person responsible for the national infrastructure program, from a political or even in lot of cases from an administrative point of view. So there is nobody that you could point a finger at.

That's a huge problem. We're accountable only to the program itself. I had to make sure, for example, in the case of the Saddledome, that they spent the funds the way they were supposed to, that their labour was allocated within the guidelines of the approval of council.

The files are open for audit. They can even verify some of the labour numbers. But there is no accountability back to the public. I am, for example, under no requirement to come back and say, here, at the end of it, is what happened in Calgary. We are planning on doing that, but there is no requirement — none.

I think there should be a public reporting component added to any subsequent programs so that the members of the public can see how the process works. In Calgary I'm relatively certain that nobody knew who to contact or how to complain if they didn't like ideas that were coming through.

That requirement should be built in to any new programs. When you have three levels of bureaucracy involved with any process that doesn't have a public component to it, there's a strong possibility of the public not being able to get full access to information. Whether there's a conscious effort to roll information under the carpet or not is subject to opinion. But I think, yes, there is that opportunity there.

To get accountability for the program, what has to happen is that the project managers at the municipal, provincial and federal levels should actually be mandated to write a report on the program itself. And they should give more than just the cursory "Here's how many projects we had and here's how much we spent." It should be honest and open about how the program operated. This will bring back to the public how the program worked.

The City of Calgary was very fortunate in the approach that the province and the federal government took with us — with the exception of the time frame. We saw it as being tied back to what they could say to their constituents. They could say, "Here is what we brought to you for this." It's tied into other agendas that we're not necessarily a part of.

In the future all three parties have to be able to sit down and agree on the terms of the program. What happened in this case was that we were sent a copy of the contract for the program, which said, "Are you in or are you out?" There was no opportunity for change or input. In reality we are putting in our one-third of the program without any say or any power.

I think the politicians were selling it to the public as free money. They had to downplay the power side of things, the fact that they weren't able to influence the program and the fact that they didn't set the timelines.

The public was not the primary consideration in this program. It's rather ironic. What a lot of the politicians were selling it as was a leveraging, saying "For your one municipal dollar, we're giving you $3 worth of facilities." But in reality the federal and provincial money is also theirs. The challenge is just trying to convince the public that it's not really coming out of their pockets.

RON HAYTER

Former President, Federation of Canadian Municipalities

Ron Hayter has a background in journalism, trade shows and Alberta sports associations. He was first elected to Edmonton city council more than 24 years ago. He served as president, in 1993, of the Federation of Canadian Municipalities, an organization that advocates for and lobbies on behalf of cities and towns.

I was a member of the Edmonton city council for 24 years. As part of that involvement, I was on the board of the Federation of Canadian Municipalities (FCM).

The Federation of Canadian Municipalities is essentially a lobby group for municipalities. It lobbies the federal government primarily because that's the jurisdiction of the FCM, to lobby the federal government. But we also have in the past gone to the provinces to get their support. For instance, on the infrastructure program, one of the main objectives when I was president was to go to the various provincial premiers and try to get them to buy into this program of a national infrastructure renewal. And we did. We succeeded. The first premier we got was John Savage of Nova Scotia. He then went to the next meeting of the premiers and he got them to agree to the program.

So that was another important consideration when we were dealing with the federal government — that we didn't just have the Federation of Canadian Municipalities as a lobby group for local government saying this is a good program. We also had the provincial governments on side.

It was the FCM that really initiated the idea of a national infrastructure program. That goes back to 1986, when it was obvious to municipal members that the infrastructure across this country, the basic infrastructure — streets and roads and bridges and so on — was in need of repair. If you don't repair it, you're going to have a lot of trouble. The program that was devised at that time was called the "Big Fix." Unfortunately we weren't able to get the support of provincial governments or the federal government of the day at that time.

That particular program didn't make much headway because we concentrated on the basic infrastructure — roads, streets and bridges. That stuff isn't very sexy. Most of it's underground where people don't see it. So you can tell them there's a problem, but a lot of people don't realize this is a problem because they can't see it.

When we went to the provincial governments they said, "Well, this should be federal." So of course we went to the federal government of the day and they looked at it and said, "Well, yes, we understand there's some problems with infrastructure in some parts of the country, particularly in the older parts of Canada like Montreal and Vancouver, but it's not a common problem across the country." Many municipalities have developed only recently and their infrastructure is quite recent as well.

We weren't able to sell them on the idea that there was a serious problem. So the Federation of Canadian Municipalities decided to go back and revise its approach. That approach took from 1986 until about 1988 to put into place. That was to change the focus, to broaden the focus and to point out how important it was to have good infrastructure. Not only because you wouldn't have water-main breaks and you wouldn't have potholes, but also infrastructure was important in other ways.

At just about that same time the federal government started becoming very concerned about this whole question of being competitive in a global marketplace. We saw Germany and Japan and the United States spending great gobs of money on rebuilding infrastructure. When you are trying to attract business and industry, one of the first things that you look for are those things — basic infrastructure.

The program that we put together was three-pronged. We would concentrate on the importance of repairing the crumbling infrastructure in Canada. That was absolutely essential. Secondly, we were in the midst of an economic downturn in Canada, so we wanted to emphasize the importance of doing this work to create jobs at a time when a lot of people were out of work. Thirdly, we wanted to emphasize the fact that a good infrastructure in your community was important from the standpoint of attracting industry and business to your community. It was a part of making Canada more competitive.

So that was the three-pronged approach that we used. It was a lot sexier than the earlier approach that we used in 1986, where we were concentrating only on the traditional basic infrastructure. That was the strategy that the Federation of Canadian Municipalities adopted for its next thrust at the federal and provincial governments, broadening the original approach in order to make it more attractive and also to sell it to the public.

I think it's one of the best examples of federal, provincial and municipal co-operation since Confederation. It's pretty hard to get any kind of co-operation these days between the federal and provincial governments. And when you add the municipal government into the mix, it makes it pretty difficult. Now, we know that the program was treated differently in every province. But I think the outcome is what you have to look at. The outcome was that we did get the money channelled in the direction that we wanted to get the crumbling infrastructure repaired.

In order for this program to work every one of the three parties had to do their part. They had to make their contribution, one-third from each of the municipal, provincial and federal governments.

Money was certainly a big factor, that and the tremendous support that the public gave this program during the election campaign. The federal government of that day didn't support the program. I was president of the Federation of Canadian Municipalities at that time and I talked to the prime minister, Kim Campbell. She said, "This program is simply too expensive and the public won't support it." Well, you saw what the results were. The public really got onboard with this particular program because it was to their benefit at the local level, all across the country. It was a benefit from Newfoundland to Vancouver Island.

At that time there was a great concern about employment across Canada. The work that the repair of crumbling infrastructure would provide was pretty obvious to people. So you could bring it down to a level where the average citizen could understand it. Even though they couldn't necessarily see all those problems, they knew that if there were problems there, then it would take people to correct them.

We also used the argument, why pay out money in unemployment insurance and social welfare when you could have those people doing meaningful work? That also had a big, big appeal. There were studies done by the Federation of Canadian Municipalities which clearly showed that this program could be neutral, as far as the costs to the federal government, by creating jobs that would eliminate the need for unemployment insurance and social welfare costs.

When you got into the campaign, the Conservative government just couldn't see the forest for the trees. It was insulting, the government's characterization of the program, particularly when the Conservative government knew that there was a serious problem with infrastructure across this country. In fact, in 1988 the priorities committee of the Conservative government had this as one of their major items, this whole question of how do we deal with the infrastructure problem. But it bogged down because they thought the costs would be too high. They didn't realize the other benefits that would accrue from having very strong and stable infrastructure in this country.

At that particular time I was crisscrossing the country, speaking wherever I was asked to, from Newfoundland to Vancouver Island, and I brought that message home at the local level. I said, "This is good for you at the local level. This is good for you." And they saw that. They got that message. I really was proud of how municipal governments all across this country responded to the challenge. They put the onus on the political parties seeking office. They held forums. They invited the candidates to their council meetings to respond to this issue. As a result, the public interest was galvanized. They suddenly realized that this was an issue in the campaign. It was a very important issue because not only did it correct the problem, but it created work at a time when work was necessary.

One of the major gripes that I have with the program is the fact that there was not municipal representation on most of the selection committees. They had a selection committee in all provinces. This was mandated by the federal-provincial agreement. The federal government simply wanted to make sure the criteria were met.

In some of the provinces the municipalities were involved. They had input. They were consulted. But they didn't have a vote. That's where the process broke down. If the province decided not to listen and not to approve a particular project, that was within the authority of the provincial government. To the best of my knowledge, the only province that allowed direct municipal representation on the selection committee was Alberta.

In Alberta the lead was taken by municipal government. In most cases, as far as I know, there was no interference from the province. I recall the deputy premier saying to me, "You're not going to have any problems with the province. We're going to approve everything that comes forward from the municipalities, as long as it meets the criteria. We have faith that the municipal governments will make the right decisions and that they're going to be accountable for the decisions that they make." That's why it worked so well in Alberta — because of the principle that if the municipalities thought it was a good thing, then why stick our nose into it? As far as we know, none of our recommendations were overturned by the province or by the federal representative.

If you talked to other provinces, they would tell you that the process worked very well: "We consulted with municipalities. They provided the information on the various proposals that they had. And we worked very well with municipal government." But when it came down to selecting the projects, making the final determination of where the dollars would go, there wasn't a municipal representative at the table. That was the big failing of the program.

In the infrastructure program we ran into a fundamental problem. That is that municipal government is the bedrock of this country, but it has no legitimacy, no recognition. Under the Constitution there are only two orders of government: the federal government and the provinces. Municipalities are the creatures, the children, of the provinces.

The Federation of Canadian Municipalities has been arguing for years that there has to be a revamping of the Constitution to recognize the realities of today. Municipal government is the most important order of government in this country. If municipal government for one day decided to withdraw all its services from across this country, Canada would absolutely be at a standstill. There has to be recognition of the important part that municipal government plays. You'll hear federal and provincial leaders talk about the importance of municipal government, but nobody wants to give them the independence and the power, particularly the fiscal power, that they need to continue to do a good job.

There's only one taxpayer, but the different orders of government have different sources of income. The federal government has the most important growth tax in the country, the income tax, which is shared with the provinces. Municipal government, on the other hand, doesn't have that flexibility. They rely on property taxes and business taxes. Property is not a growth tax because property doesn't always increase in value. Secondly, it's not based on the ability to pay, so it's a regressive tax. If you're a single parent living in a large house, you're going to pay the same taxes on your property as a wealthy person with the same kind of house.

The Federation of Canadian Municipalities and provincial municipal associations have been arguing for years that there should be a revenue-sharing system in this country. Municipal government would get a share of income tax. There are all kinds of reports that clearly demonstrate that this is a proper way to go. But of course the federal and provincial governments have resisted any revenue sharing. If you start giving municipalities a little more fiscal freedom, then they're probably going to look better than the province.

The infrastructure program was to the benefit of the municipal governments because the funding would be primarily covered by two other orders of government, federal and provincial. This lessens the burden on the municipal taxpayer, who's already strapped because the municipality doesn't have the resources that the federal and provincial governments have.

One of the criteria of the program was that you could not use the funds for projects that were already budgeted. You had to use them for new projects. That was a good criterion because it made the municipalities really think about what projects would qualify.

I was critical, to begin with, of some of the projects that were proposed by the municipalities. I saw them as somewhat frivolous and I wanted to make very clear that the position of the Federation of Canadian Municipalities was that the bulk of the funding had to go for traditional infrastructure — roads and streets, water and sewer systems, water treatment plants and things of that nature. I was concerned that maybe projects were being approved that didn't fit that definition. But I know from reviewing the statistics on the program that most of the money did go for traditional infrastructure.

In my city we had a $125-million budget under the infrastructure program and about $110 million of that went for traditional infrastructure. In the case of the other $15 million, it went to an area which I think was important as well, and that was to make our city more attractive to business and our environment more competitive.

We spent money in Edmonton on refurbishing the Coliseum. It's somewhat difficult to justify. And certainly there was a lot of criticism of council's decision to put infrastructure money into the Coliseum. There's no doubt that the approval of projects like the Coliseum and the Calgary Saddledome did create some negative reaction to the overall program.

The whole discussion was all debated publicly. That process was transparent. Once that decision was made it went down to the selection committee. The judgment was made by the municipal leaders, in conjunction with the province. I was a member of the council that made that decision in Edmonton. I don't regret it one bit. It was a good decision. The money was well spent. The Coliseum needed those repairs, needed the refurbishing, and building a new baseball stadium was a great thing for the city. Not only did it attract the infrastructure funds, but the city's portion was put up by the owner of the baseball team. Yet the facility belongs to the citizens of Edmonton. It doesn't belong to the owner of the baseball club. He gets the right to use the facility, but that's all.

I suppose you could argue with quite a few projects across Canada that were approved and that fell into a similar category. But some of the people who criticized the expenditure of funds on those projects had other projects which fell in the same kind of category. You know, it's "I want *my* project, rather than this one." I can't recall too many people saying, "Let's take the money that was spent on the Coliseum and put it into more sewer pipes." That wasn't the argument. They had some of their own pet projects that they wanted to spend money on.

While I initially had criticisms about some of the projects approved, I'm proud that the final assessment of the program shows that most of the money went for the purposes that were intended. When you're dealing with different municipal councils, different provincial governments and a different perception of what the criteria were for the program, you're going to get a few projects that you could argue about.

I don't think there were any major disagreements on the Alberta committee that I ever heard of. In other provinces the provincial government did exert their influence because there was no municipal representation on the committee. Well, you know who won the day: it was the province. As I recall, in Saskatchewan and, I believe, in Ontario there were complaints that the province was putting their priorities ahead of the municipal governments.

Having said all that, we did achieve a tremendous thing. We did have a jointly funded program that did bring us our objectives. The program did succeed on all accounts, providing work in particular. There's no doubt that this program created jobs — a lot of jobs — but I can't give you any firm statistics on whether the program was revenue- or cost-neutral, which was the original intent.

It was demonstrated to my satisfaction that the infrastructure program's three goals were achieved. One, we got money for infrastructure. Two, it created jobs. And three, because of the improved infrastructure, Canada is in a more competitive situation.

This particular program was a success — but it is only the start. The Federation of Canadian Municipalities and some provinces are saying we've got to continue this program because the job has only started. If we let this process die, in a few years we'll be right back where we started because infrastructure continues to deteriorate. You've got to keep on top of your infrastructure.

In the last couple of years we've seen a very bad trend. We've seen the federal government downloading financial responsibilities to the province and the province downloading those responsibilities to the municipality. And of course the municipality is the one with the least resources, the least flexibility and the least ability to raise funds. Municipal government is at the bottom of the totem pole. They're trying to find more innovative ways of raising funds, but there's only so much latitude for them.

This particular federal government has been very responsive in many areas. There has been a much better working relationship between municipal governments and the federal government. For instance, a lot of the programs that have been instituted by the federal government were done so with municipal input and local participation, which did not exist in the past. This government saw the benefit of working with not only the provincial governments, which they are required to do, but also with the municipal government. There's much more consultation now than ever existed in my 24 years on the city council.

The Conservatives, or Liberals in the past, simply did not give much priority to municipal government. The Mulroney government did not respect municipal government either. The prime minister would not even come to the annual conference. You know, that's the kind of thing that really bugs municipal leaders, when they don't get any acknowledgement of the job that they do in keeping this country together. If you don't have strong municipal government, you won't have a strong nation.

JIM SILYE

Former Reform MP, Calgary West

*Jim Silye holds a Bachelor of Arts degree and is a former businessman
and football player. He represented the riding of Calgary West from
1993 to 1997 and served as one of his party's associate members on the
House Standing Committee on Finance. Silye later resigned from the
Reform Party.*

As a member of Parliament I spent a lot of time criticizing the infrastructure program and objecting to its use as an election ploy, as
opposed to a true infrastructure effort.

To bribe municipalities and the provinces, and to coerce them, and to
make them believe that they are actually getting a good deal — in that
two-thirds of the moneys that they spend at whatever level is coming
from other levels of government — is a fallacy. There's only one taxpayer.

For instance, provincially we are responsible for highways here in
Alberta. It's up to the provincial government to set aside those amounts
of money that are required to fix up our roads. And in good times,
which we had 10 years ago, that's what Premier Don Getty's government

did. They fixed a lot of roads. We don't need Ottawa to give us one-third of the money to do that. So that's why I call it a bribe; that's why I call it an election ploy and that's why I call it deceptive.

I'd say that there are three reasons to do the infrastructure program. One, to get elected. Two, to get re-elected. And three, to create jobs and a feel-good attitude. Chrétien has pulled this off. When you can convince two levels of government to forget there's only one taxpayer — which they did, and a lot of money was spent in areas where it didn't have to be spent — this gets to some of the seedier parts or the weaker parts of our political system.

Our democracy is such that we freely elect a democratic dictator and this person, one person alone, Jean Chrétien, made the "jobs, jobs, jobs" theme his focal point. He hit a nerve. He said, "Well, I'm going to spend $2 billion and I'll match up to $2 billion with two other levels of government." That's $6 billion. Out of an $800-billion gross domestic product of goods and services that we produce, how is that going to create jobs and take unemployment — where were we at, about 11.5 percent — down to any realistic number?

If that job cannot exist without the government giving it a subsidy, then we shouldn't let that job be created. If that service is needed, somebody with enough brains and intelligence will create a company to provide it. One of the first rules of economics is supply and demand. If there's a demand for something, somebody will supply it. The government need not do it to become popular and to become elected.

Government should be working with the private sector, with various sectors of the economy, to see what they can do to create less red tape. If Chrétien just spent the $6 billion at three levels of government to create less red tape, Canada would be the leading country in the G7. That's where that $6 billion could have been better spent.

I really believe that government has a role in infrastructure, so I was trying to balance that against what the role of the federal government was. I was in Ottawa to either compliment or criticize the federal government — not municipal and provincial governments. If bridges were deteriorating, if highways were eroding, if sewage systems and plants needed upgrading, I feel it's up to the level of government closest to those citizens to make those decisions, not the federal government.

This has been the legacy of the Liberal government: they're not responsible for anything. If things are great, they take the credit. If things are bad, it's the global economy, it's the provinces or the municipal government that spent the money. They always want a scapegoat: "It was the province that cut money on health care and education." Their spin-doctors and their media people are exceptionally good at getting the story out from their perspective as opposed to, say, the opposition's perspective.

The federal government made one rule that made them look good: "Here's the criteria, which is generally infrastructure, but we'll give it a broad definition. If you fall within that broad definition and you get the agreement of two levels of government — provincial and municipal — then we will just sign off." The two levels of government had to agree, municipal and provincial, on the projects where the money was to be spent. The list was submitted and then Ottawa would sign off. Ontario did a reasonable job of that. I think Ontario concentrated a lot of the projects on health, education and roads.

Treasury Board President Art Eggleton may have indicated in the House of Commons that MPs would be allowed to have input. But we had no input. I think if you were a powerful Cabinet minister and you were lobbying in your community, maybe you could get the money spent and participate that way. But I don't think too many members of Parliament did that.

I saw a list of those projects that had been applied for under the infrastructure program in Calgary. I did not see hockey rinks on that list (because I was looking for abuses). I did not see any Olympic Saddledome on that list. It was only after it was approved that I found out about it. Locally I'm sure that a lot of people are happy that the money was spent on the hockey rink. I wasn't. Whether I was a politician or not, regardless, I would not have favoured that.

There's a big difference between legitimate funding for infrastructure, which I feel is a government responsibility, and those dubious areas where they ended up allowing politicians, leading businesspeople and local politicians, to get their pet projects onto the drawing board and get them done. Whether it's an arena or a hall — maybe it's even named after the politician — that's not proper infrastructure. You will find cases like that across Canada.

That happened here with the Olympic Saddledome. I questioned it because I felt that was a misappropriation of funds. I did not feel that the Saddledome was infrastructure. I felt this was subsidizing private business, and I objected to it. The answer came back, "Well, your mayor agreed to it and your premier agreed to it and the rule is clear: if those two levels agree, then we don't object. So if you have a problem, take it up with them."

Edmonton got their money because they spent $12 million. So if our neighbour to the south gets money to upgrade their hockey rink, then we've got to do the same thing to be competitive. It's a domino effect that puts pressure on politicians to spend the money.

Various infrastructure that we need across this country is something government is responsible for, at whatever level. That means that infrastructure should benefit 95 to 100 percent of taxpayers. If this money is spent on infrastructure and it does not benefit 95 to 100 percent of the taxpayers, then that money is misspent.

When I ask who's accountable for the Saddledome decision — perhaps as a taxpayer who is very upset they're funding a private enterprise — who do I throw out of office?

The majority of the $12 million went to create boxes that were sold to oil and service companies to subsidize business. There were two tiers. They extended the second tier. The seating population reduced a little bit, but what they lost on a per-game basis they made up for with the $300,000 box revenue from companies. We went through a period of prosperity here the last four years, so all signed up.

Those box seats are basically sold to businesses, which can deduct the cost — which runs for a yearly, two-year or three-year contract — of $100,000 to $200,000 a year. If your company is making enough to afford them, the cost can be written off against its income.

That money, which at that time we didn't even have, should have gone to where we did need upgraded facilities. Did the Saddledome need new boxes down at the mid-level? I don't think so. The people I fault are the mayor, the council, the premier's office, for allowing this to get off the tracks and derailed into areas of spending that were just benefiting a minority of the population.

In 1994–95, well before we had the balanced budget or a surplus budget, I debated this issue in the House of Commons. We talked about bocce courts, misallocation of the infrastructure and spending when you're already in a deficit. I came back here and went to a hockey game. I happened to know some of the owners of the Flames, so I walked by the owners' box to pop in and say hello. The door was slammed in my face by one of the owners.

I was taken aback by that. First of all, I have no criticism of the owners of the Calgary Flames for applying for the money or negotiating the deal because I know that they are sound businesspeople whose intent is strictly to provide a first-class hockey team in this city. If the government wants to subsidize something, then that's the first place business will look to. It's quick money. It's not a debt and it's not a loan. You don't have to pay interest. So if they want to give it to you, there's nothing wrong with applying for it.

When I criticized the funding for the Saddledome, I was in turn criticized for not doing my homework, and the homework that I was accused of not doing or understanding was the whole nature of this deal.

This is so simple, but it's complicated. The owners applied for the money so that they could get the cash right away and speed up the upgrading of the facility to compete NHL-wise and attract more fans. With that extra revenue they could increase profits and redistribute them in helping amateur sport. In the first year or two that's exactly what they tried to do.

Now the jobs are gone. They employ a few more people because they've got a few more kiosks, but with players all wanting $1 million-plus, their profits are gone. What they lost sight of in the infrastructure program was, "Is this benefiting the maximum number of taxpayers?" They basically lied about the number of jobs created. Their own report showed that these were temporary, short-term jobs that only lived as long as the project was under construction. The lower unemployment rate in this province was a blip. It was one-tenth of one-half of one percent, created by our ability to adapt to changing times.

I feel that the whole approach of the provincial government here, given the rules that they're working under, benefited from the overall global economic growth — not from this little infrastructure program.

I can use statistics to make my partisan point of view too, if I want to. The Treasury Board is there to justify what the government program has done or is doing. If the Treasury Board came out with statistics that said that it wasn't working, those people in the Treasury Board would find themselves working somewhere else.

There are so many different agencies within the government that look after statistics as to how many jobs were created. I have more confidence in two groups I really feel come as clean as they can, given the constraints of the public politician versus the private bureaucrat.

Statistics Canada tries to be at arm's length and objective. Also, the statistics and the numbers provided by the federal Finance Department are very good.

What did we achieve with this whole infrastructure program? Now that it's six years later, what have we got? Do we have upgraded facilities? Do we have better bridges? Do we have infrastructure that is $6 billion to the good? Has it helped business generate more revenue? If we find evidence of that, then yes, it has worked. It's like lending the money and then getting it back down the road. That would be the kind of spirit of co-operation that I would favour.

Chrétien promised "jobs, jobs, jobs." The Liberal government's idea has been, and still is, that governments create jobs, that governments are there to be everything they can be for the taxpayer and to help the economy by injecting capital into the economy.

I disagree with that philosophy. I feel that the private sector can look after the economy. The government's job is just to create the conditions to make investment attractive, to make taxation as low as possible so that we can be competitive with other countries. And the government's job, with respect to infrastructure specifically, is to make sure that communications, transportation and high tech are getting sufficient funding to help create that environment.

In our taxation system we tend to punish success. We punish those people who can help us the most in the name of helping those who can't help themselves. We tend to want to subsidize and help a lot of people who can help themselves, and we tend to become a lazy society.

People forget that eventually all this can be taken away. We might have to go to more of a user-pay system and pay a greater share for utilities, for health care, for education, if we don't address how all this was created. It was through deficit financing. We have a huge debt. We need people to recognize that and run the country the way we run our households: within our means. Yes, we can borrow money, but we have to be able to pay the interest and some of the principal. According to Paul Martin, we recently started making a payment on the principal, so we're not adding to the principal debt, which is a step in the right direction.

I criticized the Finance Department when money that would be spent next year was charged off to a current-year budget. That is against generally accepted accounting principles. The auditor general and the finance minister are having a fight over that, and the finance minister is winning.

41

Paul Martin is pretty aboveboard about what he's doing and how he's doing it. But then what if we freely elect a democratic dictator five years from now who says, "Well, the precedent was set by Mr. Paul Martin," and the new finance minister says, "We don't have $6 billion."

"Well, where'd you spend it?"

"I don't have to tell you."

You have to follow generally accepted accounting principles because you never know who the next person is going to be. So he's setting a bad precedent. It might be good in his hands, but just like there are benevolent dictators, there are vicious dictators.

How do you stop this kind of spending, where it gets off track and moneys are not spent where they were intended for in the first place? How can you control government spending in conjunction with prioritizing? Other governments will come along, and it won't be an infrastructure program, it'll be called something else, and they'll spend money and people are going to question it.

Members of Parliament only have two or three weeks to look at our statement of public accounts. The moneys that they're going to spend in the various ministries are presented to us, we look at what they spent the last year, and then we criticize what they spent if it's too much, or we define priorities.

In Aboriginal affairs, for example, we were recommending a $1.5-billion reduction in that particular file because they were already getting $8.5 billion and didn't need that extra $1.5 billion. We went through it province by province. Even the Cabinet minister can't change it because there is no sunset clause.

About 60 to 70 percent of our federal government's expenditures are already legislated and they're there ad infinitum. The 30 percent that we can increase or decrease with negotiations with provinces or arbitrarily is always after the fact. If programs were to be brought forward on a one-, two-, three- or five-year basis, then we would have what I call a sunset clause. At the end of it we determine whether or not it's been successful. What else do we need to do to make it successful? You ask for more money and you justify it that way. If it has proven not successful then you cancel it, and those moneys can be prioritized and allocated elsewhere. We don't do that. It's unfortunate.

We have to start getting people that want to go to Ottawa, that want to go to Edmonton, that want to go to city hall with a specific plan. We have to have plans from politicians that lead us out. We should be demanding this from politicians and people who are running. And if they don't do it, we should get off our butts and run ourselves.

Not enough people are involved in the political process. Not enough people realize the impact that sometimes well-meaning but unaware politicians and their decisions have on our lives. It can cost us a lot of money, a lot of taxes and a lot of lost opportunities.

We can have special-interest groups and they can lobby for their case, but you have to have some people willing to say no. You have to have some people willing to say where the spending should be, and have some commonsense rules about using the taxpayers' dollars, about spending in those areas of responsibility that do the greatest good for the greatest number. We need politicians who will say, "We want to go there to do a job. It'll take us this long to do it, and when it's done we're leaving, and we'll hand off the baton to somebody else."

If politicians are afraid to talk to media, are afraid to tell people what they really think, then what they're really trying to do is just protect their jobs. I found myself under a lot of pressure in Ottawa. I tend to be blunt and direct and sometimes critical of my own party. Sometimes I was ridiculed more by my colleagues than by the opposition.

If you have a vision, if you have an idea, then you must stand up for it. There is no solution unless you have a society where people want to participate within the system. Whenever there's an election anywhere in Canada, at whatever level, if you don't participate in that election, then don't complain because you have just allowed everybody else to decide who your boss will be. That's what you're voting for — people who will spend the dollars that come off your paycheque.

We have to make people aware of the consequences of apathy. Democracy tends to be apathetic when there's an impression that everything is rosy, or that there's nothing you can do about it. It doesn't matter if you go out and vote and participate. It doesn't matter if you put your X beside the person who loses or your X beside the person who wins. Once they're there they tend to forget why they went there. That's the general attitude.

Our democracy does have some newer innovations that are being tried and implemented. I think there is room for certain issues to be debated and voted upon through referenda in conjunction with another election. For instance, in one of the last municipal elections in Alberta there was also a question on VLTs (video lottery terminals). That's provincial jurisdiction. That is something in which citizens are asked to participate between provincial elections — like in California with amendments. It's a way to get people motivated, involved and interested.

I did not go to Ottawa to get a job. I went to Ottawa to try and do a good job. But I found resentment. The majority of politicians are there for the right reason. The system is prohibitive and does not reward incentive. The system just does not inspire excellence.

I'm going to bring what I know from the West and what I know from dealing with people in the West to Ottawa. In Ottawa they're set in their ways. They're entrenched, there's a routine and there's a procedure. You have to play the game.

One thing I learned in politics is that if you're not willing to compromise, you're not going to get even a foot in the direction in which you want to go. If you're stubborn and intolerant and narrow-minded, it's extremely difficult. When I first went to Ottawa I had a certain attitude, and the attitude was that our deficit was too high — $45 billion. I wanted the government to cut spending and cut quickly. They wouldn't.

I never saw the counterarguments until I went through Paul Martin's first budget. Quietly, privately, he would come to us and say, "Keep pushing, keep pushing, stand up in the House. I'm using this in Cabinet. I'm using this in caucus. I'm using your argument." Not me specifically, but my party's philosophy. So I learned that even if you are dealing with a member who is opposite, who has a different point of view, if you are willing to compromise a bit, water the wine a bit, you'll get some wine. A watered-down wine at dinner is better than no wine at all. The art of compromise is how you get deals done. In politics you can't take the road least travelled.

In Canadian politics we get this centrist view and everybody fighting for the middle. I'm worried that this compromise could lead to homogeneity of all of our elected officials across the country, regardless of party, with everybody moving to compromises.

Paul Martin is deceiving my children and my grandchildren. I have two grandchildren who are 18 months old, and they have a much bigger burden to bear than I ever did because they have a bigger debt to pay. We had none back in the early 1960s. So these kids are going to have to pay. They'll have less net income to spend on themselves, and Paul Martin doesn't even touch on that. He's living for the here and now.

RICK SMITH

Former Alderman, Calgary

As a member of the city council, Rick Smith chaired the Calgary Saddledome Foundation from 1996 to 2002. He has also been involved in transportation and other planning issues for Calgary.

I was an alderman in Calgary from 1989 until 1995. I did support the Saddledome as a project that qualified for funding under the national infrastructure program. The government provided us with $145 million worth of projects to do in a very short period of time, funded three ways among the federal government, the provincial government and the City of Calgary. There were hundreds of projects that were worthy of consideration.

The Saddledome went under a tough degree of scrutiny and we looked at its merits. There are about 450 permanent part-time jobs tied to the Saddledome. It was determined that our major tenant, the Calgary Flames, was responsible for about $100 million per year of economic spinoff to the economy of the city.

I don't remember the specifics, but by all means there was a cost-benefit analysis. We looked at the value of our major tenant and we looked at the value that that tenant brings to the city, and we looked at what that tenant was going to bring to the complex in excess of what was being funded under the Canada Infrastructure Works Program. The cost of the renovations that were being proposed at the time was in excess of $31 million, and it was suggested that $12 million of it qualified under the program.

The money that went to the renovations was geared specifically toward the public areas of the Saddledome. The public concourse area was widened, some of the concessions were enhanced, a parking facility was built and there is an access road which was not here before. The private boxes were truly a major tenant issue and were funded entirely by their portion. They spent quite a chunk of their own money on those renovations.

The Saddledome Foundation, as part of the clause in its lease, was responsible for any improvements made to the Saddledome. But the whole issue of the contract with the major tenant was on the table at the time and was being revisited. The foundation contributed into the building. This became the city's contribution of one-third that went toward the renovations of the building. Of the remaining funding, one-third came from the province and one-third came from the federal government. But the city's $4 million came from the resources that had already been gathered by the Saddledome Foundation.

We thought it was an excellent project in terms of job creation. We saw it as an opportunity to do some work in a short time frame, to put some people to work to boost the local economy. Local contractors were going to get jobs, local suppliers were going to get work and some projects were going to get done quite quickly.

Certainly the downside was that we already had a capital budget envelope, we already had a priority list, and some of that had to be adjusted. The province had an even bigger job because their involvement was not just $145 million, as came to us, but $172 million, which was distributed throughout the entire province. It was a matter of re-prioritizing their already budgeted spending.

There were some projects that ended up being done sooner as a result of the infrastructure program, and perhaps there were projects that might not have been done otherwise. There were certainly projects that were done that were low on the priority list simply because there was money available. I'm thinking specifically of some of the smaller projects that were only perhaps a few hundred thousand dollars, which we were able to fit in because of some of the bigger projects that came in under budget. That left some funds available for smaller projects to be done.

I think the province was ultimately responsible or accountable for the decisions made. The municipalities had to submit a priority list to the province for approval. After that, presumably the federal government was involved in making sure that their dollars were spent in ways that met the criteria of the original program.

As for determining why some projects were chosen and some weren't, that might be difficult. Those debates probably aren't in the minutes of the council meetings because the only projects that would be in the true minutes were the ones that actually made the test and were on the approval list. The other projects would be on lists that were debated by various different committees and by members of council in camera.

CHAPTER 2

PRINCE EDWARD ISLAND

Can we bend the rules enough to accommodate this?

When you talk to anyone in the Maritimes about the economy, the subject of jobs is never far behind. That's certainly what we found in Prince Edward Island. Depending on whom you talked to, programs like the Canada Infrastructure Works Program were either an appreciated influx of cash and jobs, or yet another make-work scheme that was doomed to failure. Sometimes people argued both points. Welcome to P.E.I.

Our questions concerning the CIWP's job-creation element landed smack in the middle of an old debate in the Maritime provinces: do job-creation programs work? Even the program's most ardent supporters could not provide us with much evidence of any long-term job creation resulting from the CIWP. There were, however, a lot of people who liked the short-term benefits CIWP provided; it was something that a lot of Islanders welcomed. Charlie Martell and Clifford Lee are among the municipal representatives we spoke to about the program's impact.

We found strong dissenting voices too and those whose opinion of the program was mixed. Former P.E.I. deputy minister Andy Wells contended that the CIWP was in part intended to qualify people for employment insurance (EI) benefits. People would often be hired for just enough weeks to qualify and then be replaced by someone else. Former Conservative MP Tom McMillan also addressed the jobs issue and the political "boondoggle" for politicians that the program represented.

Leo Walsh, former vice president of the Atlantic Canada Opportunities Agency (ACOA), conceded that the jobs created by CIWP were short term. He argued that it was what was needed at the time, and that the quest for jobs was the main reason the program was fast-tracked by the federal government.

Charlottetown's chief administrative officer, Harry Gaudet, and the chair of Charlottetown's public works committee, Clifford Lee, were enthusiastic about getting infrastructure money. But like other municipal representatives across the country, Charlottetown's leadership criticized the federal government's efforts to take all of the credit when projects were announced. Was the CIWP just one big publicity event? The public relations campaign for the CIWP was certainly in high gear on P.E.I. We spoke to the individual who oversaw the contracts to put up the red-and-white CIWP signs which let everyone know just where the money for each project came from. He was none other than Jack MacAndrew, a well-known former P.E.I. journalist and political activist.

In P.E.I., as in many of the provinces, funding went toward projects like golf courses, community centres, baseball parks and even a bowling alley that received $200,000, raising questions about what should be included under the category of "infrastructure." We spoke to a representative from the Tyne Valley Firemen's Club who was involved in the bowling alley project and said the project fit his own definition of "recreational infrastructure," which the community lacked. Despite the use of infrastructure funds for such projects, Charlie Campbell, who represented the province in dealing with the CIWP, insisted that the lion's share of funds were spent on "hard-core infrastructure."

So who kept an eye on the project in Canada's smallest province, making sure the funds were directed to infrastructure? We may never know the details. Trying to track down how decisions were made about which projects to fund on the island, our researcher Jennifer Nunn discovered that the CIWP management committee on P.E.I. did not keep any minutes from their meetings. There is no record whatsoever of what happened at its meetings — where tens of millions of tax dollars were spent.

Jennifer said that the way she was treated as she sought answers depended on whom she was talking to. "The mayors and the chairmen of the villages around P.E.I., most of them have been around for a long time so they know how the system works and were fairly open and approachable," she said. "At the provincial level they were a little bit more guarded than that. At the federal level there was definitely a more guarded approach. I was mostly dealing with people from the Atlantic Canada Opportunities Agency. They tended to be the federal representatives for P.E.I., and they definitely were much more guarded. It's a big government organization and it's very bureaucratic."

Some officials involved in the program said in interviews that they believed the P.E.I. infrastructure money was distributed according to population. Others said decisions were needs-based. Still others suspected that political motivations affected decisions about which projects to fund. Even the program's detractors said the program did benefit the island, but they did not agree on the extent of lasting change.

After her search for answers Jennifer decided that the ultimate responsibility for accountability for the infrastructure program rested with the federal government. "There is obviously some accountability at the provincial level because they determined what projects went ahead and what projects didn't," Jennifer said. "But the ultimate decision to bring the program in place and to put so much money into it was done at the federal level. That's really where the responsibility is to determine if it was a success. I thought it would be harder to pass the buck in P.E.I., but it doesn't seem to be. Where does the buck stop in P.E.I.? I would have to say it doesn't. It doesn't seem to stop here."

HARRY GAUDET

Chief Administrative Officer, Charlottetown

Harry Gaudet has lived his entire life on Prince Edward Island. His political career started in Charlottetown in 1975. He has worked as a city development officer and city administrator. When the city amalgamated with nearby communities in 1996, Gaudet began serving as chief administrative officer for the new City of Charlottetown.

Municipal governments across the country were concerned about the deteriorating municipal infrastructure. It was the position of municipal governments that other levels of government should participate in the upgrading of the municipal infrastructure. The Federation of Mayors and Municipalities, which is the provincial organization representing municipalities throughout P.E.I., lobbied over a number of years at the federal and provincial levels to participate in a municipal infrastructure improvement program.

The position of the municipalities was that the contributions from those levels of government were justified because they were and still are collecting taxes. The provincial and federal governments are collecting gasoline tax, excise tax, corporate and sales tax. We feel a portion of those taxes should be reinvested in the maintenance of our municipal infrastructure, which provides services to the users of those streets and sewage and storm-sewer systems — all of which had increased demands, partly because of services being provided to corporations. The proposal that the Federation of Mayors and Municipalities came up with was that it should be a cost-sharing program, with one-third from the municipal level of government, one-third from the provincial level and one-third from the federal government.

I remember Prime Minister Jean Chrétien coming as leader of the Opposition to the Federation of Mayors and Municipalities national convention and announcing that his party would support this program when they were elected. That's the first thing that the federation reminded them of when the Liberals were elected, and I think that the federal government honestly recognized that there was a serious deterioration in our national infrastructure that needed to be addressed.

The municipalities knew that the most significant thing about this program from the federal perspective was the creation of jobs. The federal government wanted to show that people were going to be put to work in a period of high unemployment across the country. From these projects not only are direct jobs created, but spinoff jobs also result. In the City of Charlottetown, over a three-year period we carried out over $9 million worth of infrastructure programs — $3 million from each level of government.

Over a three-year period, that would have meant that there were in excess of 40 people employed in any given year on these projects in our community. Now, that's just one community throughout the entire country and it represented a significant input, not only into the economy because of those employment years, but also the spinoff benefits that came from the projects that we embarked upon. Equally important to us was the improvement to our municipal infrastructure system.

We didn't participate as a municipal government in the selection of the projects. The guidelines for the infrastructure program were developed at the federal and provincial levels. The Federation of Mayors and Municipalities was invited to participate on a selection team responsible for selecting projects that were submitted to them by the various levels of government. There was particular emphasis on hard-core services, like streets, sidewalks, storm-sewer systems and water and sewage systems. We had no difficulty with this because that was the area of infrastructure that we felt, in our municipality, needed the greatest amount of work.

We put together projects that met the objectives of the program. These were then submitted to the committee of council, who reviewed all the projects and determined which were more important in terms of upgrading our municipal services. We would rank these projects and submit a shopping list of improvements or municipal infrastructure projects that we wanted to get into. We would rank them in importance to us and submit them to the selection committee. The selection committee would take them and they would review all these projects. Once the selection was made the steering committee would make an announcement of what the overall projects were and the funding level to each community.

Our priority projects received top billing from this committee. The allocation of dollars, which we were a little afraid might have been disbursed on a political basis, was pretty fairly distributed on a per capita basis throughout the province. We felt we accessed our fair share of dollars, as did the other municipalities and communities throughout P.E.I. We didn't have a great deal of difficulty with the final decisions that were made as they related to our community.

One of the projects was a road going into our waterfront, which enabled us to better service our shipping facilities and all the things related to the transportation industry on our waterfront, including potatoes, fish products and oil and gas for distribution throughout the province. It enabled the cheaper, more efficient flow of these products throughout the province. Another $1.5-million project was to build a storm-sewer system that alleviated a flooding condition in a section of Charlottetown that had occurred over the last 20 to 25 years.

There's no question that elected officials, whether they're municipal, provincial or federal, want to see projects that their constituents feel need to be done. After all, they're elected by the people that are asking for these projects. It's unlikely that they're going to be pushing for projects that the people don't want. Does this mean elected officials were trying to make sure that pet projects were carried out? I don't know if I could say that.

Every time we submitted a project we would have to demonstrate in that submission the value of the project — what the project was and how many jobs we felt that project would create. As we did each progress claim for the work that was carried out, we had to demonstrate how many person-weeks and person-years were created on that project to that point in time. We had to clearly demonstrate the immediate creation of jobs.

There was an economic advantage and stimulus to our economy by spending money on our road system. We were better able to carry on business within the city corporation. Our sewage system was better able to provide sewage and water services to property owners who were moving into our community and who were investing in our community. Then there's the long-term economic stimulus. The 40 jobs may be only those 40 jobs that year, but the projects these people worked on contributed to long-term viability of businesses and the sustainability of our community. That has a long-term contribution to financial stability and the creation of jobs in our community.

The way that we determine the number of jobs created is we do a projection at the time of the application as to the anticipated number of person-years' work that will be created in any given project. Once the project is approved, we then go out to contract and we get a bid on the project. Then it's our responsibility as the municipality to fill out progress claims for the approved projects. Over the history of the projects we calculated the ongoing person-weeks of employment created in any given project and we gave them that figure in every claim we made.

We know the number of person-years that were created in the City of Charlottetown, immediate, short-term person-years of employment through the project. Less tangible are the long-term person-years of employment because that's a more difficult thing to measure. You have to establish longer-range measuring techniques to get to that. That would be up to the federal government. Certainly measuring the long-term jobs would take a more sophisticated measuring tool. It would also require a fairly detailed and probably not inexpensive study to determine the long-term jobs.

If you want to know the number of jobs created, if you want to know the number of person-years of jobs created at the municipal level, come to the municipality. We'll tell you. The provincial government should easily be able to tell you at the provincial level because they're the owners of that information on a province-wide basis. The federal government is the owner of that information on a national basis and should be able to provide that information.

I think if the money were given as a lump sum to the municipalities, the administration and disbursement of the funds and the selection of projects would have happened a lot quicker. There's no question that if only one party has to make the decision, it's easier to make that decision and move ahead with your programs. You're dealing with three levels of government and three parties that are paying for it. However, there was flexibility in the disbursement of funds. They were prepared to carry the funding over to the subsequent year and they extended the program. We're all in this together. We're serving one taxpayer. Our objective is to get those tax dollars to work for the people as quickly as possible.

ANDY WELLS

Former Deputy Minister

Andy Wells has served his home province for many years. After a term as deputy minister of transportation and public works for Prince Edward Island, Wells joined the province's Workers Compensation Board in 1992 as its chief executive officer.

You can criticize the infrastructure program on several levels. Principally it is not a program that has been properly researched and properly designed to deal with the long-term economic and social needs of an area. It is simply a knee-jerk reaction to an immediate problem of high unemployment. If the government were planning longer-term, more useful activities, then you could understand that and accept it. But all they do is talk about another infrastructure program.

As I recall, the federal infrastructure program was established because the Liberal Party, in 1993, coming into the election had raised employment and jobs as being a major issue. Having been elected, somebody said, "Well, what are we going to do about it? How are we going to respond to our promise to create jobs?" The easy answer, and unfortunately not a very satisfactory one, was to set up this big program and run it across the country. That would satisfy the local and provincial politicians because they had a say in how the money was to be spent. That is a very powerful tool.

The major commentary we've had to date on this program has been from auditors general or the auditor general's office, in the case of the federal government. These people are very cautious; all auditors are. They don't normally come down hard on anything unless it's against the law. If you read between the lines of our own auditor general's and the federal auditor general's reports, they're really saying essentially the same thing: that this program was hatched too quickly. It did not have clear guidelines, the criteria were not properly laid out and the delivery was suspect in many cases.

There were programs that were appropriately set up and operated under the infrastructure program. But a lot of the projects just simply didn't meet the criteria or were sufficiently off that they shouldn't have been established or accepted. I'm not aware of any serious study that's looked at and evaluated the successes in terms of creating work and fixing infrastructure. You will find that by and large what was done need not have been done. It hasn't contributed in any major way to improving the economy or the employment situation in areas like Prince Edward Island.

As our auditor general said in his report, the $42 million that was put into the program had a marked impact on the economy of P.E.I. Of course it did, but the question is, was that the best place to put $42 million? Were there better ways of investing that money to achieve the kind of results that were stated as being desirable?

If you were able to look carefully at job creation in this province, you'd find various jobs were employment insurance–directed. In many cases this was a way for the province and the federal government — but more the province — to get people the necessary weeks of work so that they would qualify for employment insurance. That was an important objective of the program for local politicians. The other thing is the recognition. If they're able to go into a community and say, "Hey, look, I've put up a baseball diamond for you," that was considered important to all the politicians.

In this particular program you got a one-third arrangement, so it wasn't as bad as some of the dollar-for-dollar federal initiatives, insofar as the provinces are concerned. But often that initial rational approach to a program that comes forward is lost. You have the individual politicians, whether at the Cabinet level or at the MLA (member of the provincial legislative assembly) level, saying, "Oh, wait now, what can I do with this and what can I do for my riding?"

I'm not condemning the thought that an MLA should be concerned about what he can do for his or her riding, but I do condemn the uselessness of a number of things that eventually come forward. They're often showy. They're in response to a public that hasn't the means of understanding true economic development or growth. The result is that you have a hodgepodge of projects that in the final analysis don't add up to very much.

Discussion about the priorities and direction and philosophical concerns, as far as governments are involved, is done less today than 25 to 30 years ago, partly because the calibre and the quality of senior public servants in Ottawa was quite different than it is today. I've seen time and time again reasonably well-thought-out programs eventually bastardized by the need to get recognition, the need for public approval immediately, rather than looking at the long term.

The roads, water and sewer projects were very visible, labour intensive and by and large male intensive, in the sense that most of the people hired are going to be males. Most of them are going to be in construction of one kind or another and that activity is something that everyone sees. There were a lot of infrastructure program dollars that probably would not meet the classic definition of infrastructure. If you stretched your imagination, the definition would meet the curling rinks and the baseball diamonds and so on.

In the infrastructure program, often the criteria and the methodology are so vague that it would be almost impossible to do a rigid cost-benefit analysis because you didn't know what your benefits were supposed to be. In some cases you don't even know what your costs were. The result is that the governments and the politicians who have brought forward these programs would just as soon not have any rigid or careful scrutiny made of the program.

Look at the methodology used to arrive at the number of jobs this program created. If they're looking at person-hours, for example, and then trying to somehow or other translate that into jobs, that's a very questionable method of arriving at a useful answer. If you look at how many permanent jobs were established and track those jobs, I think you'd find a very different kind of answer than what we're hearing. Even if you looked at the part-time jobs, you'd find that in many cases, and certainly in this province, people would work just enough weeks to draw their employment insurance. They would then be laid off and somebody else would be hired who needed additional weeks to get on EI.

This is a game that the provinces, particularly the Maritime provinces, have played for years. The reason they do it is because EI is not out of their pockets. The alternative in many cases is welfare, which is out of the province's pocket. So the information that you get from any analysis of this kind of program I would say is very suspect. You would want to have that information scrutinized very carefully and analyzed very carefully before you'd start accepting those numbers as being very meaningful.

The numbers indicate spending of $42 million to create 900 jobs. I'd first want to ask whether or not there was a better way to spend it. Would the money have been better spent in a way that might have created more full-time jobs, rather than in this way, which simply put a number of people on EI? Those are the kinds of analyses that are required both before and certainly after the expenditure. Time and time again in the last two decades, the answer has been to throw money at the problem, see what happens and hope you get re-elected.

As a program designed to meet the promise of the federal Liberals to consider the problem of unemployment, it was ill designed and ill delivered. The municipal and the provincial and the federal authorities conspired to spend money on pet projects that in many respects they hoped would have an impact on their electability. And it seems like they did.

The concept of service to the public by the elected politician and by the public servant is no longer as clear today as it was 30 years ago. I worked for a premier at one time who, prior to running for the leadership of the party, had no idea in the world what he wanted to do. He just wanted to get elected. I'm of the old school who believed that you were in there, whether as a politician or as a public servant, to serve the public. That is your first responsibility. Unfortunately in the last number of years I think that has turned around.

As long as we're stuck with party politics as being the prime mover and shaker of the electoral process, we're going to end up with four-year horizons. We need to have a system that will put people in the government that are prepared to go beyond the four-year horizon, with the understanding that their success is not going to be dependent upon the success of the political party.

TOM MCMILLAN

Former Conservative MP, Hillsborough

In 1979 Tom McMillan entered federal politics, continuing a Progressive Conservative dynasty on Prince Edward Island. He served as environment minister and represented the Hillsborough riding until he was defeated in the 1988 election. McMillan ran in the 1993 election and was defeated by the Liberal incumbent.

The Federation of Canadian Municipalities (formerly the Federation of Canadian Mayors and Municipalities) had a mammoth lobbying campaign for an infrastructure program, which they triggered as soon as the Mulroney government was elected in September of 1984. It fell to me, as the minister of the environment, to be the target of much of this lobbying. The efforts were geared to having the federal government open the treasury to fund waste-water treatment plants and water delivery systems, wrapped in the garb of environmentalism, which was probably more salient politically at that time than practically any time since and certainly any time before.

When I became a Cabinet minister, the very first meeting of Cabinet involved a high-level briefing by the most senior officials of the Department of Finance, led by the minister of finance himself, Mike Wilson. It was like a cold shower. The finance people said, "Ministers, there's no money. The cupboard is bare. Worse than that, there's no cupboard."

One dollar in three raised by the federal government through taxes in all forms was going toward the interest on the accumulated debt of the country. The first message we got as Cabinet ministers was that at the rate at which the federal government was spending — and mis-spending and overspending — by 1988, instead of one tax dollar in three going toward the interest payments on the accumulated debt, that ratio would be one dollar in every two.

The inference clearly was that ministers were not to embark upon new programs involving great expenditures, much less one of the sort that the municipalities had in mind. The price tag for that program was into the tens of billions. My role, in part, was to tell them that there was no money. The federal government didn't have the money to fund those projects and programs and policies within its own jurisdiction, much less embark upon a new multibillion-dollar program for projects and policies and programs in somebody else's jurisdiction, in this case the municipalities' and the provinces'.

Municipal infrastructure, local works and undertakings are specifi-cally, in the Constitution of Canada, within provincial jurisdiction. Municipalities are creatures of the provinces. So all of these things were purely and exclusively, with very few exceptions, within provincial juris-diction. The federal government had no role in this area. No jurisdic-tion. No responsibility. No mandate. And certainly no money.

The municipalities and the mayors in their naiveté thought the gov-ernment would open up the treasury to them. I told them in every pos-sible and available form that we weren't even going to consider it. The public had become so inured to a federal government that said yes to almost every request, racking up huge annual deficits and adding tens of billions of dollars to the accumulated debt of the country, that it was a little like a heroin addict being denied a drug. It was cold turkey. And the public didn't like it. The mayors and municipalities were no exception.

The Federation of Canadian Municipalities is a very powerful and influential source of political pressure. It is made up of many hundreds of communities, from the smallest borough to the largest metropolis. They'd been in this business for a very long time, so they had fine-tuned their lobbying and pressure tactics to a great art. They had to create the impression and the appearance that this was a national problem, that the state of infrastructure had reached the point of disintegration and disrepair and that the federal government had to come in. The case was made that the roads and water systems and sewage treatment plants were in such a bad state of repair that if something were not done, the consequences would be apocalyptic, cataclysmic, and the price tag attached to the total job to be done was into the tens of billions of dollars. It was a price tag which they expected the federal government to pay a very large share of.

The Federation of Mayors and Municipalities didn't take "no" easily. In fact they didn't take "no" at all. Throughout the entire first mandate of the Mulroney government I was personally hounded, I was heavily lobbied. Other Cabinet ministers were heavily lobbied, courted, threatened and certainly approached with the possible dire consequences of not responding favourably to these pressure tactics. The federal government didn't take the view that it had no interest in or any responsibility at all for the infrastructure of the country from one coast to another. Obviously we were heavily in airports, in pollution control, in international and interprovincial waterways. We were indirectly funding municipal works and undertakings through our spending power, through transfer payments. We were especially sensitive to the regional disparities.

The fact that some municipalities were less able to fund their infrastructure than others was taken into account through regional development grants, through transfer payments from the federal government to the provinces and through the provinces to the municipalities. So we weren't saying, "No, we're not interested in the infrastructure of the country." We were saying, "We've already paid at the office. Don't ask us to pay twice."

It was clear that a lot of money had to be spent on municipal infrastructure because the municipalities had neglected this. They had spent only six percent of their total budget on something as important as water delivery, wastewater treatment and pollution control. In Canada we undervalue water and we undercharge for it. Municipal residents pay less for their fresh water to homes than is the case anywhere else in the world. The answer is to charge more to the users and the consumers of what is ultimately a scarce resource.

Opposition parties, as a general point, favour spending money because they are not accountable. At the end of the day they don't have to answer to the taxpayers as to how the money was spent. It was very easy for the opposition parties to link arms with the mayors and the municipalities in pressuring the federal government to spend money in this area, money which it didn't have. The same is true no matter what the policy area was — health, education — the mantra of the opposition is to spend, spend, spend, to support to the hilt all of the public-interest groups and the special-interest groups that are campaigning for their respective hobbyhorses.

I was invited quite frequently to speak to municipal groups in big cities and small towns alike, in practically every province and territory. Quite frequently the major umbrella organizations that represented the municipalities invited me to be a guest as a clever political means of putting me on the spot. I noticed that there was one woman in particular, a rather elderly, benign-appearing woman, who seemed to be popping up all over the place like a mushroom after an acid-free rainfall. Every time I spoke and told the municipal leaders that they couldn't have the billions of dollars they were seeking for infrastructure, when the camera lights went on and the media swarmed around me, she seemed to be there, available for interviews to express a view.

At first I thought this was just an interested, community-spirited elderly lady who was worried about roads and sewers and wastewater treatment plants. But even I noticed after a while that it was too much of a coincidence to believe that this was entirely from the bosom of community-spiritedness. I subsequently learned that she was a municipal politician who was very active in the federation. This was one of their clever and to some extent, I must admit, subtle and nuanced efforts at applying pressure. They were making sure that their message was telegraphed to the Canadian public through the media that inevitably followed a Cabinet minister when he was making appearances of this sort.

I was always aware that a program like the Infrastructure Works Program in 1993 was a highly attractive boondoggle. Politicians love to cut ribbons. There's not much political credit at the ballot box for foreign aid, for national defence, for research and development, for bilingualism. Excuse the pun, but roads, bridges, sewers, wastewater treatment plants are concrete, they're up-front. People can see them. Politically speaking, it's a gift that keeps on giving. It is superb marketing. It is wonderful electioneering because it's geared to the next election. But it is certainly not good public policy.

That isn't to say that infrastructure by definition is not good; obviously it is and it's required. But the way in which it's done is probably the last way that you would devise if you were doing it primarily from a sound, logical, public policy point of view.

JACK MACANDREW

Former Journalist and Political Activist

For more than 40 years Jack MacAndrew has worked as a Prince Edward Island writer, performer, political commentator and radio news contributor. He owns a graphic consulting business in P.E.I.

One of the things about practising journalism in Prince Edward Island is that if you have strongly held opinions, they're probably best kept to yourself because you never know whose brother, cousin, uncle, aunt or grandfather you may be insulting when you come down heavily on some subject or other. Everything is interconnected in Prince Edward Island. Everybody knows your business. And most Islanders tend to be very circumspect about what they express in terms of politics or economics or social matters.

When I was recruited by the late publisher Jim McNeil to write for *The Eastern Graphic*, there really were no rules at all. I was free to comment in whatever way I wanted to. I have been doing so for the past 15 years, often to the anger and disgust of segments of the population, particularly politicians. Even though Islanders may be inhibited in expressing ideas themselves, they do like other people to do it. So you fill a certain spot or a certain role and it seems to work out.

When I first heard about the infrastructure program, it seemed to me to be simply another attempt to hire as many people as possible on the short term. At the same time this would enable them to get on the employment insurance rolls and use another chunk of federal money as yet another short-term program to alleviate the unemployment problem. It would make the numbers look good and get the government geared up for an election campaign. In that sense it's the usual system of buying us with our own money. Governments go for very pragmatic, short-term solutions, which do nothing for the long term and simply perpetuate the conditions that they seem to be trying to alleviate.

Securing federal funding meant that the municipalities didn't have to levy taxes to the extent they might have otherwise. So in that sense you have one level of politician serving the next level. But when you roll it all back, everybody is being bought with the same dollars.

Now this is not to say that some good didn't come out of the infrastructure program. The fact is, there are a lot more sewers and sidewalks and refurbished community halls in Prince Edward Island than were there before. This is not to say that a few people didn't get long-term jobs. But if you're going to measure one against the other, and measure it against the backdrop of the economic past, present and God knows what the future is in Prince Edward Island, it certainly is no panacea.

There was a very fundamental economic difference between Prince Edward Island and the rest of the country. This is a province which has three major industries, all based on seasonal employment. That is an inescapable fact of economic and social life. Traditionally people here did a little fishing, did a little farming, cut some wood, lived on the sharp edge of poverty, and most of the young people had to go elsewhere to find work. That has been the history in the Maritimes since Confederation.

The federal government has regulated fishermen out of existence. Economic conditions and the changing technology have ruled subsistence farming out of existence. You can't farm anymore unless you do it big. The trees are being cut down at an alarming rate.

The infrastructure program is a good way to spend some money, but if you stop short and say, "That's our contribution for this year, folks," what have you left? You've left another bunch of people who can go on EI to get through that year. But you haven't changed the social conditions or the economic conditions that might provide some kind of long-term benefit to any degree.

My company has a standing offer with the federal government. That's just a system whereby companies like mine arrange with the federal government a certain pay structure for any jobs that come up under the things that I do. Over the past winter we were called by the federal government, through ACOA (Atlantic Canada Opportunities Agency), to put up about 50 signs across Prince Edward Island. My function was essentially to arrange a little contract bidding with three or four of the people who make signs and to administer the program and make sure the signs got put up on time. We put up these signs, or at least the sign company did, all over Prince Edward Island, saying that this is a joint federal-provincial project.

Clearly the federal government once again is very interested in taking as much credit as it can. They spent about $17,000 on signage across P.E.I., as I recall. I could never fundamentally see the reason for all these signs in the first place — except pure, crass credit-taking, which amounts to vote-buying. It makes sense as long as you're not spending your own money. So as long as governments can dip their hands into the public purse and use the public's money to aggrandize themselves as a political party, well, it's easy to do. Hundreds of thousands of dollars were spent on signs all across the country. Hundreds of thousands of dollars.

We have four MPs from P.E.I., all Liberal. The infrastructure grants were fairly evenly distributed across the province because, I'm sure, the four politicians worked it out that way. To me that's just another little piece of evidence that the four Liberal politicians decided where the money would go, not according to municipal need, but according to their own needs. They all wanted the same number of pictures taken, handing over the cheques, I guess. It doesn't surprise me. A sum of money was allotted to Prince Edward Island and the four politicians carved up the barrel. It's just that simple.

I think it is just as valid to build baseball fields or bowling alleys or parks as it is to build sewers. Each of them makes a contribution to society that is as valuable as flushing down the drain the refuse of society. Indeed, who knows? Building a ball field in a rural area just might give kids something to do that would keep them out of trouble a little bit. We have a rural society in Prince Edward Island which doesn't have a lot of money and doesn't have a lot of facilities.

It depends how you define infrastructure. That definition can be as narrow or as broad as you want to make it. If you want to say that it is valuable to have a community hall in a community where people can have cake sales, where they can run village days, where they can improve the quality of life, what's the matter with that? That's as important, I say, as being able to flush your refuse down the sewer.

When any kind of a program like the infrastructure program is announced, the reaction of people is, "There's a big sow and how do we get on the teat?" So you look at the rules and you talk to your local MP, and you say, "This is what we want to do, can we bend the rules enough to accommodate this?" Then you try to get done what you think is most important to you and your community. And I don't see anything wrong with that.

CLIFFORD LEE

Chair, Public Works Committee, Charlottetown

Clifford Lee began serving as Charlottetown's chair of public works after the city amalgamated in 1995.

Since April of 1995 I've served as chair of the public works commit-tee for the City of Charlottetown. That was around the same time that the federal infrastructure program actually started. I led the city, from the infrastructure perspective.

We developed the long list of things we wanted. Then, of course, as in any project, you end up with a shortlist. That shortlist ended up being submitted to the provincial-federal committee on the island here for selection of what projects they were prepared to support.

The infrastructure program was a great asset. The major part of our projects was roadwork. The biggest one was the creation of the water-front access road on Water Street, which allowed the harbour-area roads to be used for more heavy industrial traffic without affecting the adja-cent residential areas. What we ended up with is a new access road going right to the working wharf. So now instead of travelling up through a residential area, there's a new road that takes them right out to the outskirts of the city and on to the Charlottetown bypass system. The waterfront access road cost in excess of $4 million to be constructed and everything was replaced in the street system in that area. If the infrastructure program hadn't been there, chances are that project wouldn't have happened.

Another big project was the replacement of a storm-sewer system in an older part of the city that was causing real problems for the residents. It seemed every time it rained, the whole area would flood. That new system has replaced a smaller system and rectified that problem. The rest of it was an upgrading of sidewalks and streets throughout the whole city.

Charlottetown went through an amalgamation process back in April of 1995. As a result, it went from a community of 16,000 people to 32,000. When amalgamation happened a lot of tax rates in the old parts of the community, which became a part of the new city, went up. I expect that the citizens wanted to see something for their increased tax dollars.

The infrastructure program allowed us to triple the amount of major work that we would have undertaken. The infrastructure was really paid for in 33¢ dollars, but Charlottetown didn't reduce its operating budget by two-thirds. We continued on and said this is the money that we would normally spend on streets and sidewalks and this type of thing. We just added on the federal and provincial share. So if you had $1 million in 1996 under operating budget, you ended up spending $3 million that year. Obviously some of the projects that were done were projects that normally would have had to be capitalized.

City council sent its short-listed applications to a selection committee which had representatives of the three levels of government. In P.E.I. the municipal representative was the executive director of the Federation of P.E.I. Municipalities. That committee made the recommendations to ACOA, that these are projects that should be funded under the infrastructure program.

After the application went in there were all kinds of rumours of what happened. There have been all kinds of stories that some federal politicians were right in the middle of the selection process. Is that real or not? I don't know. It seems in P.E.I., whenever any project of this type becomes available, the perception certainly is created out there that it's sort of like a slush fund and the politicians use it to get themselves re-elected.

In some parts of the island there were major renovations or new community halls built. In the long run I'm not sure that those communities will be able to sustain the operation of those buildings. I'm not sure if a lot of that down-the-road approach was considered. Nobody thought of the operating cost. These buildings are going to continue to operate on their own with no subsidy from any level of government? That just doesn't happen. Quite honestly, it's one thing to take $1 million and put it into a street or into sidewalks. But when you take some of these buildings that have been almost closed down over the years and suddenly have them revitalized, I don't honestly believe they'll serve in the long term.

There was a general understanding that the money awarded to the province of P.E.I. was going to be split among the four federal ridings. I don't know what the total dollar values were. So if $100 million was spent through the infrastructure program on the island, my understanding was that the four districts were to receive in the area of $25 million each. The reality is politics was a part of this process. The infrastructure program was instituted, I think, to assist some federal MPs to reclaim their seats. I can tell you, for example, that if there was $100 million spent in P.E.I. and Charlottetown didn't receive any of that, I would suspect that our MP for Hillsborough would have a real difficult time maintaining his seat. The public expects their politician to deliver the goods.

The infrastructure program extension was granted, as I understand it, because the Federation of Canadian Municipalities kept pressuring Ottawa. It probably had something to do with the federal election campaign that was about to take place. The disappointing part for Charlottetown was that it was September of 1997 when we found out what projects and what amount of money were approved for the city. Well, in Charlottetown you can't pave a whole lot of streets or fix a whole lot of sidewalks after September, so basically that whole infrastructure extension program was carried over. The work really wasn't done until 1998.

We found it very frustrating to be waiting all summer, in 1997, for Ottawa — or for ACOA, I guess — to tell us how much money was coming to Charlottetown, so we could plan, so we could call tenders. It just seemed that no matter who you spoke to, they kept referring you to somebody else. There was a change in the provincial administration and the Tories were in power. But my understanding is the people who were involved from the provincial scene on the infrastructure program under the previous administration continued to administer the extension to the program in 1997. It could very well have been that the provincial government didn't want the projects because they knew the federal election call was coming and they didn't want to help the Liberals. I wasn't part of the provincial or federal political scene, so I honestly can't say.

I think the citizens of Charlottetown were aware of the city's involvement in the process because we made very public comments. I don't think council said a whole lot of things behind closed doors regarding the infrastructure program. The selection committee said to the city that they wanted to ensure that the waterfront access road was one of the projects completed under the program. It was clearly identified. In all other cases the committee came back to Charlottetown and said, "You've got this much money, council, you determine what the priorities are. Once you determine what your priorities are, send it back to the committee so that we can ensure that it falls within the guidelines of the federal municipal infrastructure program." I'm not sure if that's how it happened in all communities.

I think Charlottetown was probably treated a little differently in the process because in the end about $10 million worth of work was done through the infrastructure program. That money came from all three levels of government. We probably submitted to the committee projects totalling $100 million, though.

In today's times there's a negative perception that the public have of politicians. If there's ever anything that a politician can do, you can probably rest assured that most people think it's probably not aboveboard. Why that is, I don't know. It's a funny system. If a citizen goes to a politician and the politician says to that person, "I'm not involved in that process, I shouldn't be involved in that process," then that citizen is upset with the politician because it's perceived that he or she is not representing their constituent. If they do get involved in the process, then people don't say they're representing their constituents, they say that they're interfering.

There was no political interference that I'm aware of in the choice of projects for the infrastructure program. Generally I'm very happy with the infrastructure program that came to P.E.I. My only wish is that it was extended for a few more years. I'll sit back forever and let somebody else take the credit as long as they keep sending the money in to us. But that's probably not going to happen.

CHARLIE CAMPBELL

*Former Provincial Deputy Minister
of Intergovernmental Affairs*

Charlie Campbell was provincial deputy minister of intergovernmental affairs from 1993–94. He was the person in charge of dealing with the federal government when it came to writing the infrastructure agreement. Campbell died in 1999.

As deputy minister of intergovernmental affairs, my role was largely to work with federal officials to try to get the right wording for federal-provincial agreements that could be signed by the respective ministers. This is how I became involved in the infrastructure program.

The actual agreement was already drafted in terms of most of its major features, calling for cost-sharing by federal, provincial and municipal governments of one-third each, and was sent out to the provinces for reaction. Our work and discussion focused more on administration than it did on principles. In January of 1994 we were able to make a recommendation to our provincial Cabinet that the province enter into such an agreement.

Normally an agreement with the federal government takes much longer, particularly if the province is seeking something and takes the initiative. In this instance the feds wanted it to happen as fulfillment of a *Red Book* promise. In fact it wasn't necessary to deal with the traditional federal line departments because, in their wisdom, they established a special task force which was headed up by a gentleman by the name of George Anderson. He was under the direction of the Honourable Art Eggleton. This does prove that when the federal government wants things to happen, they can happen. I think they made progress because they didn't want to listen to what might be the traditional objections inside the federal departments. We were dealing with a group that would quickly get back to us with answers to our concerns. I don't know why all governing can't happen that way.

The speed with which it happened was not unusual in terms of the new federal government's objectives. These were in three areas. One was to assist municipalities in putting needed infrastructure in place. Another was the economic and social objective of trying to create some new jobs, lower the level of unemployment and create some economic industrial activity. And obviously the government also had some political objectives. The first two sets of objectives were rather well spelled out in the agreement, and I think even the political objective, although not explicit in the agreement, certainly wasn't all that well hidden.

The agreement called for things to be fast-tracked in order to create an immediate profile as a government of action. The time frames within the agreement for spending were indicative of this since 35 percent of the budget was to be spent by March 1995, and 85 percent by March 1996. So the objectives of the federal government were fairly explicit. The program addressed some municipal needs together with job creation, and with very low federal expenditure it gave them a very high profile in the 24 months leading into the next federal election.

I think that the government probably was sincere in wanting to increase employment and economic activity as well as address the concern of the Canadian Federation of Municipalities with respect to infrastructure. After all, the federal government previously had been in the infrastructure program and some of the provinces had objected. So this was a way around the provinces to assist the municipalities. Obviously in addressing these two objectives they were conscious of the political objectives. This is not to suggest that they were primarily politically motivated, but there was certainly a positive political outcome.

It was also indicated within the agreement that there had to be a high degree of signage, with the result that as the agreement got carried out, there were lots of red-and-white signs in communities all across the country six months or a year prior to the 1997 election. As political strategy it was masterful. They achieved their results.

It certainly helped to see these signs in local communities, fostering the concept that the federal government, as a partner, was doing something in the local community. It worked much more effectively for federal politicians than municipal or provincial politicians because whenever we Canadians see a federal government sign, we tend to think it's largely federal money due to the 90/10 funding practice in the past — even in this case, when it wasn't.

One might question whether or not the signage practice was fair. Obviously the other levels of government wanted the federal participation so badly they didn't seem to object. Certain provinces that were not Liberal had their own political colours. I doubt whether signs helped any municipal or provincial officials gain any profile or get re-elected. Provincial governments changed in that period of time, and many councillors and mayors were defeated, so they didn't get much value for their 33-and-a-third cents of the dollar, while the feds got a lot of value for theirs.

Prince Edward Island has four Liberal members of Parliament, but I doubt whether any of them had a great deal of involvement in the infrastructure program. As a matter of fact, I think the strategy was pretty well centralized and that perhaps there was even some disenchantment on the part of the local MPs that they did not have enough input or control because of the fast-tracking. They may even have felt that the provinces and the municipalities had a greater degree of say over which projects would actually go forward. I cannot speak from the perspective of a member of Parliament, but I would assume that they would have liked to be seen responding to a particular group applying for a project. However, the projects submitted by P.E.I. went through a screening committee which included the provincial officials and representatives of the Federation of P.E.I. Mayors and Municipalities. I would say the MPs' opportunity for direct input might have been more limited than they would have liked.

The P.E.I. government primarily wanted to ensure that the program could be modified to address the greater infrastructure needs in municipalities, and there were several provincial criteria in addition to the federal criteria that were established and accepted by Cabinet. One was that project submissions would be prioritized on the basis of need and what they would solve in terms of environmental problems. Secondly, what would be the economic spinoffs for the island? How many jobs would they create? Could the required equipment and materials in some cases be produced locally? Could the municipalities actually operate it? So projects such as building new edifices, which might have great operating costs, wouldn't get a high priority.

The final consideration was that projects should be spread geographically across the province. I think that the province, no less than the federal government, wanted to ensure that it wasn't putting all of its dollars into just a few municipalities. However, it wasn't really necessary to impose a geographic distribution because the projects tended to fall that way. Charlottetown may have thought that it had great needs but there were communities like Murray River, in which the river itself was being polluted by raw sewage and the shellfish industry was being placed in jeopardy. On the basis of the more objective criteria, it just so happened that geographically the dispersion was there.

The first round of projects was largely things that most Islanders considered necessary and that were high on the list of municipal objectives. Throughout the life of the project, 90 to 95 percent of the funding did get spent on what we would call hard-core infrastructure. There may have been a few very small projects in the first round like community halls, parks and recreation facilities. Recreational facilities such as arenas were not excluded, but were not high on the priority list, at least in the first round, as I understood it.

The federal government had draft agreements prepared in the fall of 1993 which they hoped all provinces would sign. These agreements were sent by federal officials to provincial governments. Provincial governments were asked to react and go to Ottawa to meet with the task force officials. The feds were fairly rigid on the basic principles of the agreement — that the funding had to be one-third, one-third, one-third and the definition of what constituted infrastructure projects was pretty firmly fixed.

There was some room as to how the level of funding would be calculated. For example, originally it was thought that it would be by population across Canada. In our discussion we were able to modify that to take into consideration the unemployment rate in the provinces, since job creation was one of the objectives. We asked, along with some other provinces, that it be calculated on the province's percentage of the total unemployed in the country, as opposed to the percentage of population. Under straight population statistics, P.E.I. would have received 0.5 percent of the total available funds. We were able to up that to 0.6 percent. Under the new formula the province's percentage of the total population and its percentage of unemployed workers were added together and divided by two.

Another modification we were able to achieve was with respect to the actual time frame for spending the money. The feds originally wanted to fast-track even more than what we finally agreed to. We indicated to them that because of construction problems in the winter in P.E.I., the kinds of projects that were truly infrastructure — such as the laying of sidewalks, sewer and water pipes — from a practical point of view could never meet the targets. We gained some flexibility in those areas.

The infrastructure program certainly met the political objectives of the federal government. On the positive side for the province and for municipalities, there is a lot of infrastructure in place today that otherwise would not have been there. The capital balance sheets of a lot of municipalities, particularly their utility commissions like sewer and water, are in pretty good shape as a result. They have many additional capital assets, which may not be disposable, but the liabilities against them are not great because they only had to pay one-third. So both from the federal point of view and from the municipal point of view, I think they were beneficial.

The long-term economic job creation and national and regional economic benefits may be a little bit more questionable. It was as though the municipalities were invited to a dinner and they got the appetizer but they didn't really know what the main entrée was going to be. We have the question of ports and airports and other forms of infrastructure which are not supported by the federal government. It may appear hard to justify spending money when there is going to be a payback at election time, but then allowing airports to close and things to be privatized. When something is being offered, people have the responsibility to ask questions about what is coming down the pipe and what the implications are. There is a tendency for people to say a bird in the hand is worth two in the bush.

LEO WALSH

Former Vice President,
Atlantic Canada Opportunities Agency (ACOA)

Leo Walsh has served in many capacities related to development in the Atlantic provinces. He was vice president from 1987 to 1993 of the ACOA, the federal government's development agency for the region. He was appointed secretary to the Council of Maritime Premiers in 2000.

The Atlantic Canada Opportunities Agency was designated as the delivery agent in Atlantic Canada for the national infrastructure program. We were in the best position to get out and deliver the program for the federal government. The Atlantic Canada Opportunities Agency was set up as a regional development agency to work closely with provincial governments and with the private sector in Atlantic Canada. We had people in the field, a headquarters in Atlantic Canada, in Moncton, and regional offices in the four provincial capitals. We had ongoing working relationships and other agreements with the provinces and were familiar with federal-provincial agreements. It was just a very logical extension to bring in the municipalities as a third partner and put us in charge of delivering the federal program.

We were the vehicle to transfer federal moneys. I think that other departments were identified in other regions of the country to deliver these funds in that region. You could say that the national program was regional in nature because it put infrastructure or development into each region. The program had been debated nationally in the political arena. An election had been held. The new government had made a commitment, a very public commitment, to put this program in place nationally — and quickly.

Central agencies in Ottawa are key partners in the management of government, and their intent or desire is to farm out — if I may use the expression — responsibility to various departments. Much of our discussion was about transferring the moneys and the authority out to somebody to deliver a program at the community level. A small community in Kings County is a long way from Ottawa.

We did our best collectively to identify a simple process. We tried to draw on our experience from delivering other federal-provincial agreements and our model was similar to those we had used for other programs. Our responsibility was to recommend. Final approval was beyond our level. Ultimately a decision was made. That's the way democracy works. That's the way government works, and we are lucky for it.

It was a political decision to fast-track the infrastructure program. I am not a politician, but from my perspective it seems that from time to time government looks at the economy and finds some slack or some high unemployment. They want to kick-start the economy and they look for programs. It has happened several times in the past 20 years that the government has decided to start spending public money. This time the rhetoric was that we have to create jobs for Canadians, bring down unemployment and put people back to work, and they chose this program to serve those purposes.

It certainly wasn't difficult to put this program in place. We had four members of Parliament from P.E.I. who supported the government, and they were very interested in delivering programs on behalf of the federal government. We had a new premier in P.E.I. who felt that this was an important area for provincial spending. And we had municipalities who were looking for some assistance from any level of government to improve the infrastructure of their communities. This doesn't often happen in government at any level, but this was a new government and a new program, and there was lots of enthusiasm.

When processing applications we had to try to reach consensus because there were three levels of government involved in making the decision and nobody had a veto. The important thing was to get all parties and all partners agreeing on a priority. It was that exchange of attitudes that guided you. Eventually projects were referred to the provincial system and also up the line to the federal system.

It was subjective — certainly some of it was — but there was also financial analysis and rigour and a measure of the benefits, whether political, social or economic. These things were all considered and in the end I would say perhaps 98 percent of the decisions were very good. Benefits are certainly hard to measure. What is the value of having certain amenities or facilities or improved sidewalks? What is the value of fresh, pure, clean municipal water when you have a high concentration of homes in an area where there is potential intrusion of waste and high bacteria counts? I think by and large the public got very good value for their money.

We received applications and exchanged information with different levels of government. Much of this was done in an informal manner to get some vetting of a project to see what we thought of it and to decide about its value and priority. The process was new and untested and informal. You may think that is a risky way to make decisions about spending millions of dollars, but you have to weigh that against the urgency of bringing a program forward. What is the cost of high unemployment? What is the disadvantage of taking a longer time? There had been a decade when investment in infrastructure had not been viewed as a priority.

It was a challenging job but fun at the same time. The direction for the program was not carved in stone. As a matter of fact, there was a sense that not all of the funds should go into the traditional infrastructure programs like water, sewer and waste treatment. That is a fixation or a mindset regarding investment in infrastructure that has been around since the 1970s, and there was a sense that we could be more creative in the use of the infrastructure dollar with other and perhaps longer-term benefits.

Some of these projects, like baseball fields, community halls and bowling alleys, had some short-term impacts but they have probably brought long-term benefits to communities large and small. I'm thinking of the community that built a ball field. That particular community has a wonderful reputation for hosting regional, national and even international ball tournaments. They are a destination, and that ball field has become a critical piece of tourism infrastructure that allows thousands of people to come and visit that community annually to participate in regional and national ball tournaments. There are great spin-offs beyond the ball field for the hotel operators, the restaurants and so many other people, and so it's part of our tourism business. Both short term and long term, it was a very good project.

We are always conscious of the Financial Administration Act and what the audit process requires, so we wanted to be sure that the authorities were always correct, and we could in fact go back and defend our decisions. Speaking as a public servant for probably 20 years now and as a custodian of public funds, we always have to be guided by the rules and regulations that protect us and protect the public. We ensure that the audit process is in place to account for public moneys and to hopefully demonstrate that people got good value. That is always a concern when spending the taxpayers' dollars.

The auditor general rarely writes praise. He writes observations on ways the system can be improved. The auditor's report wasn't critical about final products. He might have questioned the value, ratios in jobs created, but there is more than one way to measure and evaluate a program.

Nothing makes people happier than going to work. This program made that kind of a short-term economic impact. It created jobs for people. That means paycheques at the end of the week, which is the best test of development. It might have been expensive, as some suggest, but it achieved its objective of short-term stimulus to the economy and it created a lot of optimism. If the objective is to reduce unemployment, you push. It may be expensive and inefficient, but maybe in the end these government programs are worth it because there is an acute need.

The response to the program was certainly enthusiastic. There were numerous newspaper discussions, informal phone calls and conversations. Projects had been waiting around for a while. We had gone through a decade of significant urban growth when numerous suburbs had grown up around cities. Areas were subdivided and homes were built without the systems in place to support that residential development. So there was a need at the municipal level for sidewalks, for waste treatment, for water, for roads and bridges.

I don't share the view that when it comes to public spending, politicians and public servants have changed over time to put their own careers ahead of the public good. It would be unfortunate if that were the prevailing attitude today. I think there are many individuals who are very public-minded and very committed to serving the community. Every now and again you get the exception, or somebody is not as diligent as you might want them to be, but we should be careful not to judge the majority by the exception. I find by and large the politicians are very committed to serving the broader needs and interests of their community, and those who meet those needs have long careers.

I think in a democracy there are always political motives and political forces. That's the basis of our type of government. If we had some other kind of government, then we could look for other directions. But we are guided by political will and are responsible to that same authority. We should recognize it, be open to it and welcome it.

CHARLIE MARTELL

Chair, Georgetown and Area Development Corporation

Charlie Martell, a former mayor of Georgetown, heads the Georgetown and Area Development Corporation. The corporation receives funding from several government agencies to promote economic opportunities on P.E.I.'s eastern coast.

I was very pleased that there was going to be infrastructure money allocated for Prince Edward Island. In P.E.I. the program helped a lot of communities. I only wish that Georgetown received more money — our fair share. We tried to find out why we didn't get as much money as we anticipated. We could never get the answers.

We estimated what Georgetown needed and applied for $150,000. In the first round we applied for $50,000 for sidewalk work. We were told you couldn't do sidewalk work with the infrastructure money. Yet in the same infrastructure program the town of Parkdale got $125,000 for sidewalk work. We were asked to prioritize our infrastructure projects and they approved some of them. When the money from the first phase was allocated, we ended up only getting $40,000. I wasn't too pleased. We wrote letters to our politicians. They said to wait for the second installment of infrastructure money.

On the second application we asked for over $300,000 and ended up receiving $211,000. We were still angry. Eventually we ended up with another $200,000. The GADC (Georgetown and Area Development Corporation) applied for $60,000 to do work on a marina and a cafeteria, and the town got an extra $120,000 to do the upper room in the rink. On the second phase there was $1.8 million allocated for a sewage project in Murray River that did not go ahead. That money was redistributed. With the extra money from Murray River, we got everything that we had asked for. Had Murray River done their sewage project, we would not have received that money.

In the third phase of the infrastructure program Georgetown applied for $1 million, which was a lot of money, but they only got $13,000. The new mayor wasn't very pleased about that. Council met with the member of Parliament for Cardigan, Lawrence MacAulay. They met with the provincial officials. I think they ended up with another $150,000. I guess it really would have looked bad if they left us out. So they gave us some money to satisfy us.

I read in the auditor general's report that Seaview Estates up in Cavendish got around $750,000 to hook onto the Cavendish sewer system. That was a private business. So I went into Charlottetown to complain. I never found anything out. I didn't want to make too many waves because many times the politicians and the top bureaucrats get mad at you and I think a lot of them have long memories.

A community like Georgetown is not a fast-growing community. Our tax base is very small and it makes it hard for us. So I think a lot of these things should be taken into consideration and I think all the community wants is to be treated fairly.

When I first became mayor we had no money to operate because we owed everything. We had no money to do anything. I must give the provincial government credit because they changed the way the funding comes back to the municipalities, which gave us a lot more money. We had things to do, but we also had to pay the money we owed. I didn't want to put the community in a position where we had to go borrow a lot of money just to do work. So we lived within our means really. That's what we applied for, money that we knew we had. Well, if you were going to do $30,000 worth of street work, you could take that $30,000 and end up with $90,000 worth of infrastructure money. We worked it out that way.

In the first phase they wanted to allocate money for sewage here. At that time we didn't need any sewer work. We wanted to do other things. If you're elected in a municipality, you should know what's best for your municipality and what you want to do. I didn't like the idea of being told what had to be done. It should be left up to the municipal officials. You're elected to make decisions, so you should be able to make them.

The program certainly created quite a few jobs and it helped a lot of municipalities where normally the work wouldn't have been done. I always care about creating jobs here and especially in Georgetown. If you build buildings, you create more work than digging some sewer lines because they use a lot of major heavy equipment. As long as the products that they make for the sewer lines are made in Canada, you are going to create more work, maybe not in Prince Edward Island, but in other areas of the country.

I know we created some jobs in Georgetown. I don't know how many, but there were many people working at different jobs, small contractors. I tried to give the work to local contractors because we have no general contractors. The new building down on the waterfront was built by a local contractor that employed two people for X number of weeks. But if you asked me for a definite number of how many people worked, I'd have to look back and go over the whole thing to give you that answer. If you can create one or two full-time jobs on P.E.I., you're doing something in my book. Of the work we did, none of the jobs ended up creating any full-time jobs, which I think would be the same in a lot of cases on the island.

Over the years the federal government has spent many millions of dollars, not only in P.E.I. but also in Newfoundland, to create full-time jobs. It's not an easy thing to create full-time jobs in this part of the country. We've lost a lot of workers because of plant and fisheries closures. In two plants alone there were over 800 jobs lost. So you lose 800 jobs in Prince Edward Island; that's a heck of a big job to replace them.

In the town of Georgetown we employ people but a lot of them don't live here. Our unemployment rate is probably about the same as in a lot of communities that are involved in fishing. We don't have that many government jobs or full-time jobs. It's like any other little community and a lot of the people work 12, 14 weeks. Some work 20, 25 weeks and then they draw unemployment. It's a way of life on P.E.I. I would like to see it change. I hope I live long enough to see it change, but it hasn't over the last 25 years since I've been back here.

I think this program was a great idea, but with any program when you're spending billions of dollars, there will be a certain amount of problems. I know after reading the auditor's report for P.E.I. there was. Government almost always moves too slowly for me. I don't know how much politics was involved in the decision making. Many people said there wasn't any but it's pretty hard to believe when you live on P.E.I. where politics revolves around many things, compared to Ontario, for example. Politics is an everyday thing here. You have to live with it when you live here.

In order to determine how much infrastructure money to allocate to a province, the government allocated on population and the unemployment rate. That's fair. I think P.E.I. was quite happy with the $21 million.

There are critics who think the whole program itself was just a way for the federal government to win some accolades prior to an election. I think it all depends where the critics live. A lot of the critics living in Ontario probably wouldn't know what it's like to live in P.E.I. They may come down here on a vacation but if they come down here and they had to work for a minimum-wage job and then try to raise a family, it might do them good. Maybe they'd have a different outlook on things in the Maritimes.

There was an article the other day which some chap wrote; he thinks employment insurance should be cancelled. I think if you take that away from P.E.I., you're going to cause a lot of problems because so many people would have to move. If you're 40 years old and you have four or five kids, you're not very well educated, how do you move to another province and get a job? Some of them think it's easy but they probably haven't tried it. People who talk like that probably graduated from university, probably have had a job all of their lives and were never out of work.

I think in a lot of cases we were just happy to get the money. I never tried to get politics involved too much in municipal government anyway. I never got involved in a provincial election, but I did get involved in some federal elections by helping people. My main concern was getting some dollars to do things that normally we wouldn't be able to do. It didn't matter to me who got the credit for it, as long as we got the work done and we were helping our area.

STEVEN ELLIS

Past President, Tyne Valley Firemen's Club

As a member of the executive of Tyne Valley's recreation club, Steven Ellis was among those who went to bat for the organization's plan to build a six-lane bowling centre.

We were very short of recreational facilities in Tyne Valley and the ones we had were pretty limited in terms of who could participate. We had a hockey facility and a gymnasium at the school, but those are physically active sports.

The club was a licensed bar and we catered to an odd banquet. We needed to hit a much larger cross-section of the population. Our participation here at the club was going down. We started looking at how we could get more active in the community and make better use of the existing facilities. We started looking at offering recreational services.

The bowling alley option came as a suggestion from the membership. We started checking into the actual sport of bowling. It appealed to us because it is available to any age group and any fitness level.

The entire project, including the renovations to the facility and everything else, would probably cost in the area of $620,000. We felt in order to go ahead with it, it was probably too expensive for us to take that kind of a commitment on. The club has been involved very heavily in providing firefighting equipment and those sorts of needs. We're looking at replacing a new pumper, and to make a commitment beyond that was just not a possibility for us.

It wouldn't have happened without the infrastructure money. We made an application to the Canada Infrastructure Works Program and an application to P.E.I. Economic Development. We did get approved for a portion of it through ACOA. It was really a two-stage thing because we get a partial approval, which is $100,000 from the federal government and $100,000 from the provincial government, under the infrastructure program.

We took our plans to the community and they supported the idea of spending this money on a bowling alley. I don't think they had done any great deal of planning on it. When we stepped in they gave us priority.

Nobody really asked a lot of questions. There were questions about funding, but we felt that if we could achieve that level of funding from the infrastructure program and P.E.I. Economic Development, then we could do it. But we had set a target number for ourselves as to our level of commitment and if we didn't get to that number, we weren't going ahead. We took a look at what our possible increases in revenue and so on were and basically set our margin of safety — what we could afford to pay.

In the village of Tyne Valley, Rod MacNeil is the chair. Rod has a bit more background on the business side of things than I do. Under his coaching I learned a little bit. With the infrastructure program, we realized there would probably be an enormous number of applications. We looked upon it as competition and developed a package that expressed our ideas. For our application we had done up a package which gave our history and a little broader range of what we planned on doing. Then we got into the actual numbers, like feasibility study and the demographics. We wanted to answer as many questions as possible.

I had some conversations with local politicians. We approached our local MP, Joe MacGuire, and we approached our provincial member.

We had to sell them on the idea of a bowling alley as infrastructure because they hadn't thought of it in those terms before. I think they were skeptical at first but we had done a lot of research. A lot of work went into this before we sat down with any of the politicians. We tried to provide as much information as possible then stuck it in the pot and crossed our fingers and hoped we'd done our homework well. And apparently we did.

Is it infrastructure? I don't know. There are a vast number of definitions on it. For most people, they say infrastructure is sewer lines, water lines and roads. For a rural community like us that's very limiting. My definition of infrastructure is dependent on the community's needs. If you have a need for roads, sewer and water, then that's what it is. But do you limit the needs of communities to roads, water and sewer? Would you build a road to nowhere? If you're going to build a road, you have to have someplace to go. We're trying to make that someplace to go. What stage of development is there in a community? Where does it start and where does it end?

Our opinion is that for our rural communities to survive, we have to provide services. We want to be able to provide services and make it a nice place to live. In the case of the municipality of Tyne Valley, they didn't really need the infrastructure money for any hard projects.

Some people may drive down the road and see the potholes and figure that's where the money should have been spent. But I think, as a non-profit organization, our willingness to invest in our own community certainly sends out a signal that we don't think that Tyne Valley's going to shrink up and go away. We think there's a good future here. It's an optimistic view.

Rural communities, we've got to fight, we've got to claw to make our voice heard. If you don't fight, then maybe somebody'll look after you and maybe they won't.

In terms of the jobs to project created, I would say the average here for the period of construction was probably between 12 and 14 people on site for an average of 12 weeks. Activity of any kind is good here. One job is good. But this was quite a large project for this community. If it were in my control, I would want to see everybody with long-term jobs, but that's not the reality. I know of nobody that wants to work only 12 weeks of the year. I don't like short-term jobs but they're better than nothing.

We've created two full-time positions here. And two part-time positions. And the two full-time positions — there's a certain amount of skill involved in them. We had five weeks of training for the maintenance person and also five weeks on the management side of it, so it's a year-round job. We're pretty pleased that we're able to do that. Hopefully it grows in the future.

CHAPTER 3

THE ACADEMIC ROUNDTABLE

If we don't take care of infrastructure, we suffer.

Our researchers set out to contact people who could comment on the Canada Infrastructure Works Program and to gain a view from the grassroots. We hoped that this research would culminate in an empirical assessment of the way citizens are treated when they approach government to ask how and why spending decisions are made. No one had tried to understand public policy issues that touched on all three levels of government in this way.

One convention that the researchers were asked to ignore was the reliance on academic commentators. We feared that the reliance on an expert's opinion might be used as a crutch that would prevent the researchers from slogging through the intensive legwork at the municipal- and provincial-government levels. We wanted to gather raw data that could be used to form our own opinions. That way we could compare the various ways the researchers were received and contrast their findings. This new method of journalism hinged on the information-gathering process as much as on the information the researchers dug up.

But the information our team obtained from those who actually worked on the CIWP, or who questioned its effectiveness, was often contradictory. It varied from one political party to another, from one province to another, and even among people we spoke to about the same project. Because of the quick decision-making turnarounds, the politics at play in almost every aspect of the program and the many questions surrounding the measurement of job creation, we resorted to experts for help.

We decided to seek out two academics who took part in studies and debates over our country's infrastructure needs prior to the infrastructure program's start-up. A third academic was approached to help us understand the government's job-creation figures and the future costs of the program.

In Montreal we met Professor M. Saeed Mirza, co-author of *Canadian Municipal Infrastructure — The Present State* (1996), a report assessing the cost of the country's infrastructure needs. The report was sponsored by the Federation of Canadian Municipalities. Dr. Mirza, Canada's foremost expert on infrastructure, was dismayed that the program had strayed so far from its original intent and instead had become primarily a job-creation program. He warned that procrastination when it came to traditional infrastructure repairs would only increase the costs to future generations and said the short-term nature of the program prevented a thorough analysis on the costs and the benefits of each project.

At the University of British Columbia we spoke with economist John Helliwell, the author of the conference summary from the 10th John Deutsch Roundtable on Economic Policy (1993), which focused on infrastructure and competitiveness. The summary is entitled *Infrastructure and the Economy: Evidence and Implications*. He warned us that there would be little government interest in assessing the CIWP after the six-year program. Helliwell said there are no rewards for identifying mistakes and exposing glitches such as the fact that theatres were competing with bridges for funding. His comments were encouraging because we realized that our citizens' audit of a spending program was unique.

At the University of Manitoba economist Milton Boyd brought home the true costs of the program. Professor Boyd questioned the benefits of these types of job-creation programs, from the expense of the signs that attached the political credit to each of the 17,000 projects, to the long-term debts that governments incurred to access their "free money."

M. SAEED MIRZA

Professor of Engineering, McGill University

Professor Mirza is a member of McGill University's civil engineering and applied mechanics department. He co-authored Report on the State of Municipal Infrastructure in Canada *(1996) and is an active member of the Canadian Society for Civil Engineering.*

Infrastructure has been defined in different ways by different people. I guess it depends on how you've been trained. A political scientist might define infrastructure much more broadly than I would, but to me infrastructure would be everything that makes us live happily, efficiently and comfortably. If you look at our roads, for example — we need roads to go from our place of living to our place of work, for shopping, etc. Water supply and sewage systems, communication systems, various transportation systems — all of these should come in. Where you could distinguish is the difference between hard infrastructure, which I just described, and soft infrastructure — places like skating rinks and libraries in cities.

That's the only distinction I would make, but I think hard infrastructure is the one that defines the quality of life for all of us and that stays with us. It just doesn't stop after a period of five or six years; it has to be maintained continuously. Therefore I think it is the responsibility of the government to state that, just as there are policies for health and education, there should be a national infrastructure policy. It should state that every Canadian citizen shall be entitled to decent roads, safe water supply and safe disposal of sewage. These kinds of policies need to be established. We realize that the funding is not there, and therefore the question would be, how do we fund this? But that's the second issue. I think that governments should perhaps get together immediately and define what we need as a society.

If you look at the surveys of the Federation of Canadian Municipalities of 1985 and 1992, they saw there was significant need in the areas of streets, bridges, sidewalks, water supplies and sewage disposal systems. In 1985 the total infrastructure deficit was $12 billion, but in 1992 it went up to $20 billion. An infrastructure deficit is the difference between the amount of moneys that are available right now to ameliorate our infrastructure, and what it would take to renovate it up to an acceptable level. At the same time the provincial premiers were trying to push the federal government to initiate infrastructure programs. But the Conservative government just did not agree, and therefore when the Liberals came to power they created the Canada Infrastructure Works Program with $6 billion over six years.

We developed a detailed questionnaire in consultation with the Federation of Canadian Municipalities. They have a technical activities committee who reviewed our questionnaire, and we asked very detailed questions on all aspects of infrastructure — financing, technical details. The return rate was 58 percent. In terms of response it was excellent. Based on that, what we found was that it would take about $1,500 per person in Canada just to bring the infrastructure up to an acceptable level. And this worked out to about $44 billion.

In our study we looked at the reasons why infrastructure is in its present condition. One of the reasons that came from all regions of Canada was that there wasn't enough money. The municipalities were short of money, the federal and provincial governments were following their zero-deficit policies, and as a consequence there would have to be other solutions to enable us to work toward the improvement of infrastructure.

The positive aspect of the Canada Infrastructure Works Program was the injection of a large sum of money at a time it was needed. Our economy was low, the construction industry was slow, and therefore it really helped. But there were problems with the way the program was brought in. They didn't look at all the issues. Of course the Liberal government was concerned about international trade, as you have seen from the various international missions that Prime Minister Jean Chrétien has led. So they wanted the infrastructure to be improved, but at the same time the emphasis was on trying to create jobs.

If the federal government, along with the provincial governments who were their partners, were genuinely concerned about the state of infrastructure in Canada, they would not have conceived such a program over such a short period. The program was implemented so quickly, all the municipalities could do was to bring in the projects that were already on their books. They didn't have any time for consultation as to what projects might be useful, or where the real needs were, and they could not involve the private sector. There was no time to bring in the innovative technologies that have developed over the past 10 years. The Government of Quebec was avant-garde in this respect, and they introduced a $25-million program where there were partnerships created to take advantage of innovative technologies in trying to improve the infrastructure.

So there were both positive and negative aspects. There was money, but at the same time the municipalities would have spent this money anyway, let's say five years or 10 years from now. So the final advantage might not be there, but the problem is that, as they say in one of the reports, it was boom and then bust.

All of the municipalities work out their needs based on surveys of infrastructure, and the visible parts like roads and sidewalks get attended to right away. There are other infrastructure facilities like water supply systems and sewage systems which receive much less attention. Unfortunately the politicians want to make their political points over their four- or five-year term, so they concentrate on areas which are visible, and what is out of sight is out of mind. The result is that the water supply and sewage systems get the least attention, to the extent that there are several provinces where the pipes are so deteriorated and perforated that about 35 or 50 percent of purified water is being lost. This is *after* purification.

That's a loss of money, so one has to look at the business aspects of it because we have spent money purifying the water. What should we do?

Why shouldn't our pipelines be in a reasonably good condition, from an economic and also from a health point of view? If there are perforations in the pipes, you don't know what is coming in, what is contaminating the water that you and I drink. If we are losing water or if our sewage is flowing out of the sewers, we don't see it. But it might come back to haunt us later on, in terms of our health. See, we have to go beyond the politicians' goals of a short-term duration to long-range goals which would come through the administration of the municipalities.

What has led to the municipalities' lack of credibility is the Federation of Canadian Municipalities survey, which stressed needs and the infrastructure deficit. When they were given this money on a one-third-share basis, they saw it as manna from heaven, and they spent it on whatever they wanted. The result is that only about 40 percent of the total money was spent in renovating the infrastructure, and the remaining 60 percent was used for building some new infrastructure.

When a city's facility department, or the infrastructure department, goes to the municipal council to ask for money, saying, "Look, we have to renovate this road this year," the first question the councillors ask is, "Can it wait until next year?" The engineer thinks about it, and they arrive at a consensus after some discussion that, yes, it could wait. It waits one year, it waits a second year, it waits a third year. Finally, five or six years from then, the deterioration has gone to such an extent that one ends up spending five or 10 times the money one would have spent initially. Deterioration is like cancer: once it sets in, it grows at a very rapidly increasing rate.

Because of lack of funding, municipal maintenance programs have been cut back, or what they call "deferred." Deferred simply means they won't do it now, but they might do it five years from now or later — or never. So that deferment has really cost us, and the costs involved have been increasing. In some municipalities the population has decreased. If we just look at the principle of sustainable development, we want to make sure that the capacity of any infrastructure is completely utilized before we build any new infrastructure. Therefore any planning and development in these regions should be such that we use up the local capacity available now, and then build anything needed. But we have to keep in mind that costs will always keep on increasing, and our total tax base, or the money base that is available, is just not adequate to deal with this.

The problem occurs when infrastructure becomes a political issue: an election is coming up and therefore a goodie has to be thrown to the voters. Now, what unfortunately happens is that the governments or the private organizations, all they think about is what kind of investment would be needed to build an infrastructure facility like a bridge, a water supply system or whatever. They give no thought to what will happen later on. How will this be maintained? Ten or 15 years from now, will there be any need for any major rehabilitation? For example, if there is a bridge and the new codes increase the load allowed on the bridge, will this bridge be able to withstand the new loads? Will it have to be strengthened, will there have to be changes? We don't think about these things.

It's very scary. Right now we are paying some municipal taxes, we are paying our taxes to the provincial and federal governments, but I'd hate to see what our children and our grandchildren will have to pay for their roads. Worse than that, our water supply and sewage disposal systems will be in much worse condition by then. We will need a lot more money to renovate and rebuild these, and the result is that future generations will have to pay. To ignore this is irresponsible of the present governments — federal, provincial and municipal — and even of the private sector.

Our banks and insurance companies, over the last few years they have made profits of well over $1 billion each. All it would take is some incentive from the federal and the provincial governments to encourage these private institutions to invest money, perhaps in a national infrastructure bank from which we could give low-interest or no-interest funds to different provinces and municipalities for various infrastructure works. And the government could provide the difference. This could cost much less than $200 million for all parties involved, for every $1 billion spent. And it could be easily handled.

To look at the history of infrastructure in Canada, let's go back to the time when Confederation was conceived. At that time the politicians wanted to connect the east end of Canada with the west end using railways, and the federal government provided most of the funds. The investment involved was very large, and the private sector may not have been able to afford that kind of risk. Therefore the government had to be involved. But now, if you look at many areas of infrastructure, railways included, in the States, for example, there are many railways that are privatized. For that matter our own CN Rail has acquired a railway line way down south, near New Orleans. So there are examples where infrastructure is privatized, and perhaps that is the way to go in the future.

If you look at the issue of cost-benefit analysis for the various projects in the Canada Infrastructure Works Program, there was no time to do it. But I think in any responsible organization this should be undertaken. You or I or any politician, if we want to run a business, we would look at the total cost and the benefits that we'll get out of it. The municipalities should have done this. The expenditure of a large sum of money without consideration for the benefits accruing on it is irresponsible.

Any civil engineering graduate from McGill, and for that matter from any Canadian university, would look at the cost and benefits right away for a given project. If you look at the private sector, which has been involved in dealing with some projects like the Confederation Bridge in P.E.I. or Highway 407 in Ontario, they have carried out detailed cost-benefit analyses of these projects — otherwise they would not have invested the kind of money they did. If you're going to spend $6.5 billion over five or six years, I think it's imperative to go through a cost-benefit analysis, even if it takes some time.

A survey in Australia shows that the total costs of business include about 15 percent relating directly to infrastructure. In Canada it would be about the same. Any large business spends about 15 to 20 percent that is directly related to infrastructure, and therefore every organization should be concerned with infrastructure. Otherwise we have a national wealth which we'll gradually lose.

So what we have to do is adopt the principles of life-cycle cost, which would mean that right from the time the project is conceived and the feasibility studies are undertaken we have to ensure that it is maintained properly. We have to ensure that down the line, when there is a need for rehabilitation of all infrastructure, that that happens. And last of all, when the facility has outlived its useful life we have to dispose of it. How do we do that? Because we have to dump it somewhere. The best thing would be to recycle; first of all reduce, reuse and recycle. For example, with roads, old asphalt and concrete can be broken up and used as aggregates. And new technologies are coming.

At the same time I think there has to be a close collaboration between the engineering community — which has to think in a very avant-garde manner, dealing with the total life-cycle costs — and the governments, who are the ones that give out the contracts. In most of North America a contract goes to the lowest bidder, irrespective of their experience. So I think one has to pre-qualify these contractors, to ensure that they are able to do a particular kind of job, and then from there on ensure the principles of life-cycle costs and sustainable development.

In terms of international competitiveness, if we have good infrastructure, the result would be that new industries would like to locate themselves in these areas. When new industries come in, of course, there's more tax base, there are other facilities, and the quality of life generally improves. For example, there is a move in Canada right now to have a highway. A fair investment in the highway is being recommended somewhere between $12 billion and $18 billion. This highway will promote the transport of goods and services from east to west, and also from north to south with the programs developed through NAFTA. This would increase our competitiveness, but if we don't take care of infrastructure, we suffer on many grounds. If we lose productivity right now, we'll lose many industries that might want to move to areas where they could carry on their operations more efficiently and economically.

Vis-à-vis the role of politicians, one point I would like to stress is what has happened in the United States. If you look at the issues of infrastructure rehabilitation and sustainable development, Vice President Al Gore has been directly involved and President Bill Clinton has been very supportive of these, and I think the prime minister and the premiers have a lesson to learn from the politicians in the States in paying more attention to the whole area. Personally I would like to volunteer to give one- or two-day courses in Ottawa and every one of the provincial capitals so that we can raise the awareness of the politicians. They just don't know.

In 1996 I wrote a fairly detailed note to Prime Minister Chrétien sort of defining the state of infrastructure to him, which obviously he must have known. I outlined what kind of investment was needed in the infrastructure — of course praising the Liberal government for the infrastructure program in the process, but also indicating to them that the needs in Canada were great, and that if we didn't do anything now, our costs would double, triple, quadruple and even increase exponentially. I sketched some curves as to how the costs would go, but the prime minister never even acknowledged my letter. I sent copies of the letter to every premier, and the premiers responded, some very warmly, stating that there is a strong need in this area right now.

Then during the last federal election, when I noticed that none of the politicians talked about the infrastructure the way they did in the 1993 elections, I wrote a detailed note to the leader of each political party, and the only one that acknowledged my note was the leader of the Conservatives at the time, Jean Charest. So I just wonder whether this is really an issue with the politicians. That's why Prime Minister Chrétien is saying that there's no money for infrastructure. Obviously they don't think it's a concern. Of course, they don't know what's going to happen in the future.

At McGill University, over five years or so we've initiated courses in the area of infrastructure renovation, debility of structures, materials, etc. And students have been taking a keen interest in it. I also give a course in the general category of the impact of technology on society. It's called "Infrastructure and Society," and we deal with issues of sustainable development, socioeconomic, legal and political issues, financial issues, how to raise money and so on. The last time I gave the course one student came to me and said, "Look, I've been studying engineering for the past seven years. Now I'm able to relate to all of the issues that are involved. This puts the civil engineering profession, or whatever I'm going to do, in the context of the needs of society and how we're going to deal with it."

I would like to see every student take this course or a similar one, but unfortunately it's an elective and some people wouldn't take it. But about 10 percent of the students are coming out with an outstanding awareness of the issues. If we can send out some people, they can propagate the word and say, "If we don't take care of our infrastructure now, what's going to happen?" They're becoming more socially responsible and looking at the issues in a global context, not just the narrow engineering context.

In this infrastructure course we spend about four or five lectures on value engineering, which looks at the various options that are available for a given project, and looks at all aspects of cost and benefits. We look at this totally, not just from an economic point of view but also from social and technical perspectives. There are some things that might not be feasible. So we look at the global picture and then try to decide what is the best alternative.

As I said, our estimate for the cost of bringing infrastructure up to an acceptable level was $44 billion. If we don't do it now and wait for five to 10 years, it could easily be $100 billion. And if you still wait, it could be a lot more. But at some stage we may not be able to repair it. We'll have to replace it, which would be a much costlier option. Our responsibility is to ensure that we look at infrastructure in a very rational manner so that future generations don't end up paying 10 times what we might end up paying now. We may eliminate our federal deficit 10, 15, 20 years from now. We may eliminate the provincial deficits. In the process we are creating a monster — the infrastructure deficit.

JOHN HELLIWELL

Professor of Economics, University of British Columbia

As a past president of the Canadian Economics Association, John Helliwell has done a great deal of research in comparative macroeconomics, including growth and international linkages.

There's an essential "short-termism" that you find everywhere among people who are responsible for important, big decisions. They want benefits soon. They don't want long-delayed benefits. Typically the returns from a clear-cut evaluation project will allow you to more clearly define the long-term benefits, but not the short-term ones. The short-term ones are often as plain as the nose on your face. The real ranking of projects changes when you look out further into the future. That's what takes more effort, but looking back at past projects would repay.

The thing about infrastructure spending is that a piece of road or a building or an education is bought and somebody expects the benefits are going to be widely spread. To evaluate it is inherently difficult because some of the benefits are never priced. They're never charged to anybody, so you can't measure them as revenues. You have to go and take some often rather complicated steps to try and figure out just what the overall advantages are.

Sometimes the more difficult the assessment, the better the investment because the gains are very widely distributed. When serious attempts are made to look at the costs and benefits of a number of physical investment projects — human investment projects — often you can see very sharp rankings from the top to the bottom. Unfortunately it's possible, once these assessments are done seriously, to discover a great deal of dross in the mix.

A problem is bound to exist where each jurisdiction's got its own shopping list. Sometimes they're almost accidental differences. You could find somebody midway up in your decision chain saying, "I think this project's got a better chance of going through on the infrastructure grant. We'll handle this other one on some other device." Some projects could end up getting support when, if you'd put everyone together in a room and ranked these projects from top to bottom, you might have got a different answer.

Something about the CIWP decision process I don't understand is how they got re-ranked differently at the upper level. I have no way of knowing because I wasn't on hand when the decisions were made. I've had a lot of experience in the transportation sector on the evaluation of various projects. Typically the decisions do not depend heavily on the assessments that are made of the costs and benefits. In the transportation sector it's very easy to make those assessments. You know almost kilometre by kilometre which highway projects have the high return and which ones don't. In the national highway system, which was an important part of the shopping list for those who wanted support under the infrastructure program, there are some very high-return components and some very low-return components.

To make a judgment that this decision process wasn't political, you'd have to have evidence that all the high-return investments were done and the low-return investments were not. You need to go back afterwards and compare how they really looked. Then you could make an easy judgment about how political the process was.

Usually difficulties about assessing the costs and benefits are raised by those who don't want to see the answers, who are throwing up their hands and saying, "This is too tough a job" — not by those who are seriously trying to do it. The reason is that the ranking curves for the projects often turn out to be so steep that you can take almost any of the uncertainties and double them or triple them, then attach it to this external benefit, and you still leave the rankings more or less unchanged. Some of the bottleneck-removing investments — third runways at Vancouver and Pearson airports, for example — measure way, way up there. If they don't get done, it is politics. It's not because of the cost-benefit ratio, even taking into account any measure of noise-reduction costs. There are other major highway expansion schemes in areas of low traffic where there's nothing you can do in terms of the advantages — accident reduction or anything — that will convert those into anything but bad uses of the taxpayers' dollars.

To achieve transparency is not simply a question of having disclosure of information, rules that mean all questions have to be answered. What you really need is a system that produces enough information about decisions — information that usually ends up in dry library files or in an Internet site — plus reports after the fact that allow anyone who's interested to see what the consequences were.

The standards of documentation before the decision are usually pretty limited. Assessments of projects afterwards are almost nonexistent. This is not a question of bad government. The same is true throughout the business sector. I once did a very extensive study of how capital expenditure decisions on corporate infrastructure are made in the business sector. I found very similar things. For example, detailed rates-of-return rules that were continually overridden because something was thought to be strategic or important or fitted in with somebody's idea of what needed doing. Post-audits, whereby the actual rates of return were looked at afterwards, were almost nonexistent. These were, after all, in companies whose main objective was a bottom line. Is it any surprise that there's even less of this in the government sector, where the bottom line is much less easy to define? They're providing a whole range of things that aren't priced services.

Systematic pre-evaluation of expenditures and post-evaluation of returns is done very little in both the public sector and in business. Now, is that a good thing? No, it isn't a good thing. The people who make decisions would make better future decisions if they spent more time looking backwards and finding out what the consequences were of past decisions.

It has essentially been a question of lack of incentives. People make their own cost-benefit calculations. Where am I best spending my time? Do I really want to look at all those old bridge projects and discover that I was only right two times out of 10? Or am I better to try and get a sharper pencil and look at the projects more carefully this time? People only think about things as hard as they're forced to. After you've pushed these projects through, somebody should go back and look at past projects. But when do you have the time to do it? The immediate pressure is to make the next decision.

One way of judging fairness might be that each block of population ought to get back their share of the federal dollars. That's one way of dividing the kitty. Infrastructure could be located in one city but really serve the whole province. You might regard tertiary-care hospital facilities that way, or provincial airports and so on. You might want to think of that benefit as if it were coming out of the share of the whole province's citizens rather than just the people where the physical facilities were located.

It doesn't surprise me that you see fewer roads and sewer investments in the big cities. It doesn't surprise me that you'd find hard items — roads or sewers or waterworks — appearing at the top of the list somewhere and further down somewhere else. The newer communities are more likely to be strapped for the cash for the hard facilities. The major cities with a good established tax base have regular programs for their roads and sewers and they have a reasonably good tax structure to raise the money to do it. There's no particular reason why they need new outside funds in order to get those things happening. For them there's more appeal to launch a project that will be partially funded from outside investment, something they would have trouble getting fully out of their own property tax dollars.

I take a very broad view of infrastructure. Ideally you want money put where it'll last a long time. It doesn't matter so much whether it's theatre building or roadway building. In the past infrastructure has included all public assets, whether they be roads or buildings. Increasingly it's more broadly defined. It is no surprise that when the time came to think about renewing it, the government said, "Let's talk more broadly about infrastructure and talk about knowledge infrastructure."

I don't think they've even gone far enough yet. They should really be talking about knowledge in terms of what's in people's heads, not the nature of the repair of the buildings that they're taking those classes in. You've got theatres competing with bridges. That poses some complications for people who hadn't thought of a theatre as infrastructure. But then they're in a different province, where theatres weren't included in the list. So you get these non-comparabilities that are inevitably part of what a federal system's going to produce.

If there was a narrowing in the definition of infrastructure as the program developed, it probably was in response to some of the projects that were wider. It may be that the broader you get, the harder it is to do good assessments. Or it may simply be that it's easier to make fun of some of the broader projects than some of the narrower ones. Some of the examples that were made fun of in Phase I were not classic infrastructure, in the sense of the municipal building.

If they really had a narrow base in the first place, then it's unnecessarily and unfairly complicating to then sneak something in the back door. If it looks too much like it's benefiting the cronies of somebody making the decision, then that's going to cause a political backlash. That's what politics is for. The politics are a good part of the game for everybody.

Even if assessments are made, it's often hard to get them taken seriously. You end up finding a lot of actual infrastructure projects — whether part of a special program or just done as a run-of-the-mill part of the department's operations — putting the taxpayers' money to not very good use. It didn't get raised in public debates in a way that I ever saw. Typically the more understated and objective a piece of research is, the less likely it is to get a lot of camera time, and in turn, public discussion. Nuts-and-bolts evaluations of infrastructure are much less discussed.

The systematic evaluation of projects is always much easier when there's a single decision maker. If your job is to build the most effective road system and you've got to raise money directly from the taxpayers to do it, you're going to watch your pennies pretty carefully. That way you make sure you can go to the voters or the gas buyers or whoever is paying for the system and say, "Look, we've done a pretty good and effective job for you," and you can be convincing about it.

Once too many people start sharing in the financing, it gets pretty complicated. There would probably be at least one or two of the three parties involved who didn't want too much of a detailed evaluation of investment. In a better world than the one we're in, this multiple decision making would have led to a more formal set of rules. Then everybody could go away happy and say they'd done a good job for the taxpayers. They would make sure that none of the really good projects are being sacrificed on the altar of somebody's special treat.

I'm really optimistic that the assessment of the infrastructure projects is being done in a sensible way. Most of the serious attempts to value their benefits show that there is a lot to choose between the best projects, the average projects and the worst projects. It is possible to find some wonderful projects and to get funds invested in them.

The pessimism comes because often there are a lot of other projects that have more politics going for them — local supporters and bad numbers. That means a lot of people don't want to see a methodical assessment of the cost and benefits. Nobody wants too many auditors chasing around because inevitably it's much easier for the media to focus on the ones that didn't turn out, not the ones that did. There may be a bit of a fear that detailed evaluations will end up causing all the emphasis to be on the bad projects. Indeed, you might say that some of the more casual evaluation of the infrastructure project has focused not on average returns or on whether the projects generally were good. They focused just on particular features of the process that may or may not be very widespread, but that caused people some grief.

People who look at these things say that if you didn't make any really stupid mistakes in the past, you weren't doing your job. It meant you were being so safe that you almost surely missed huge ranges of really good investments in order to stop yourself from making one bad investment. If the assessment process eventually turns out where you get so much blame for the bad ones, and that you don't get proper credit for the good ones, then that's an additional reason why people will be afraid of a systematic post-evaluation. They'll say, "Let the people just look at the average and see whether they're happy with life and their role in it. They elect us."

MILTON BOYD

Professor of Economics, University of Manitoba

Professor Boyd's research centres around futures markets and risk management.

I t's very difficult to determine how many jobs were created in the infrastructure program. As economists we don't have good enough formulas to produce these numbers. We also have to ask, are all jobs created equally? In other words, if we pay someone to do a short-term job for a few months, is that different than providing a job for 30 years or so?

Another question that we have to look at is the productivity issue. Is job creation our goal? Or is having a productive economy our goal? If having a productive economy is our goal, then we put the consumer needs first. We ask the consumer how they would like their dollars spent. When they vote and spend their dollars as they wish or when they pay their taxes or however they spend their money, then they have made their decision. In that process jobs are created. So if we simply make our goal to create jobs, we may be misallocating our resources and not creating the industries that we desire.

Many people have job-creation formulas and you'll get a wide range of estimates on any given program. In other words, if you spend one dollar, how much does this create in terms of jobs? It's very controversial. Taken to an extreme, I think we could see that the more money you spend, the more jobs you create. Ultimately we would be spending 100 percent of our income toward taxes for creation of jobs, possibly through the government. Taken to an extreme, we have a complete socialist-type economy with the government running everything. Through an extreme of spending some money to create some jobs and then more money to create more jobs, it breaks down at a certain point. Then we have the government as too big a part of the economy.

Whenever there's a public-spending project available, all other things being equal, we would like that project to create as many jobs as possible. Many of these formulas have been criticized for being overly optimistic in the numbers and the quality of jobs they'll create.

You have to look at what opportunity cost is. This is the idea that if we spend a dollar on one thing, then we can't spend it on another thing. So my generation spends a dollar today but has to borrow it. Then the next generation has to pay it back. So if I haven't spent that borrowed dollar wisely, I've done a disservice to future generations.

In terms of the national debt, we have come to the point where we're taking in as much money each year as we're spending. We've built up the debt over the past 25 years or so to $600 billion. If we divide that by 30 million people in our country, we come out to about $20,000 each. Thinking of that another way, a family of four would have a mortgage of $80,000. Or when a new child is born in Canada, they come with a stone around their neck, a mortgage that they drag around of $20,000.

If you borrow a dollar today at an interest rate of eight percent, in 30 years you'll have to pay back $10. When we borrow that dollar it's very important that it is invested and not consumed, so to speak. So when we approach infrastructure projects, it means that we want a building or a road that will be around for future generations to use. We have to be able to justify the debt we've run up, in terms of the life of that road we'd be building.

One of the problems with infrastructure spending is that we don't have as good a set of priorities as we should have. When a business spends money on capital, on its infrastructure, they know that the plant will last a certain number of years, and after that plant's life is over they will have to build a new plant and facilities for manufacturing. So they do planning and cost-benefit analysis.

We need to consider the cost-benefit analysis and planning for an infrastructure project, just as the private sector does for its projects. We need priorities. We need to see how much the public wants these projects. What is their ranking of them? Then after they're built we want to perform an audit — at least on some of the larger projects — to see if they were built, how well they were built and how well they've been received by the public. What the public is often looking for is more transparency, more opportunity to see if their tax dollars are being spent on the infrastructure in the ways they wish the money to be spent.

The government faces the same question that we do as families or individuals. We have a dollar and what are we going to do with that dollar? Are we going to invest it so that in 30 years we have something to show for that dollar? Or are we going to consume it now and enjoy the short-term pleasure of that dollar? As individuals we strike a balance and each of us strikes that balance differently. But when it comes to the government, we have an obligation to future generations. If we take a dollar today and if we spend that public dollar, the future generations have only a debt for that dollar that we borrowed. We have consumed everything. On the other hand, if we're spending that toward investment, then future generations have a bridge or a building that they need. They have something to show. It's a long-term product rather than short-term consumption. We tend to think facilities we use for leisure more as consumption goods than investment, whether it be a tennis court or a golf course.

Our true goal should be to please the consumers' needs. The consumer has to decide how they want that money spent, how much infrastructure and public spending they want. Job creation becomes the result of what the consumer wants or desires, not the goal.

If we were a family planning to cook dinner, we would first decide what we want for dinner. Then we could calculate how many people we need to cook the dinner. In a family we have other responsibilities. The house needs to be cleaned. The yard needs to be cleaned. We don't want a whole bunch of people in the kitchen cooking dinner when they don't need to be. They could be doing something more productive, and we'd prefer that. The same analogy applies for job creation and the economy. Job creation cannot be our goal or we will misallocate our resources.

We have to go back and look at what the forefathers of our country intended originally. I think they intended a smaller form of government in this country. As a result, a lot of controls were not put in to police the spending. They never envisioned that half of our economy would be geared toward government spending. We spend half of our year paying taxes. I think in the future we'll be called on as citizens to emphasize controls on spending. It could be a constitutional limit of a certain dollar amount or a certain share of the economy. After we have spending controlled, then we have to establish priorities and decide how to spend that money.

Our forefathers did not foresee that we would need to police this so closely. That's why today we can't. So it's left up to politicians to allocate spending as they see fit after we elect them. Unfortunately, as citizens we're unable to account very specifically for how our dollar was spent.

We have it backwards to some extent. We have made job creation the goal of our society rather than making a productive economy the goal. If we make a productive economy the goal, the jobs will result. If we make the jobs the goal, then we'll misallocate the resources. We will have the wrong types of jobs, or jobs in the wrong area.

We have it backwards because we want as high a standard of living as possible in Canada. People have to be working in certain sectors of the economy in order for us to achieve that. But if we allocate them to a certain part of the economy or to a certain job that we as individual citizens don't choose, then this will lower our standard of living.

In a market economy, a Western-style economy, our goal is a high standard of living. Jobs are the result. The fewer people that we have, for example, making cars, then the more we can have making computers or TVs or producing food. So business starts with using as few people as possible to produce a good. Then those excess people can go to other industries and produce goods that we need. On the other hand, if we take a socialist or a planned economy, their goal is to create a job for everyone. The only problem is, they're not employed according to a high productivity scale. So society has a low standard of living, even though everyone has a job. You might say that in our society we are unequally rich. In a planned economy they tend to be equally poor.

The cost of the individual signs erected at infrastructure program project sites has been calculated at roughly $1,000. When you build another sign, you're going into more debt. So that sign costs you $1,000 today at eight percent interest. If you pay that sign off in 30 years through more government borrowing, it will cost you 10 times as much as today. That $1,000 sign, it becomes a cost of $10,000.

If you take that across the country, you can multiply it by roughly 15,000 signs. If you assume an interest rate of eight percent over 30 years, you'll multiply the figure by 10. So the initial cost of $15 million then would become $150 million. That's what would have to be paid back in the end. The taxpayer has to take a look and see how much of their dollar they want spent on signs or on sandcastles or whatever they want built. At some point they have to draw a line in the sand, so to speak, and make their decision.

We can take the equation even further and apply it to the cost of the entire infrastructure program, which is $8.5 billion. If you assumed an interest rate of eight percent and you take that over 30 years, you will have to pay back $85 billion for your infrastructure.

CHAPTER 4

MANITOBA

Politics played an enormous part.

Our efforts in Manitoba brought us in contact with one of the more interesting characters we met during our travels. Bill Comaskey is the mayor of Thompson. He had had a huge battle with both the province and the federal government over what he saw as their efforts to cut him out of the loop when it came time to take credit for a big Thompson infrastructure project. The question was, who would get their name on the plaque celebrating the renovation of a sewer system for a subdivision?

From what these interviews tell us, it seems that all levels of government, particularly the federal government, were very interested in capitalizing on the public relations benefits from the Infrastructure Works Program. Comaskey's interview paints an unflattering portrait of a federal government that vied aggressively for what it saw as its right to cut the ribbons, turn the sod and take a lead role in all of the good photo-ops. It invested a lot of time and money putting up signs and plaques testifying to the government's generosity, raising the question: did more planning go into the CIWP public relations effort than into the process of project selection?

Dan Kelly from the Canadian Federation of Independent Business gave us a "big picture" perspective of the CIWP. He said the idea for an infrastructure program was a good one, but the CIWP had allowed itself to become far too broad in the types of projects it approved. Manitoba had permitted a wide variety of projects to go ahead which didn't fit the traditional infrastructure mould. Items like golf courses and community centres received a large piece of the CIWP pie in Manitoba, despite the fact that Winnipeg's sewer system was springing leaks all over the place.

Jae Eadie, a former president of the Federation of Canadian Municipalities who was active in getting the CIWP off the ground, spoke about how the infrastructure program evolved and how it played out in Winnipeg. Juergen Hartmann explained how Winnipeg used infrastructure money to revive an existing program, providing short-term jobs for unemployed construction workers.

Anette Mueller was our Manitoba researcher. She was just finishing her journalism degree at Red Deer Community College in Winnipeg when she joined the project and brought an abiding interest in politics to the table.

Anette thought researching the Canada Infrastructure Works Program would provide a crash course in the Canadian political system. "I didn't know what I was getting into," she admitted. "I couldn't get any answers and I didn't know why. I felt like a failure. I'm a very normal, average Canadian. I had some background knowledge on this program. I think I asked the questions everyone would like to know. But still, in the end I can't say that I know the whole picture. I still have a lot of questions that I would like to have answered."

Did the crash course answer all her questions about government's inner workings? "It's even less transparent to me now than it was before," Anette found. "It was like I had tried to walk through a political maze. I felt like going out and telling all my friends, 'Do you know this? Come on, do some research yourself.' I had to draw the conclusion that the lack of facts was telling the story itself."

BILL COMASKEY

Mayor of Thompson

Bill Comaskey is the mayor of Thompson, Manitoba, and is active in the Federation of Canadian Municipalities. Thompson is the province's third-largest urban centre and an important source of nickel ore.

We had a bad experience with our CIWP project. Back in the 1960s, in Thompson we had what was considered a boom and there was a great need for housing. A temporary solution to the problem was to open a mobile-home subdivision. It was to consist of 100 mobile homes, but it developed into over 330 mobile homes.

The project that we applied for was to replace collapsing sewer and water lines and to provide fire protection in the way of fire hydrants in the Burnwood Trailer Court. These were not there before because the area was privately owned. We inherited the problem when the deal with the developer expired and we had to buy the land back.

The City of Thompson was very supportive of the infrastructure program. We participated with the Federation of Canadian Municipalities. I sit on the national board of directors, and we were very

pleased when the Government of Canada accepted the federation's recommendation to have a nationwide infrastructure program to repair
the crumbling roads, sewer and water services, and bridges and walk-
ways. We had four projects that we wanted to apply for, but we felt that
it would be fair to apply for the one that was most needed.

We applied for the Canada–Manitoba municipal infrastructure
project, then waited for an extended period of time for approval. When
we finally got approval it was not what we had anticipated. The federal
and provincial governments would pay a smaller amount and we would
be expected to pay the lion's share of the project. We applied for the subdivision project based on the one-third/one-third/one-third formula of
the infrastructure program. We actually commenced some of the work,
expecting to get the same level of funding from the other two governments. We were very surprised that we did not. They approved the project, but the City of Thompson would pay $2.4 million, the Government
of Canada would pay just over $860,000 and the Government of
Manitoba would pay the same.

We communicated back and forth with the Infrastructure
Secretariat and government officials. They applauded this great project
that had commenced in Thompson. The explanation from the
Infrastructure Secretariat for the funding we received was that they did
not have the money to approve the project in full. If we wanted to go
ahead with it we could, under the conditions that they had outlined, but
they were not going to be paying a third, a third and a third. We had to
complete it; you can't stop it halfway through.

It was a difficult project for us. We had to move some of the mobile
homes in the subdivision, the lines were about to collapse, and we did
not have any sort of fire-protection system in there. This project desperately needed the support of the infrastructure program. While some
communities didn't know what to spend their infrastructure money on,
we couldn't get full payment on our project.

The province had approximately $204 million to spend. They allo-
cated a large portion of that for the City of Winnipeg and they held a
large portion of it for Canada and Manitoba projects. The rest of it had
to be distributed amongst every other municipality across the province.
It became very, very competitive.

Many of the projects that were funded were in my view grandiose
projects. I don't believe the Calgary Saddledome project should have

qualified for the infrastructure program. I know of many projects across the country that were in the arts and entertainment sector. Even in Manitoba they had a project in Assiniboine Park that certainly did not in my view qualify for this basic Infrastructure Works Program.

I wish that the Government of Canada would have accepted the rules as presented to them by the Federation of Canadian Municipalities and not tried to use the program for political gain. Politics played an enormous part. Corporations had great influence. The program was never intended to be a boost to the owners of the Calgary Flames. I believed the National Hockey League should be able to look after their own business without having to tap into a basic infrastructure program, and I use that as an example. Influence had a real bearing on why the program turned into this gift idea. I was on the FCM board of directors, and we never expected these programs or these projects to be approved.

The Government of Canada and the Government of Manitoba decided on the formula. The Government of Manitoba then decided that they would have some municipal representation on the selection committee, using a per capita formula. So the Manitoba Association of Urban Municipalities and the Union of Manitoba Municipalities had representation on that panel. One of our councillors was president of the Manitoba Association of Urban Municipalities at that time and sat on that panel, but was unable to budge on any conditions with respect to the cost of our project. The other governments would say that they give municipalities a voice in the programs when in fact we were hamstrung on how we would fund it, short of paying the rest of it ourselves.

Many of the northern and rural communities felt that they were shortchanged in this program. Many of the projects that some of the smaller communities applied for were not approved. The governments would say that they were trying to include all the rural and northern communities in the program, but that is not so. Some of the smaller projects were approved to appease the rural and northern communities, but some of the projects that desperately needed funding were excluded.

When projects are going well, or when the municipality is paying more than their fair share, then they are recognized as an order of government. This did not happen with the infrastructure program in Manitoba. When other levels of government want to download to us, they will consider us a level of government. When they have a project that they see as popular, they want to take the credit for it, and that's what I saw happening with the Infrastructure Works Program.

Where do we go to lodge our complaint? The people of Thompson, the people of Manitoba, the people of Canada have got to get the message to the federal government and to the provincial government that they are the stewards of the taxpayers' purse. They are not doing us a favour or drawing money out of a treasure chest when they give us their contribution to these projects. It is taxpayers' dollars and government is expected to be fair. I did not see fairness in this program.

I don't believe the citizens of Canada really understand the spending habits of governments. Politicians have a poor image, and I believe that we have earned that. Canadians need to ask more questions and receive answers. When you ask a question from the federal government or the provincial government, it's almost impossible to get an answer. You will have to spend some money and go through several hoops in order to get the answer. I encourage people to ask the questions from their member of Parliament, from their MLA and from representatives like myself to ferret out that information for them.

The Government of Canada wanted to take most of the credit for the Thompson infrastructure project, and the Government of Manitoba wasn't far behind. The municipal level of government was left out of that. We weren't doing the project because we wanted to get credit for it. All we asked for was fairness, and we don't believe that we got fairness in the overall project.

We received a sign. The sign was quite colourful. It had "The Honourable Lloyd Axworthy, Minister Responsible for Western Economic Diversification" on one side, and "The Honourable Eric Stefanson, Minister Responsible for the Project in Manitoba" on the other. In the middle it was blank. The other partner, the City of Thompson, was left out. We were told we had to put the sign up, where it had to go, and we had no say in the matter whatsoever. The cost of erecting the sign was ours. We had to pay the labour cost to have the sign installed. When the project was completed there was a plaque made to commemorate this great project. The Infrastructure Secretariat told us that the city would not be on it. It would say, "Canada–Manitoba Infrastructure Works Project." There was an exchange of information. I said that if the city was not mentioned, the plaque would not go up. This is a tripartite agreement. After several discussions they agreed to put the

City of Thompson on the plaque. They told our engineering department that they don't usually do this.

The official ribbon-cutting ceremony took place in the winter. We were saying that we were not going to participate unless the City of Thompson got recognition. Our MP, Elijah Harper, was scheduled to participate at that particular opening. He did not attend. Lloyd Axworthy was expected to attend the official opening. He did not attend. The provincial minister, Eric Stefanson, did not attend, but he did have then MLA David Newman represent the Government of Manitoba. Quite frankly, we could have had the official opening in a phone booth.

The way I see it now is that the two other levels of government owe us money. If they want to take the credit for it, fine, but they should have paid their fair share.

JAE EADIE

Deputy Mayor of Winnipeg

Jae Eadie has lived in Winnipeg all his life. He represents the St. James ward and has been on council since 1980. He was president of the Federation of Canadian Municipalities from 1997–98.

I think, generally speaking, the outcome of the national infrastructure program has been very good. Number one, it showed everyone that three orders of government in Canada could come together and work co-operatively for the common good. Number two, in many jurisdictions across the country, including my own city of Winnipeg, great advances have been made on the renewal of aging municipal infrastructure. So I think generally it provided positive benefits to all Canadians.

There were varying degrees of success. My understanding is that, for example, in Newfoundland and Labrador there's reasonable satisfaction with the program. Nova Scotia, I understand, had some pretty good success with it. There might have been a few problems in Saskatchewan, but it wasn't all rosy everywhere.

I heard that there wasn't very much co-operation between the provincial government and municipal governments in British Columbia. Therefore the program didn't work as well there as it did, for example, in Manitoba or in Alberta, where municipalities were actively involved in the selection and prioritizing of programs to receive funding under the tripartite arrangement. So every province has its own story. I know there was some discord in British Columbia because the money didn't get to the municipalities that well. Other than that, I think generally the program has been very well received.

Manitoba and Alberta municipal governments were directly involved in prioritizing the projects that were going to receive funding out of the program. Every municipality that was prepared to get involved had a long list of projects. My city was no exception. A committee consisting of government representatives from all three orders of government in Manitoba and in Alberta went through the list of projects, prioritized them and approved them. Generally municipal governments in Manitoba were very happy that we had a presence in the selection of projects.

In a number of other provinces the municipalities were not even allowed to come to the table to have some say into the projects. Their money was certainly wanted but their presence at the table was not, and that caused a lot of discord between some municipal governments and provincial governments. The B.C. government had its own arrangement with the federal government. It's an unfortunate occurrence as far as the tripartite municipal infrastructure program is concerned. A number of my colleagues in B.C. municipal government were very unhappy, not with the program per se, just with the cavalier way they were treated by their provincial government.

All provinces got some say in project selection because the agreement was between the federal government and the provincial and/or territorial governments. In turn provincial governments made their arrangement with their municipality. The federal government still does not recognize municipal governments officially and therefore cannot directly negotiate with municipal governments. I hope someday that attitude will disappear completely in Canada.

So the feds and the provinces directly negotiated their individual agreements, and then the provincial governments could do whatever they wished with that money.

The agreement that the federal government reached in Manitoba split the infrastructure dollars. A good portion of the dollars were a three-way split, so on any of the infrastructure projects the signage indicated the contribution of all three orders of government. A portion of the money allocated to Manitoba was reserved for what were deemed federal-provincial priorities to which municipalities did not contribute. Any of the signage on those projects indicated the contribution of the provincial and federal governments. The signs for projects in which our order of government was involved show municipal contribution and presence.

At the very beginning of the municipal program in Manitoba, the first few signs that went up in Winnipeg on shared projects did not recognize the city's contribution. I raised a little hell with our own administration on that to get them in touch with the provincial and federal bureaucrats, and the signage was immediately changed. So in any project in which the City of Winnipeg government was involved financially, the city's contribution was recognized in the signage. We had to change the culture of the other two orders of government right at the very beginning. Typically they wanted our money but did not want to recognize that it was contributed by us. That has changed.

There was criticism, from the auditor general among others, that some of the programs financed by the three orders of government were not traditional municipal infrastructure. There was some validity to those criticisms. However, the Federation of Canadian Municipalities always said that the projects financed by the three orders of government have to recognize municipal government priority. If an arena or a fountain or a concert hall was deemed by the municipal governments to be one of their priorities, so be it.

In most Canadian cities, including Winnipeg, almost all of the money that we contributed was for traditional infrastructure. A very small portion of our contribution went to local community centres. All of our projects were included in our five-year capital program. We didn't pull them out of the air.

The baseball diamond at The Forks was the result of an agreement that was worked out between Manitoba and Ottawa and a private sector consortium. The City of Winnipeg was not involved financially in that, at least not with a direct contribution, other than $1 million cash, which had nothing to do with infrastructure. There's quite an involved arrangement between Ottawa and Manitoba with respect to the ball diamond. I'm not privy to all of the details. The City of Winnipeg indicated right from the get-go we would shut the door on any attempts to get this city's government into megaprojects that had nothing to do with infrastructure.

The Federation of Canadian Municipalities and its board of directors had some harsh words with Minister Eggleton when the federal government announced the infrastructure program because we thought the definitions were far too broad. That was an arrangement made by Ottawa. I guess they were trying to satisfy a broader constituency than we were. Mr. Eggleton certainly took it on the chin. He served on our board, he had been mayor of Toronto and he was a strong proponent of the municipal infrastructure program.

All governments of course are held accountable for the money at the end of the day. I'm quite satisfied, as we've reached the tail end of the general election here in Winnipeg, that the majority of citizens will believe that their municipal government channelled the money in the right direction.

I think most municipal governments in Canada would like to see a new program focused again on infrastructure renewal. When I met with Minister Marcel Masse earlier this year, he indicated he would be prepared to consider having the federal government invest in a renewed program, provided the terms of reference clearly state that municipal priorities are the only priorities that are recognized in the program. The provincial governments would have to sign on to that.

Municipal governments can't be taken for granted any longer. If provincial or federal governments are going to expect municipal governments to take on some of their responsibilities, then they either have to loosen the purse strings or give municipal governments the constitutional authority to get into revenue sources other than realty tax. We have to get the other orders of government to recognize that they can't cure their taxation or spending problems by sloughing them onto the municipalities. We have to pay for our police, our fire, our basic services. As these costs go up, property taxes go up. Realty tax is not a good way to finance operations any longer. If municipalities had some flexibility when it comes to revenues and expenditures, most Canadians would see a vast improvement in the property tax situation.

Change is about to happen. In Alberta, for example, they have the most advanced municipal legislation of anyone in the country. Municipalities are now being given much broader authority. A municipal council essentially can do anything it wants to do unless the legislation specifically excludes them from doing it. They can get into other sources of revenue by passing a bylaw through their council, unless the act specifically states that they cannot.

Those changes are beginning to happen slowly across the country. The Ontario government is talking about empowering its municipalities. The Yukon and the Northwest Territories are going through that. Manitoba is slowly getting there. The Federation of Canadian Municipalities has asked to be there when the federal government meets with Aboriginal peoples and talks about creating Aboriginal self-government because we don't know what that means. We don't know what that means for Aboriginal groups living in municipalities; we don't know whose laws will be recognized.

Municipal governments were here before provinces were invented. We were here long before Confederation. Sir John A. Macdonald began his political career by getting elected to Kingston city council some 34 years before he became the first prime minister of Canada.

People are beginning to recognize that municipal governments have always had to operate with balanced budgets. We've had balanced-budget legislation for over 100 years. The other orders of government are just starting to recognize what balanced budgets really are and are starting to work toward balanced budgets. They are recognizing that municipal governments have been pretty financially prudent for a century or more. The other orders of government have huge deficits. They pay their bills with borrowed money.

DAN KELLY

Director of Provincial Affairs,
Canadian Federation of Independent Business (CFIB)

Born and raised in Winnipeg, Dan Kelly served as policy advisor to
Premier Gary Filmon before becoming the vice president of the Prairie
region for the Canadian Federation of Independent Business. He works as
a government lobbyist and media spokesperson for 18,000 federation
members in Alberta, Saskatchewan and Manitoba.

When Canadians think of infrastructure they think of the hard projects — bridges, roads, sewers, waterworks projects. That is their general definition of infrastructure.

I don't think Canadians view cultural centres or upgrades in parks and community clubs as being the infrastructure they thought they were buying when they bought into the infrastructure program. What they did not buy into was the fact that the government was going to spend money on multicultural projects or pavilions and parks or little piazzas on avenues and those kinds of things. That really tests the definition of infrastructure.

They want money spent on the things that are crumbling. If you drive through Winnipeg, we have roads that are falling apart, we have

potholes cars are driving into. And we need some substantive improvements to our capital infrastructure — things that allow Canadians to get
from place to place and get their products to market. Those are the types
of infrastructure projects that Canadians view as being important. But
I don't think there's a lot of sympathy among Canadians to use their tax
dollars — and in fact borrowed money — to pay for projects that don't
fit their definition of infrastructure. In Manitoba a pretty massive chunk
of the program was dedicated to those sorts of projects.

The Canadian Federation of Independent Business conducted a
survey on the infrastructure program in 1996 which indicated that the
majority of Canadian small businesses were not in favour of renewing
it. Canadians, and in particular small businesses, view job creation as
being the responsibility of the private sector. Reduce the staggering levels of personal and corporate taxation in the country, reduce the levels
of paperwork that are required in small business, and then allow private
business to create jobs for Canadians. Don't use tax dollars or borrow
new dollars and then try to spend them as a means of job creation. That
is why Canadian small businesses did not support the renewal of the
infrastructure program.

I think the federal government used the word "infrastructure" very
deliberately. Infrastructure is something warm and fuzzy. They decided
to use the term infrastructure because it had that broad public policy
acceptance. The word infrastructure is something that most people feel
positively predisposed toward. They use the term to justify programs
that are perhaps being used to improve the fortunes of Canadian governments and Canadian political parties, rather than to improve the
lives of the constituents they serve.

The infrastructure program far outstripped its core definition. It
was used to pay for a number of projects that really fell out of the traditional infrastructure definition. If governments want to use infrastructure dollars to pay for multicultural programs, let's call them
multicultural programs. Let's not try to use infrastructure to justify
some spending and then use the funds for other purposes.

If you look at the real reason behind a lot of the spending, it
becomes obvious that insiders that are on the boards of some major
charitable organizations got money thrown their way through an infrastructure program. Some businesspeople got money to benefit their
own local interests through the program. I think the Infrastructure

Works Program was used very deliberately to improve the federal government's *political* infrastructure rather than the infrastructure for Canadians themselves.

In some cases the infrastructure program could be defined as a subsidy because it was used to try to attract a specific business. I think it was used to subsidize some private entrepreneurs, in some cases to embark upon projects that they viewed as important. There was a huge debate in Winnipeg about the use of the infrastructure program to provide money for the Winnipeg Jets, a hockey team.

Any time you have a group of politicians — particularly politicians of a variety of political stripes — coming together, you get into bargaining and tradeoffs. That's what we see far too often among Canadian governments, especially for a tripartite program such as this. It's even more prone to that type of abuse.

CFIB has done a variety of surveys on effective and ineffective ways of job creation. Our members are small and medium-sized companies and are responsible for 80 percent of the new jobs created in this country. They are telling us that what doesn't work is heavy-handed government programs. They say that programs that have the government take the lead seldom, if ever, amount to the number of jobs that are being forecast in the first place. They often result in more abuse to the system and higher taxes for us for the future, rather than long-term job creation.

The Infrastructure Works Program borrows money or uses existing tax dollars to pay for heavy government spending that seldom will live up to its job-creation potential. The money that was used on the infrastructure program could have been far better used if it had been used to reduce employment insurance premiums or reduce the growth in the Canada Pension.

Infrastructure may be a positive use of tax dollars, but let's do it when it's affordable. Let's do it because it makes sense to improve our infrastructure, and let's make sure it's actually paying for infrastructure. Unfortunately we have financed an infrastructure program that is now going to mean that future generations of Canadians will pay for improvements that are going to be enjoyed by people today. We're leveraging our children's future to pay for quick political fixes in the present day. That to me is not the best way to stimulate job creation.

JUERGEN HARTMANN

Manager, Employment, Training and Education,
Social Services Department, Winnipeg

Working in the Social Services Department, Juergen Hartmann was already involved in a short-term job creation program for Winnipeg when the infrastructure program was introduced. He oversaw a one-of-a-kind infrastructure renewal program that used infrastructure funds to hire welfare recipients for short-term jobs.

As manager for employment and training services, my responsibilities include developing programs, forming partnerships with other organizations in the community and directing a staff of 60 to deliver those services.

The community infrastructure program grew out of our collective experience in Social Services and other civic departments. As far back as the mid- and earlier 1970s, we had worked with pilot projects to put people on social assistance to work on projects of lasting value to the community.

When the Chrétien government announced the Canada Infrastructure Works Program, we were successful in getting moneys allocated to us. The contracts essentially were in terms of seasonal work and ran around 20 weeks, 22 weeks. There were in the neighbourhood of 17,500 people on social assistance in the City of Winnipeg, which is near six- to seven-fold of what it had traditionally been. The kind of work that they were doing had to do essentially with street, sidewalk and some sewer construction. For the most part it's heavy-labour work, cement finishing, shovelling, laying pipe, laying concrete, those kinds of things. The wage rates ranged between $9.50 an hour to as high as $13.00 an hour.

There were 141 jobs actually created in 1994. I believe that an additional 84 were created in 1995 and I think there were another 47 in a subsequent year. The actual numbers that we finally ended up creating were limited by the amount of money we were able to get under the infrastructure program. The jobs that were created in all the years under the infrastructure program were seasonal full-time jobs. They were covered by union contracts because all civic employees of course are covered by union agreement.

In terms of the 1,500 jobs that were supposed to be created in Manitoba, I can't comment accurately on the entire province because I am not aware of the numbers outside of the City of Winnipeg. I think the province probably came very close to that and my feeling is that in fact it exceeded it.

At the same time that the community infrastructure program was operated, there was a complementary program in the private sector. The city put up some of the work for a private bid. That proportion of the infrastructure program provided employment to a whole number of people on employment insurance. So in addition to the community infrastructure program, which was essentially an in-house program that the city ran, there was also another one that was run by the private sector.

How many dollars would go to the program run in-house by the City of Winnipeg, and what portion would go to private contractors? That was an item for negotiations. I believe it was $10 million for two years, for 1994 and 1995. I can't recall the amount that was set aside to be used by contractors that bid on city projects. It was a negotiation. Essentially a political decision was made.

Did the need to create jobs come first, or the need to have work done? In the infrastructure process the need for the work was established beforehand, and then it was, well, some people would say a happy coincidence that there was some labour available. Of course, it was serendipitous that we were in an economic crisis in terms of labour supply and labour demand. It just happened to be a fit.

To create employment for employment's sake only, without having a long-lasting community benefit come out of it, is in my opinion of little value. In other words, to contrive to create work that's really not of long-term value to the community would not be sound or fundamental in terms of employment creation.

In terms of long-term effects of the infrastructure program, they were actually quite good, according to the follow-up studies, up to 1997. In Winnipeg the infrastructure seasonal work for the most part was much longer than 10 or 12 weeks. It was from 20 weeks and longer. Some folks in fact worked for 24 weeks. The benefit for those individuals was that they had a longer term of reasonable-paying jobs for a good portion of the year. We also found, when we followed up year after year, that it's much easier for persons to find new positions when they have not been out of the labour market for very long.

The numbers of people working on the infrastructure program decreased from 1994 to 1995, and again in 1996, because the federal government chose to put, in Winnipeg's case, less money toward that particular program. The work was certainly required, there were certainly people that enjoyed working on the program, but for reasons that only federal spokespeople can explain, there was less money assigned to that program.

As part of the agreement, the community infrastructure program that the city entered in with the province and the federal government required that there was regular reporting. We had to report on the number of people hired, on the work completed and so on. We supplied those to the Infrastructure Secretariat of Manitoba, which was the co-ordinating group for the province of Manitoba with the federal government. There are some reports that were publicized and are available to the public at large.

The connection between infrastructure renewal and job training was really quite wide under this particular program. The definition included such things as development of the Internet, in 1994. There was some work done in that particular area and it was included as infrastructure work. This is an example of how wide that definition actually was. In retrospect I think that the definition was sometimes too wide because it didn't really help to clarify things for the interested public.

In terms of accountability, I think constructive criticism can be made. In Winnipeg we limited ourselves to the community infrastructure program expenditure and the work that was done on streets, sewers, sidewalks. Some people chose to call infrastructure renovating a community centre or building a public fountain. Our core infrastructure — which we consider the roads, sewers, water systems — we believe those things should receive priority for infrastructure money. But I'm not particularly concerned about infrastructure program money having been used to build community centres, if the projects employed Canadians who were on social assistance or employment insurance. One could argue over which "infrastructure" is a higher need.

The Infrastructure Works Program could be described as a short-term fix. A short-term fix is better than no fix at all. In Winnipeg we never sold the infrastructure program as a long-term solution. When you have a situation of high unemployment and people are available to do the work, then you must pay those people. We have done that in Canada.

CHAPTER 5

QUEBEC

We played the game, like everyone else.

Unique though the province may be, in Quebec our researchers encountered the same patterns that were present in the other provinces. Quebec being Quebec, these patterns were played out against the backdrop of La Belle Province's desire to guard its jurisdictional controls and its cultural identity. But when push came to shove, Quebec had no philosophical problem taking the federal money that was up for grabs.

The Montreal area produced an extremely controversial CIWP project: the Outremont Theatre. This project was fraught with complications from the very start and was held up for years by a number of lawsuits. The City of Outremont bought the rundown theatre with the intent of refurbishing it using CIWP money. Its proponents thought it would give an economic boost to the area and revitalize the cultural scene. Jacqueline Clermont-Lasnier, then an Outremont councillor, opposed this move for a number of reasons. She argued that the area's outdated sewer system could have been upgraded using the same CIWP funds, preventing the devastating floods that occur periodically in the area.

Even the CIWP, designed to fix roads and sewers, was immersed in the federal-provincial bickering that characterizes the relationship between Canada and Quebec. On close inspection our researchers found that Quebec's agreement with the federal government was slightly different than the other federal-provincial agreements. The other agreements noted a fairly standard clause, that they were subject to the rules of the Financial Administration Act (FAA). This was absent from the Quebec–Canada agreement. Also absent was the clause confirming that the final resolution of the agreement fell to the federal courts. It seemed that the Quebec government did not want the agreement to appear to be subject to Canadian law ahead of its own laws.

We were not permitted to see all the documents related to the Quebec agreement, but we did have access to two people who help to keep the Quebec government accountable: the auditor general of Quebec, Guy Breton, and Jacques Chagnon, the former chair of the Quebec Treasury Board and Liberal member of the Quebec National Assembly.

Breton criticized the Quebec government for its so-called "fourth envelope" of infrastructure projects. He argued that these items encompassed a loose interpretation of infrastructure. The Quebec government actually approved a number of church renovations under the CIWP fourth envelope.

Under the administration of Claude Ryan, the Liberal municipal affairs minister, Quebec's CIWP management was tightly controlled, Chagnon said. When the Parti Québécois was elected to lead the province in September 1994, funding decisions took on a new tone. Projects were approved, Chagnon said, to court the favour of cities in the province. This led to approval for projects that were not new, as the CIWP required, and also for projects designed as much for self-promotion as infrastructure.

The Jarry Tennis Centre in Montreal is one project that some said fell into that nebulous category. A privately owned facility, the Tennis Centre received $20 million to upgrade its facilities. The facility upgrade included adding public indoor courts, a fact that likely aided its chances of program approval. Brigitte Pellerin, one of our researchers in Quebec, contends that this desire to "appear international" was a factor in the CIWP funds being granted to the Jarry

Tennis Centre. Much of Brigitte's experiences are chronicled in her book *Down the Road Never Travelled.*

We spoke to one of the people directly affected by the Jarry funding: competing club owner Peter Malouf. The director of Tennis Canada for Montreal, Richard Legendre, supported the Jarry funding and made a familiar argument in support of "soft infrastructure" projects: that the upgraded facility would have far-reaching, but admittedly incalculable, economic benefits for the City of Montreal and the province of Quebec.

The search for answers about CIWP projects proved too much for one of our Quebec researchers, Philippe Forest. An ardent follower of Canadian politics, Philippe was intrigued by the documentary project. "I just wanted to dive into the Infrastructure Works Program, to understand it, to be able to better criticize it and maybe along the way influence or be responsible for some kind of change," he said. "I had the idea in mind that at the end I would get that politician on his knees, saying 'Yes, I did it! I'm guilty!' There was this tiny flame of optimism that maybe I could change something. Boy, was I wrong."

After seven frustrating weeks — weeks spent feeling mistrusted by politicians and bureaucrats, Philippe developed an odd sense that he was living out a Kafka novel, in which dense and absurd rules take on a surreal element. Philippe felt so dejected that he resigned.

"I couldn't take it," Philippe said. "It was oppressing me. It had really infected me. I was angst-ridden. I'm not just saying that government is impenetrable. There are a lot of secrets, a lot of closed doors. I can say it because I've tried. That experience is invaluable to me. If a lot of people ask questions, then eventually the barriers will have to come down, and government will have to open itself up. Perhaps I'm dreaming when I say that, perhaps I'm looking for a utopia. I don't think I can ever be free of what I've learned."

It is important to note that the Quebec interviews were conducted in French, then translated into English. Some phrases may seem awkward in their English translation. In addition to these language idiosyncrasies, another important point to note is that in Quebec there are municipal "critics," who function on city councils in a similar way to federal and provincial "shadow Cabinets." For example, when she was interviewed, Jacqueline Clermont-Lasnier was the local "critic for infrastructure," and thus brought her own expertise to the discussion.

JACQUELINE CLERMONT-LASNIER

Former City Councillor, Outremont

Jacqueline Clermont-Lasnier was on the council of this well-to-do Montreal suburb — now part of the amalgamated City of Montreal — when the infrastructure funds were assigned.

How are public moneys managed? There is not one taxpayer who likes to see his tax bill increase, so we have to spend the moneys responsibly and to the city's advantage.

It's a question of deciding which projects have priority. It is the municipal council that establishes priorities. We ask the civil servants to report on the various aspects of the city and we decide which projects — such as streets or recreation — should have priority. For example, snow removal is very important in a snowy city like Outremont. It's really very simple.

The infrastructure program was like pennies from heaven. There could not have been one municipal council across Canada that wasn't delighted with this program. If I remember correctly, Outremont received $6 million to $8 million from both federal and provincial governments. Our city was to invest a third, or $3 million to $4 million more.

I had great expectations. I was responsible for public works for eight years, so I knew the state of the sewer system, the streets and the sidewalks. We have century-old brick and wooden sewers in this city that are about to crumble. I had assumed that this would be a priority project.

To choose the infrastructure projects, the mayor asked our civil servants for a list of projects to be submitted to the city council. Some of the items were containment basins — the basins of Parc Prêtre — which are unique on the Island of Montreal, and all the basins were deteriorating. There was also the library, repaving projects and the Outremont Theatre restoration.

The dialogue between the opposition and those in power on the topic of the theatre project was like a dialogue of the deaf. Our priority was the streets. There was a storm in the mid-1980s. Outremont was badly hit and basements were flooded. In Outremont we have no containment basin. We are at the foot of a mountain and rainwater flows directly down into our city. Our sewers were built in 1901 and 1902, so water flows into houses and the sewers cannot contain it. Containment basins are very important, but they were not accepted as a project by our council.

The council decided with a majority vote that the theatre, the library and Mont-Royal Boulevard would be covered by the amount allocated to us. These were the only three projects to be undertaken under the infrastructure program.

Personally I never understood the choice of the Outremont Theatre restoration under this program. I thought that because the project would be submitted to the other two levels of government, it would be rejected. To my great surprise it was accepted. It was a totally illogical choice, but it was accepted by both Quebec and Ottawa. I protested to the council. A city shouldn't get involved in the entertainment business.

It was all politics. The theatre had been closed for a few years, and we had declared it a historic site so that promoters couldn't develop a commercial outfit. There was a petition with 3,000 to 4,000 signatures circulated. These signatures were certainly not those of the property owners of Outremont; they were either tenants or people who frequent the area. Of Outremont's 23,000 inhabitants, only about 2,000 are property-owning taxpayers, so how could we justify buying a theatre? Retailers on Bernard Street hoped it would bring them more customers. But frankly, when you go to the movies you don't go shopping and bring your bags to the cinema.

The theatre was restored and rented to Spectra, who was managing it. How can this choice be explained? It was purely political. I'm not aware of how the decision was made at the provincial or federal levels. What was the debate in the council when the project went through? I don't know what went on behind closed doors. I have no idea what transpired between Jerome Unterberg, who was president of the budget and therefore in charge of this type of project, and our mayor at that time, Mr. Pomminville.

The restoration fulfilled an election promise. The elected councillors represent the majority of the citizens, which in our case is the tenants who don't pay tax directly. Frills such as a theatre are more appealing to them. For them it was more political because when the infrastructure program was announced, the theatre was for sale. They were eager to buy it so they could fit it into the program and benefit from federal and provincial moneys. I don't know if there was pressure from the provincial or federal governments to launch the theatre project.

In the decision process there was some talk of job creation. Job creation was not a first consideration for selecting the Outremont Theatre project. Only temporary jobs were created, private sector jobs on construction sites. In the end the projects created no jobs at all. Our library went from 3,000 square feet to 28,000 square feet and not a single new employee was hired — on orders from the council. Contrary to other town libraries, like Ville Mont-Royal, where their library opens in the morning, ours only opens at 1:00 p.m.

If memory serves, a consulting firm was hired to do a cost-benefit analysis on the Outremont Theatre project. This ended up being totally inadequate. Just to build the theatre now will cost two or three times more than forecast. When you buy an old building there are always nasty surprises.

The purchase was made with the city's money, not the money from the infrastructure program. To purchase the theatre, the money came from the budget: the reserves and the surplus. The City of Outremont had to share a third of the total cost of the project. It was the same for repaving Mont-Royal Boulevard and building the library. We didn't have to borrow this money; the citizens of Outremont would not have accepted that. Recently the city tried to borrow $14 million, and the Outremont property owners voted against the loan. Our city has one of the lowest debts in Canada.

The motivation behind the Outremont Theatre and library projects, especially the theatre, was political in nature. Outremont has one of the highest percentages of educated citizens in Canada. We have a lot of artists and writers living here. In a nutshell, we deserved better. Our old library was too small. A good library is part of a city's infrastructure; it is part of community life.

The Outremont Theatre project was aimed at pleasing the general public, not the intellectual, cultural elite. You have to understand that Outremont is divided into two parts: Upper Outremont and Lower Outremont, as the newspapers call them. In Upper Outremont you have the property owners who were not so hot on buying a theatre and turning it over to a private company for operation. But the project pleased the majority of Lower Outremont.

Studies done on the feasibility of the theatre project suggested we should have a little money coming in, but in how many years? There was very little money in it, for the first years anyway, because of tax exemptions and so on. For this theatre to be successful, a parking lot had to be built. We already have parking problems in Outremont; the city was not built to accommodate large theatres. The only suitable location was under the St-Viateur tennis courts, which are some distance away. Many proposals were submitted to the council. Private developers took over the construction of a parking lot under the tennis courts and cashed in on it.

The portion of the annual budget devoted to infrastructure is unfortunately only five or six percent. Half of our municipal budget goes to the CUM (Communauté urbaine de Montréal). Let's say we have a $30-million budget. Fifteen million goes right off to the CUM for such services as police, Métro, public transport and water purification. The remaining $15 million pays for the rest of the city's needs. About five percent of that goes to public works, and the majority goes to paying our civil servants.

Should the province of Quebec have become involved? What was the municipal-provincial relationship? As I said, I was in the opposition and not privy to what went on behind closed doors. I imagine it was a question of the mayor convincing his counterparts that this project was valid. Mr. Pomminville, being a lawyer, was undoubtedly convincing and succeeded in doing so. But it was utter nonsense.

Jacques Chagnon

Liberal MNA;
President, Committee on Public Administration

After serving on boards of education for several years, Jacques Chagnon was first elected to the Quebec National Assembly in 1985. He holds a B.A. in political science and was head of the province's Treasury Board from 1989 to 1994.

I saw how the infrastructure program was launched after the federal election. I also saw how it was received.

In Quebec there were negotiations with the Municipal Affairs Ministry, where Claude Ryan was minister in charge, and the follow-up was done with the Treasury Board, of which Daniel Johnson was president. The finalization of the agreements between Ottawa, Quebec and the municipalities was done so that Quebec was solely responsible for choosing the files that it would agree to.

We decided to keep this control because we wanted to avoid being caught in projects like Perspective Jeunesse or Horizon Nouveau, where the federal government would invest in the creation of an agency which then required an operational budget. As soon as the agency was in place,

Ottawa would go home, saying, "We did our part." The Quebec government would then have to finance the daily operation of the institution. So we kept control over the choice of projects, with the final approval from the federal government. They weren't thrown out — they still kept a veto over Quebec's projects.

This federal program made a lot of sense since it arrived at a point when unemployment was high in Canada, particularly so in Quebec. We financed a ton of projects with this. There were local needs, and we used the money to solve infrastructure problems.

We asked the municipalities to send their capital budgets for the next three to five years. Usually they gave us their three-year plan. The municipalities told us which projects were tabled and which ones they wanted to add. If the project was already part of their municipal budget, it was refused, and if it wasn't, it was considered. We already had our infrastructure program in place, our capital budgets for hospitals, cultural projects, health sector, education sector. If we had used that money for projects that were already planned, we would not have created any new jobs.

That's how it worked until we Liberals lost the provincial election on September 12, 1994. Later the federal auditor general noted that only two provinces had really understood the intent of the project, and those were Quebec and Saskatchewan.

Soon after winning the election the Parti Québécois (PQ) government dictated new rules. They let municipalities integrate their infrastructure projects, as they themselves integrated government infrastructure projects, into the federal program. This really ended up substituting federal dollars in provincial or municipal projects. This was denounced by Quebec's auditor general, and with good reason.

We called in the deputy minister of municipal affairs, and he answered our questions. He was a little uneasy on the question as to why they had changed the standard. He said he did it because he had orders to. It was obviously political, which everyone understood. You can't reproach a civil servant for following orders. He was just doing his job. He hadn't invented this new rule, the politicians had.

The political order could not have originated from anywhere other than the municipal affairs minister and the government that accepted it. It was in the minister's interest to please the municipalities, which could then include part of their existing capital budget in the federal infrastructure program. Municipalities would then have a third of their capital budget paid.

But that was not the purpose of the program. It was intended to create new jobs, to create new economic activity over and above the planned projects by each municipality, such as those that were already included in their annual or three-year budget. Same thing for the Quebec government.

The "fourth envelope" of the program was a little bit on the wild side, as it included projects other than those that the municipal, provincial or federal governments could come up with. For example, the Quebec tourism centre and the Centre des congrès de Québec fell into this slot. When I was education minister I personally managed to get $5 million or $6 million from this to finance the new École de Technologie Supérieure in Montreal, which is a great success.

There were some vague definitions in the fourth envelope. In its defence, this imprecision created a less rigid frame that otherwise would have hindered the capital expenditures. This vague definition allowed me to do things I wouldn't have been able to before. We would not have the École de Technologie Supérieure, or the new engineering school at McGill or the new programs at the UQAR (Université du Québec à Rimouski).

The infrastructure program met its original goal — to accelerate the renovation of rain sewers, sanitary sewers, sidewalks and so on. But given the fourth envelope, Canadian cities were also interested in sports centres, cultural centres — economic projects that would benefit them in one way or another. That was the reason for this fourth envelope. Again, the imprecision was deliberate since neither the mayors nor the governments stood to benefit from too rigid a frame.

It might seem overly vague, but there are no real horror stories. I think every municipality had a project that was outside the standard. The analyses have been made, and even the auditor general would say that no money was wasted — nor was there any question of the quality of any project. I don't recall any project that was considered a waste, in either infrastructure program.

Some projects have been questioned, such as the Jarry Tennis Centre. About $20 million was spent on that project. You could say that tennis is not the most important thing for a city, but Montreal had a strong interest in the project because it had a direct impact on tourism.

Now tennis events in Montreal are widely attended, and hotels get filled up more than they would be otherwise.

The cost-benefit ratio for most projects from 1993 to 1997 was based on the requests put in by the municipalities. The municipalities function with three-year budgets. We required that in addition they make decisions about their infrastructure needs. Did the cities pick the bridges, the access ramps that needed the most work? It was a judgment call. We could only presume that they had made the best decisions for their cities since they were paying their share.

There are many different ways to review cost-benefit numbers. Was the cost of digging sewers within the infrastructure project more expensive than it would be with regular city projects? At the time there were many projects competing with each other, which made it difficult for contractors to undertake new projects. Costs could climb, so we were careful. It's also difficult to assess the importance of a cost-benefit analysis for the $5 million that we invested in the École de Technologie Supérieure. A cost-benefit analysis would have been difficult. But we did some studies.

It's fair enough to say that you can't question decisions after the fact. Six years ago when I came to St. Catherine Street here in Montreal, it was described to me as being like Beirut: devastated, with unoccupied stores everywhere. The $14 million we invested on St. Catherine Street between Atwater and Bleury has revitalized this street. Now it's a lively place to walk. What is the cost-benefit ratio of this project? I think it's very positive. I can't put a number to it, even five years later. But I can see that it's good. I have to have faith.

Quebec is a little behind on the subject of accountability. The question of accountability at the highest level sparked a heated debate in the previous legislature. With Robert Bourassa's Liberals, I was not in the Cabinet then, but my colleague Henri-François Gautrin from Verdun and I strongly campaigned within our party to make changes within our institutions.

As much as we preached a balanced budget, we also preached that the highest-ranking civil servants must be required to account for the management of their sectors. At that time the Cabinet was not too favourable on accountability, nor was the Opposition. An Opposition critic, Jacques Léonard, now president of the Treasury Board, was completely opposed to the very concept. He thought it went against the principle of ministerial responsibility. I argued the opposite. Finally Premier Bourassa let us present a bill on the subject. But it took two years before we managed to create a process of accountability. Now our process goes a little further than in other provinces.

The role of the public administration committee is essentially twofold. First we study the auditor general's report. The auditor general is named by the Quebec National Assembly. Twice a year the auditor general submits a huge report to be analyzed by the members of my commission. The second role is to analyze all expenses of $25,000 or more from each of the ministries or government agencies.

The commission is more or less non-partisan. The members of the commission are elected MNAs. There is a somewhat similar commission in other provinces, even in the federal government. It is usually called the Public Accounts Committee. One of the features of a British-style parliament such as ours is that the presidency of these commissions is always given to a member of the Opposition. So I am a member of the Opposition, and I was named president of this commission. Most of its members belong to the party in power. Then there are a minority of non-government members, among whom you find the president of the commission.

When they come before the commission, the government takes the opportunity to allow the deputy ministers to announce some new solution to an existing problem. Because of its public nature and all the media attention, the commission has more power when it's sitting than when it submits its report to the National Assembly. So many times before the commission was due to sit — a few days before, or even the morning of — decisions were reversed. It was really funny. Even the MNAs thought it was a little too obvious.

This kind of thing didn't happen with the infrastructure program because by that time it was too late. We suggested that the government change the process for the third phase because when the new PQ government arrived, the minister of municipal affairs had made a request to the Treasury Board to have the previous rules changed.

The Cabinet accepted the changes, and that was the end of that. The municipalities had no more obligation to submit their three-year capital budget to the selection committee of the Quebec government. Quebec later had to back off so that the Canadian program could offer as many services as originally planned. The idea, again, was to create employment with new projects. So unlike Saskatchewan, Quebec ended up, along with all the other provinces that had modified the basic rules in the first year, creating a cost increase, which was denounced by the auditor general of Canada, Mr. Desautels. That may be why Quebec backed off.

The question is, were the right choices made? Some decisions are good, others not. When you make a decision you're usually assuming that it's the right one. Good faith is also part of the assessment process. We try to make the best decisions for the future, for the younger generation and for those who are going to follow them.

Should we not invest in infrastructure programs today to prevent the existing infrastructure from costing too much to replace in the future? We hear numbers that are beyond reality. In one report the cost of redoing infrastructure was estimated at $44 billion across Canada. But the Federation of Canadian Municipalities estimated about seven years ago that it would cost $10 billion. There are still wood pipes in many places in Quebec, and they still work. The future in Canada will certainly be to replace the infrastructure in urban areas.

There isn't enough investment in infrastructure maintenance. When there is no maintenance, major construction or repair problems occur. Managing a government isn't that different from managing your own house. When you don't want the roof to leak, you fix it before it springs a leak. Otherwise the damage spreads all over.

It's a truism that politicians don't pay as much attention to long-term, low-profile projects. On the other hand, a municipality without water for its citizens, or whose water supply is of poor quality because the water mains are damaged, is a municipality in serious trouble. It happens in the case of a boil-water advisory. It's in a municipality's best interest to avoid this.

Is there a problem of accountability? Yes and no. I admit that the commission could have greater powers. We review the file that the auditor general studied. We study the file more from a management point of view than a political one.

Accountability certainly has its limits. It's not a matter of rediscovering the philosopher's stone. At some point, if you don't catch up to events, the concept of accountability loses its purpose and its importance. And it can incapacitate your ability as a legislator and public auditor to make changes quickly. But such is life. We only live for 75 or

80 years. If we had 200, it would be a lot better, but this won't happen any time soon. It's the same in public administration.

We took a great step with Quebec's accountability — it was a revolution, almost a cultural revolution. The concepts of accountability and transparency are becoming more and more important in public administration, and they will continue to, under our scrutiny. In the future you can expect us to dig deeper and deeper. Eventually we'll organize an accountability chain, starting at the deputy minister level, down to the service manager, right down to the foreman.

RICHARD LEGENDRE

Director, Tennis Canada, Montreal

As the head of the Montreal section of Tennis Canada, Richard Legendre oversaw the group's request for infrastructure funds that would help to solidify the city's place in international competition. Legendre is currently the Parti Québécois minister of tourism, recreation and sport; he represents the Blainville riding.

Tennis Canada runs two tournaments, in Montreal and Toronto. These events are our main source of revenue, and we use the profits to reinvest in the development of tennis throughout the country. We develop players and coaches and also organize events to promote the sport. We have resources that most national sports organizations don't because we're not dependent on government funding. Government funding represents only three to four percent of our total budget. Our total budget now exceeds $16 million, and hardly $350,000 comes from Sport Canada.

You have to understand that the Canadian internationals are at the top of the list on the international scene. We are part of what is called the Group of Nine, or the Super Nine, both in men's and women's competition. Because of the alternating process, the women's competition is in Montreal when the men's is in Toronto, and then the following year it's reversed. To remain among the top nine in the world, the old stadium had to be renovated, and funding was a priority.

The tournament has a big impact on tourism and on Montreal's visibility around the world. We argued that we needed money from the infrastructure program to renovate Jarry Stadium. Otherwise there was a risk of losing our tournament status — maybe not of losing the tournament itself, but of being considered in the middle instead of at the top.

I don't think this project could have been financed from the private sector alone. We got $8 million from the federal government, $8 million from the province and $4 million from Montreal. We argued that we needed to make this investment or be out of the circuit. Twenty million dollars of public money out of $24 million is enormous. There was a strong public appeal to the project, although obviously there was also an interest on the part of Tennis Canada.

We were very confident about asking for public funds for this endeavour. There were many arguments and criteria for receiving infrastructure funding that were in our favour. First of all, it's not like we sprung into action on the day the program was announced. We'd already been soliciting for this project for two or three years. The governments would say that it was a nice project, but they just didn't have $24 million stashed away somewhere. So when the infrastructure program came to be, the governments were already aware of what we needed.

Our first argument was to defend and protect our tournament status. But we knew it was risky to put all our eggs in that basket because it would have meant spending $17 million to $18 million for renovating a stadium that would be used for two weeks a year.

So we thought it was extremely important to build a facility that could be used all year. It might cost a little more — $24 million — but it would serve the greater public. This was a very important argument, but it wasn't self-evident because of all the private clubs around Montreal. But there were few, if any, public indoor tennis centres. We don't operate at all like a private club. No one needs a membership here, and they can play outside as well as inside.

The great accessibility was a key element. And obviously so was the economic impact of the tournament. Like most big events, it brings in out-of-town visitors — 20 to 25 percent of the tournament audience is from outside the Montreal region. You have to maintain a product as it is.

Jarry Park was already a Montreal landmark. That was important because we were maintaining a part of Montreal's heritage. It was a huge renovation project, granted, but we kept an important part of the old Jarry Stadium, which saved us close to $4 million.

Job creation was a natural consequence. Of course we created jobs with the construction to be undertaken, but there were jobs created everywhere. We could almost guarantee 15 permanent employees. But we were conservative. We didn't want to flash big numbers in people's faces if they wouldn't mean anything in the end. We talked about numbers we were used to, important figures like the $10-million impact on tourism and the number of real, permanent jobs created. We proved that a certain level of operating budget would translate into so many jobs. We played the game, like everyone else who applied, and we put in the same numbers as everybody did.

No one was more surprised than we were to see how many jobs we created. It would be exaggerating to say that that was our key argument. We had to meet the requirements like everyone else, but I don't think the 300-or-so jobs estimate was the driving force of our projects.

I don't think it was any one argument more than another that convinced them to fund the project. I felt that we were competing against many projects, and the pie wasn't big enough to share with everyone. It was a hard enough sell in 1995, just before the cutbacks in health, education and so on. We came right before these cutbacks; otherwise public opinion would have been against us. With elections at the federal, provincial and municipal levels throughout the process, we had to deal with six different governments, so we needed public support.

If people felt it was a risky investment of government money, that's totally legitimate. People react first and foremost as citizens. But after two years of operation I can safely say that Montrealers and Quebecers are happy with the Jarry Stadium and the Tennis Centre. I don't think it was a mistake.

The tournament is now seen in 150 countries, and Montreal is on every tennis fan's lips around the world. It's difficult to measure this impact in numbers, but it's obviously an important one. So you can see that we had an impact on many areas — tourism, international visibility and community service. Now our position is guaranteed. Since this investment in Montreal people on the international scene are very happy with the quality of our facilities. We want the international organizations to give us long-term contracts. I think it's going to happen.

Peter Malouf

Owner and Operator, Rockland Sport Tennis Centre

As a private tennis club owner, Peter Malouf fought for years against plans to put public funds into the Jarry Park Stadium.

Back in 1989, I think, there were rumours of Tennis Canada wanting to upgrade the facilities at Jarry Park and at York University, to be able to hold the international tournament known as the Canadian Open. The reason they wanted to do it was to keep up to date with existing facilities around the world. They wanted to have an established facility that could be presented as world class, and they thought that players would feel that this was fantastic.

It became a much larger project than what was originally foreseen.

A study had been commissioned in 1986 by the indoor club association, formed by the various indoor tennis clubs here in Quebec, to determine what type of negative impact could occur on the tennis industry if an indoor club facility were built on Île Ste-Hélène. What we learned from the study is, number one, we had too many indoor courts to serve this population. Number two, the industry was actually starting to see a decline, an aging population of people taking up alternative sports. The impact study showed that Montreal had the highest per capita number of indoor tennis courts of anywhere in North America. There were so many indoor courts, they weren't being filled up. Ultimately the City of Montreal, which had plans for building these indoor tennis courts, changed its mind and said, "Fine, we won't build them."

What happened in 1989 is that the government decided it had a high-profile project that the public would say was wonderful. But I was absolutely amazed and astounded that they would go ahead with a project like this. They'd already had a failure on their hands with the Olympic Stadium. They already had problems with hospital closures at the time. And yet they still had the gall to go ahead and spend money for an event that would take place two weeks out of the year.

At the time the Quebec Tennis Federation had its offices at the Olympic Stadium, and I said, "You know what, this is a very underutilized facility — what a great way to justify its existence. You don't even have to fix the roof. Instead of spending $50 million on a roof, we should bring the tournament over to the Olympic Stadium." They said, "No, it's going to conflict with baseball." I said, "Baseball is dying in this city." They would have nothing to do with it; they wanted to hold the Canadian Open at Jarry Park. I told them it made more economic sense to hold the tournament at Olympic Stadium, and they wouldn't have to spend a lot of money.

I took the time and corresponded with several provincial ministers who were involved in the infrastructure program in Quebec. I communicated with the premier, the federal ministers and the actual ministerial agency. Essentially what I got back was, "Thank you for writing us, and we will take your concerns into account." But that was the end of it.

I think they were just placating me until they got their funding in place. I had spoken to the media. There had been articles in the newspaper. There was an editorial in *The Gazette* about it being another white elephant. Even though there were several articles, it didn't really matter. Once the project was in motion, once the people concerned were out there for their own interest, once it got into the ministerial hands, it didn't matter — the money was spent. I thought there was hope at the time, I thought I was making some progress. Well, forget it. Once it's over, it's over. You can't compete against them.

They ended up having the largest number of indoor courts in one club in North America — 20 indoor tennis courts. It's very difficult to steer the *Titanic* away from an iceberg, right? A smaller boat can veer off real quick. But if you have 20 indoor courts and they're empty, how do you keep paying for it? This club, perhaps due to their complacency with Tennis Canada, decided that there was a need for *more* courts.

People have less time for tennis. That's just what's happening. What are clubs doing? They're converting their existing facilities to alternative uses. For example, Carrefour Laval took one building with 15 tennis courts and put fitness facilities on two of the tennis courts, badminton on another two, and a golf driving range on another. Now they're down to 10 courts. That's what people want.

We belong to an organization called IHRSA, International Health and Racquet Sports Association. The publication that we get monthly used to be mostly about racquet sports. In the past five or six years, it's only about fitness. You've seen a decline in a lot of racquet sports. Racquetball is pretty well dead. Squash has declined considerably.

Indoor clubs are going to have to innovate, change or shut down. Clubs have been shutting down in Toronto and in Montreal; several clubs are suffering. Some of them have even considered becoming warehouses, public storage facilities. We make our club popular to the young by offering exciting programs for kids. We offer teen nights. But they really only want to play indoors for a maximum of six months. What do you do with the building the rest of the year? To keep your doors open you have to cater to the youth. But the youth is saying that once they get to an older age, they drop tennis and go into the gym.

In my opinion the Jarry Park facility hasn't had a positive impact on bringing new blood into the sport. What it's done is cannibalized the indoor clubs, whose members are looking for a less expensive venue to play at. Even the youth have been approached to go and play at Jarry. Why? Because they can be offered courts at a subsidized price. They get into programs where the court costs are not included. So it's very interesting for families whose kids play tennis, to send them to Jarry Park rather than a private club.

The private clubs are the ones who are really committed to the industry. As an owner I have invested in this club — acquiring it, renovating it, upgrading the facilities. Where does it come from? Not from government grants. It comes from my pocket, or from profits generated from the club. I'm the one at risk; if things go bad, I'm the one that loses. If things go bad at Jarry, where they spent $24 million of the public's money, none of the people on the executive of Tennis Canada will be affected by it.

I've been to Jarry Park several times during the course of the summer months, just to go and look around. And I don't see anything going on. I see a lot of lights that are turned off. I don't see anybody playing.

One of their objectives back in 1990 was to bring all the talented juniors from across the country to Jarry Park for a high-performance training program. I asked them who would house, educate and feed these kids coming to train. To bring them all here for one central training centre doesn't make any sense. For all the money spent and the operating costs, would it not make more sense to take that money and subsidize the existing clubs, get it to the grassroots level where the people are?

We worked very hard for five years to build up the business and put our heart and soul into it. You work seven days a week and you do everything you can to give the best service, in spite of the market conditions and people doubting. We're used to being accountable. If we don't pay our bills, our creditors will be down our throats.

What's frustrating is that it's my money. The government comes along and says, "We'll just take some of your money, build an indoor tennis facility because we have a reason for it, we got some tournament that happens once a year. Too bad for you."

All of the efforts that I made lobbying against it, trying to educate the officials, trying to educate the ministers about the statistics, the change in the industry, not only here in Quebec but globally, about the negative impact that it would have — nothing happened. It was very discouraging. So it goes to show you, if you haven't got your hand in the government, controlling somebody or something, you can't get anything to change.

The private sector is supposed to be creating jobs, not the government. We create the long-term jobs, we give the incentive for people. For all the jobs they create, I have to let people go and streamline my operation because I have to compete at a very low court rate against the public facility. So they're not creating more jobs. They're just taking jobs away from the private sector.

160

We have to ensure that people use their imagination and creativity — we encourage them to do so. This is where you have the life of a nation. If you don't, and it's all government-run, it is basically a socialistic concept. There's no incentive for anybody to achieve.

I think Jarry will just continue to exist. Look at the Olympic Stadium. What's its raison d'être at this point?

GUY BRETON

Quebec Auditor General

An auditing professional since the 1960s, Guy Breton was first appointed auditor general of the province in 1991 and served in that post until 2001.

The report on the Canada–Quebec Infrastructure Program for the year 1995–96 was one of many we did that year. The program had already existed for a number of years, and it seemed the right time to look at it, to ensure that it was being properly run.

Auditing the effectiveness of government programs follows something we call "deficiency identification." Every year we audit the financial statements of all government ministries and organizations and half of its businesses. During this financial verification our staff examines whether an organization is being run well. If it's not, we look at how much effort will be needed to better understand the nature of the problem, the impact of the problem and, most importantly, the benefits to be derived from correcting it.

We then put these analyses aside. Once a year we plan our work, 60 percent of which involves financial verification, while 40 percent goes toward ensuring effective management. This 40 percent is divided up among the files in which deficiencies were identified over the past year. This is how we ended up taking a look at the infrastructure program. Our personnel felt that everything wasn't entirely clear.

To identify deficiencies we rely on the accumulated expertise and experience of our staff. The staff on site may have a sixth sense that something isn't right. The best way to uncover problems in a business is to spend some time in the cafeteria, which is where people discuss current problems. If you really listen, you'll find out what's happening. This is an idea I got from Max Henderson, a former auditor general.

We don't have a five-year calendar scheduling visits to each of our clients because it would actually take 15 years. It pays to go where we're sure to get positive results. If we went systematically to each business, we could waste money on work that would be better spent elsewhere.

When a staff member identifies a deficiency, he is following a systematic work process. He needs proof to begin with, either through declarations, interviews with people, signed documents or external events in which the impact of the weakness was felt. We want to ensure that people are managing with a concern for economy, efficiency and effectiveness.

A lack of economy is sometimes quite obvious. Sometimes the employees readily identify it; they may feel that recent decisions are very costly and not really justified. A lack of efficiency refers to too many resources being used to accomplish something, resulting in waste. A lack of effectiveness is trying to kill a fly with a cannon, for example. It's putting too many resources toward finding a solution to a problem, or throwing the same solution at a problem that no longer exists just to keep people busy.

Some audits are done to set an example. When we report that a manager or a business does something improperly and this comes out in the press, we can assume that the next day any other managers doing the same thing would stop, to avoid appearing in the papers a year later for not having learned their lesson.

The auditor general's office performs a cost-benefit analysis of the weaknesses we presume to exist. We avoid going to places we think are generally well run. If we simply prove that it is well managed, how has money been saved and public administration improved? Giving out medals for good management is not very profitable. Our role, by law, is to report problems to the National Assembly. Then members of the Assembly, if necessary, can demand changes to the law or prompt the minister to bring about money-saving changes.

The auditor general's office doesn't have much difficulty collecting information. In fact, our right of access as auditors is upheld in the law; we have the same authority as an officer in charge of an investigation. Up until a few years ago we had the right to incarcerate someone who refused to give us information. If someone opposes us, the worst that can happen is for us to denounce him in our annual report. The newspapers usually get a hold of this, and the parliamentary committee invites this manager to explain his position. It's a rather uncomfortable situation.

Because we have this right to information, our staff works with absolute discretion. The documents that come into our office never leave, and no one else has access to them. This is how we gain people's trust; it makes it easier to ask questions and get complete information. The only thing that leaves our office is the report, which is published and submitted to the National Assembly. People are aware that the report gets published. Without credibility our audits would be a sham. Credibility also implies that we may withhold information to avoid making false claims. To protect our credibility, our printed matter is always supported by at least two separate sources, written or verbal.

We became interested in the infrastructure program because during the audit the team on site became aware that some procedures needed to be examined more closely. In reviewing the infrastructure program, we concentrated on why one project was chosen over another in the decision-making process. When the project was complete, we checked that the money was spent, that there were a certain number of employees and that there was a tangible result.

There was also a political aspect to this. The program involved the distribution of federal funds to many municipalities, with Quebec and the municipalities contributing a portion. Quebec had to report either its final or ongoing contributions, depending on whether the topic was on the minds of the public and receiving media attention.

On the one hand it was important to see how the funds were being managed, and on the other hand it was a subject that interested members of the Assembly. They wanted to know whether the program was well run and whether the money was well managed. When we see that all of the members are leaning in the same direction, we try to bring them an answer that they could not get themselves. A parliamentary commission would not bring all the information out on the table because it's a more political and public environment in which people guard their words. We often have other corroborating information and the facts come out more easily.

We were looking at the program, first, because there were weaknesses and, secondly, because it was a subject of general interest. Thirdly, when the program is short term like this one, there's no point in concluding three years down the road that it was poorly run. At that point it's too late to do anything about it. We would prefer to give recommendations before it's over, and if there are corrections to be made, we can save or improve the program before it ends. The short-term programs in the public eye are made priority.

After studying the infrastructure program file, we arrived at a number of conclusions. First, we were not satisfied with the way the minimum annual limit of engineering assets was prepared. To Quebec's credit, it is the only province with this criterion. The program was intended to create jobs through infrastructure projects. So imagine that a municipality intended to invest $500,000 in roadwork and requested an extra $200,000 through the program. To receive the benefit, Quebec would have to prove that the total cost of the project would be no less than $700,000, and that the $200,000 was not simply added to the project to reduce the municipality's $500,000 investment. In the other provinces we didn't demand this calculation.

Some parties benefited from the system, while some were penalized by calculating too strictly. It was a good concept that was generally well applied, but there were two extremes: those who were a bit too strict and the majority who were a bit looser, hoping that they could get a larger amount and save on their base spending. This subject was important to us. It was surprising because it was a good concept intended to improve the administration of the program. But it's difficult to seek perfection.

There was also the discretionary aspect of the fund allocation. Many requests were well structured, but there were a few instances that were more discretionary, where lump sums could go to either one place or another.

We noticed that the minister would use his discretion to decide that the money would go to the left rather than to the right. So we asked whether he had the authority to do so, and yes, he did. Must he provide an explanation? This is where it was not very clear. In this case he chose not to explain why he sent the money left rather than right. It was a ministerial decision; it was his right and that's what he did, end of story.

We would have preferred that he explain his decision. But at the time we were in the midst of researching ministerial discretion and the information was not in the report. We could theorize that when the subsidy is relatively high and the disbursement of funds is well structured, a minister may use discretion to choose between several well-structured plans and is not required to explain his decision.

However, what happens when the disbursement of funds is not well structured? We've seen some municipalities who receive a lump sum and are then asked what they did with it. There are two lines in the minutes of the municipal council meeting stating that the funds were used in roadwork. Well, we need a bit more precision than that. So we say that the less a project is structured, the more we expect a minister to explain his choice. Otherwise we don't know on what basis he has used his power of discretion.

In such unstructured cases, once the money is gone, it's much more nebulous. Therefore it would make sense if we specified that when a program is really well structured, it doesn't matter whether you have chosen A, B or C, but when it's not structured, we would like to know why A was preferable to B.

In all of these processes the minister relied on recommendations. In theory the budgets were divided up by region and within the regions, and the deputies, the municipal councils could decide how they would allocate this lump sum.

The regions would report the results of their internal discussions or their chosen projects to the minister. Then the minister would say that he had enough information from all of the regions to make an informed and rational choice. And he wouldn't have to say anything more. But we felt that he should have gone one step further and said that on the basis of a certain region's rational arguments, he favoured this region over another because of the economic fallout, or the impact, or the long-term effect, or another reason.

These were the comments we had. To say that there was falsehood is going too far. But when a project is well structured, there is no need for an explanation of a discretionary choice.

At times people submit a file in which they've calculated their expenses high, and the minister must review the figures. I think each file is validated; the files are not accepted at face value. When files are reviewed, the details of each revised calculation may not be given. The people who experience this kind of setback in their submission are not necessarily happy. They tend to say there was a problem and that their file was not properly processed. Occasionally there is no documentation in the file about how the costs were lowered, leaving the impression that the measures taken were not transparent enough to be written down.

It's not easy to prove. We know there were decreases that were not written in the file, but I don't think we can go further and assume that this was done dishonestly or that there was manipulation. An undocumented decision leaves the door open to a certain lack of transparency. When a civil servant is transparent, all his actions are known and his motives can be interpreted. When he is not open, we cannot understand his motives. So people have doubts.

I think that in general people are honest. Some feel the need to prove their honesty by being open. Others do not, but that doesn't mean they are dishonest. Sometimes they are in a hurry and don't complete all the documents they need to. That doesn't prove that they're being dishonest.

In the auditor's report the purpose of the infrastructure program is described as creating jobs and improving municipal infrastructures, in that order. The Federation of Canadian Municipalities and the federal Liberals' *Red Book* put these concepts in the reverse order.

For the report there was no debate to determine the order. It seemed to me that the program's main thrust was to create employment, and the excuse was municipal infrastructure. The definition of municipal infrastructure was greatly extended, and money was put toward digging an aqueduct or a sewer or redoing asphalt.

If the word "infrastructure" had been the key word, we would have been more strict about the definition. But in my mind the key words were "job creation" because we had to generate economic activity. The excuse was infrastructure, and luckily it needed labour. The government came running to save the infrastructure because it had fallen into such disrepair. In my mind the government's purpose was not saving infrastructure but handing out work and money to people. If the infrastructure needed work, so much the better. But it could have been shipbuilding, for all it mattered. Of course there was always the possibility of creating jobs that squandered public funds. Jobs can be created if you ask people to do menial jobs, but is this the best way to use public funds?

You must look at each case individually. In the list of projects there is often no explanation of the number of jobs created in relation to the investment. For the job-creation projects we did not attempt to validate how the number of jobs for each project was calculated. The number of employees is not a figure that warrants complete accuracy. We did make sure that the total number was recorded. We may be told there were 42 employees, but we only certify this if we have at least two forms of proof. We rely on the work of the internal and external auditors, and we will do surveys if necessary.

There may have been 42 employees at the height of the project, but if we were to divide the total project hours into person-hours, we may not arrive at 42 for any given project. It's unlikely that we can determine the size of each project as a whole; in fact, we didn't even try. It's very relative. This is why the government now speaks of "full-time equivalent," and we're trying to establish a universal rule.

How do Statistics Canada or the Quebec Bureau of Statistics arrive at the full-time equivalent? If we need to understand the application of these formulas to understand the file that we are analyzing, we will not complete the analysis until we have understood the formula. People often simply accept an actuary's calculation at face value. But we don't. If a statistician maintains that we don't have the intelligence to understand his system, we will hire another statistician to do the same calculation with the same raw data. If his answer is different, the two will sit down together and figure out why. We don't let this slip by when we think it's important. Whether a number is 42, 46 or 40 is not important, but the process that results in the figure is.

Quebec was the project manager of the infrastructure program. Did this affect how the program was managed? Being project manager means being in control, and this did have an effect. Everything was decided through the Ministry of Municipal Affairs, who centralized the requests, managed them and ensured that the funds went to the right places. As far as I know the federal government was not equipped to deal with the municipalities as closely as the provincial government could, so it would have been wrong to set up a new structure to do this.

In Quebec there are many more municipalities than in Ontario or the other provinces, where there are fewer municipalities of greater size. The management and communication infrastructures to deal with these municipalities are not comparable. Quebec works with thousands of municipalities, whereas the other provinces only work with hundreds. Already the number of people at the ministry is different.

The 1995–96 report on the infrastructure program discusses a huge urban project in which the criteria were not precise enough to ensure that the program would be properly managed. This is the famous $300-million envelope. After trying to define a certain number of investments and projects very precisely, "envelope four" was developed to deal with large infrastructure projects. It was like a "miscellaneous" envelope that allowed the greatest leniency in the definition of the word "infrastructure" and allowed big projects to be done without getting hung up in a restrictive definition. To prevent civil servants from making all the decisions, the government allowed a committee of ministers to examine the files, or at least follow them closely. But we realized that because of the size or the nature of the projects, the decisions were not always completely justified through documentation.

For example, there was a water purification system involved. In Quebec we had already put $6 billion toward water purification through an existing program. So should this have been included in the project? You could argue that it's already covered in the minimum service. But you could also argue that we needed to create jobs in this region, and this was the perfect excuse. This project was on again, off again. The arguments that finally pushed it through, the whole reasoning process, are not indicated in the file.

The higher school of technology (École de Technologie Supérieure) is indeed an infrastructure in which people work, but normally the Ministry of Education would have something to say about it. There is nothing in the file to indicate that the Ministry of Education was consulted. This does not mean it was not done, but it was not documented. This is why we were interested in these big projects where the definition was less stringent. We wanted to see the rationale behind the decision, but we didn't always find it.

With a big project like moving a school of technology, it may be the parties who profit from the materials or the construction who are dishonest. In my mind the transparency must be found in that initial decision to spend so much on moving the school in the first place. People can always question the reasoning behind a project, but there is always a political aspect to the decision. Although there may be legitimate reasons for doing a project, it may also be the first step of a larger, long-term plan that is not currently on the table but which will be announced in a year or two.

In politics that's how people work. They can see beyond the end of their nose toward long-term objectives, and they work progressively to achieve them. The first step may not seem transparent, but if the long-term plan is rational, I wouldn't call this a lack of transparency. Lack of transparency is a long series of steps without explanation or justification; it's too much discretion.

As auditor general I never question the appropriateness of a political decision. Administrative decisions cannot be touched — this is written in the law. Or to look at it another way, the law states that we are not obliged to give a verdict on the efficiency of administrative measures. Efficiency means that the solution is appropriate to the problem. For example, if the problem has disappeared, then no solution is appropriate. We may be technically able to demonstrate that the situation is not appropriate, but then what happens? The government would be forced to change the situation, even if it dovetails with other plans. It's the opposition's role to show that the government is behind in its actions. Then, of course, the government will counter that everything is going according to plan and the results will show in due time; that's the whole back and forth of political rhetoric.

When an auditor presents his measurements and his conclusion, there is no way of arguing against them except to say that the auditor is incompetent. As of today, no one has ever wanted to go on the attack. If you take the auditor off the case, there would be no one left to speak for it and no way of knowing what is going on. No one criticizes the government for waiting too long, and the government doesn't criticize the auditor for making it lose face. It's accepted that there may be programs that are no longer appropriate and that should be discontinued. If the auditor spent a year systematically examining all the programs people felt were less effective or useful than others, every page of his report would state, "Money was wasted to solve a problem that no longer exists."

The auditor does not need to examine efficiency: it comes out in the report. What the auditor must do is establish whether the results are real, reliable and properly gathered. If they are, the reader can draw his own conclusions without the auditor's comments on efficiency.

When the auditor's report comes out, one of the first questions journalists ask me is whether there has been an improvement over the previous year. And yes, there is always improvement because every year we have more difficulty finding files to verify. As time goes by, people learn to manage better and there are fewer glaring errors, so we must do more research to find files. The second question is always whether the report has made a difference. Indeed it does. Four or five years ago 75 percent of our recommendations were corrected in the same year. The rest were corrected in the following year or two.

Quebec is the only province whose infrastructure program text does not include the Financial Administration Act, the federal law on public administration. We did not stop to consider this exclusion or look outside of the agreement. Its absence is undoubtedly due to the negotiations that took place between Quebec and the federal government. This type of agreement is always the subject of negotiation, whether we like it or not. They would have had to discuss how they planned to communicate when there is a rendering of accounts.

There are certainly minimum rules to be followed before the federal government lets go of its money. I presume that when the program was presented to the different provinces, Quebec demonstrated that adding this text of federal law would have created a duplication of Quebec's management tools. I presume this, but I think it was undoubtedly the argument that the political representatives invoked when the time came to say that they were in.

The procedures are already in place, the working methods already established. Quebec's parliamentary commission on public administration is specifically mandated to invite the manager to respond to the auditor's recommendations a month and a half or two months after the report. This is followed by a public meeting before deputies. Most of these projects are done in conjunction with municipalities, which have their own accounts, external auditors, and internal auditors if they're big enough. They will not create accounting methods specifically for an infrastructure project as opposed to another project.

Responsible management of public funds for the benefit of future generations is a subject that is close to my heart. Our high level of participation in affairs of the state through taxes gives us the right to the intellectual satisfaction of knowing that this money is being well spent and not wasted. And the only way to be sure of this is not to be told by a government that everything is great, but for each manager to be open.

We need to hear that the government found a solution to a problem, applied it through a set of objectives, evaluated its success at the end of the year, and decided what to do better next year. The government recognizes this need, which is why we are moving toward management by results and creating structured, autonomous units of service. We engage a ministerial department and its manager in a contract that is a public document. In it the manager pledges that he will run the business in a certain way, reduce expenses by a certain amount, speed up processes, improve results, reduce the percentage of bad debt and so on. He establishes success factors and measures and re-examines them at the end of the year. Normally a third-party internal or external auditor determines whether the results are reliable. Then the manager writes a report outlining his success and his plans for the future.

Such a document demonstrates that our taxes were put to good use in that particular department, but we should have these documents throughout the government. Accountability is the only way of ensuring on an individual basis that government is being well run. We have the right to know this given the price we pay, and I think the government has understood that it must tell us.

There are already 18 autonomous units of service and many more coming. Even those that are not autonomous units of service are starting to think that they should report on their activities using this approach of objectives and results. Openness is increasing and will become a necessity.

CHAPTER 6

ONTARIO

You go for the glory projects.

As the largest province in the country, Ontario received the biggest allotment of infrastructure money. Ontario also had one of the largest, most spectacular projects funded under CIWP. The National Trade Centre (NTC) was the jewel in the crown of the Ontario program, and it came with a whopping $180-million price tag.

Many of our sources told us that the choice of a huge project like the NTC was just another example of Toronto desiring a larger-than-life symbol — "municipal boosterism," if you will. We examined the funding of the NTC in detail, along with some of the more unusual projects to appear anywhere in the country. Among the most interesting were a number of bocce courts in the Toronto area. A lawn-bowling game, bocce would never be mistaken for a road or sewer.

Toronto city councillor John Filion told us a candid story about his attempts to get a community centre funded with infrastructure money in his constituency — giving us the flavour of some of the horse-trading that goes on among city councillors when a pile of money is up for grabs.

The funding of the NTC raises a number of important issues, including how funding priorities were set and whether or not government should be involved in competing with private business. We talked to Gail Bernstein, who managed a trade centre that was in competition with the new NTC. Bernstein explained the important differences between trade centres and convention centres — differences that can determine whether a facility will become self-sufficient or require long-term subsidization. We spoke to a wide spectrum of Toronto councillors on both sides of the Trade Centre issue. Many argued that the Trade Centre project was so big that it ate up most of the infrastructure money allocated to Toronto during the first phase of the CIWP, leaving many worthwhile projects on the drawing board. Some also pointed out that there was no guarantee that the NTC would actually be economically self-sufficient.

We spoke to Shekhar Prasad, a budget analysis expert, about the real costs of such large projects as the NTC when things like borrowing costs are factored in. He spoke to us about how debt financing will escalate the true cost of the Trade Centre project for years to come — a factor that many municipalities failed to calculate in their infrastructure plans.

Councillors Ila Bossons, Jack Layton, John Filion and Joe Pantalone commented on the NTC and other Toronto-area infrastructure projects, some of which more closely resembled traditional infrastructure, such as storm-water and sewage treatment facilities. Former Ontario environment minister and NDP notable Ruth Grier spoke to our researchers on a wide range of infrastructure issues, including the western beaches tunnel project. The tunnel was a "lightning rod" for environmentalists and others concerned about how Canada's largest city deals with sewage and storm water. Grier's interview gives the reader an insider's perspective on a number of matters, including the public relations effort that the infrastructure program elicited.

Geoff Scales provided much of the legwork for us in Toronto. He was part of an economic public awareness group called Mission Zero and had studied political science for his undergraduate degree. He took on this project because it sounded like an exciting way to gain work experience while seeing his government in action.

"Actually seeing it in action was a different story," Geoff said. "I knew that government wasn't necessarily an easy thing to access all of the time. You're given the go-around and you meet a lot of lulls and obstacles in trying to get an answer at the bureaucratic level. The right hand doesn't know what the left hand is doing."

A lack of accountability for how it spent taxpayers' dollars was an unpleasant facet of his government that Geoff hadn't expected. "Money was being spent for various reasons, with shaky foundations and assumptions. Some of that was very political, some wasn't. It was being spent because it had to be spent. I still have many questions and perhaps this documentary (*Secrets in High Places*) will bring those questions to the forefront, where they'll have to be answered sometime down the road."

GAIL BERNSTEIN

General Manager, International Centre

Gail Bernstein oversees operations at the International Centre in Toronto, which is a multi-use building that opened near the Pearson International Airport in 1972. More than two million people visit the trade shows, conventions and other events at the centre each year.

When they started to develop the National Trade Centre, the story that they told was about the opportunity for new business. Words such as "new business" or "international trade" are very attractive buzz-words. Almost everybody has a positive emotional reaction to those buzzwords and they were used to help sell the National Trade Centre.

I'm not saying those aren't admirable objectives; I'm just saying that does not reflect the reality of the trade and consumer show business. It reflects the reality for conventions, but not for trade and consumer shows. The reality is, there has been very little new business and there has been no international trade.

The Metro Toronto Convention Centre had an expansion simultaneously with the National Trade Centre. There is a difference between what the Convention Centre did and what the National Trade Centre did. Both of them quoted sources of new business. Both of them used as an excuse for not naming the new business the fact that they "weren't at liberty to say" because this was privileged information. Yet the Convention Centre opened with new business from day one and has continued to enjoy new business, while the National Trade Centre has never had a new piece of international business. They cannot name any international business that they have been able to secure. What they talk about is vague, in the future and mysterious.

The National Trade Centre was not intended to cater to the convention market. The Metro Toronto Convention Centre does that and will continue to do that. It is ideally suited for that business by virtue of where it's located and how its services are arranged. The National Trade Centre's mandate was to go after trade and consumer shows. But there are no huge international trade shows that are going to relocate to Toronto, even on an incremental, once-in-a-blue-moon basis. That's not how the business works. It flat out is not how the business works. Anyone who understands the business knew immediately that was a red herring and that was silly. However, that's what they used to get that project off the ground and to sell it to politicians and to people who absolutely did not understand this business.

Just because we built a building doesn't mean they're going to come. Politicians and bureaucrats don't understand that there's a regional aspect to trade shows. For example, the shows that run in the World Trade Center of Chicago are there primarily because the trading market within a 500-mile radius of Chicago is, I believe, 70 million people. If you were running a show in Chicago and you were going to have 30,000 attendees walk by your booth, versus running that same show in Toronto and having 3,000 attendees walk by your booth, which show are you going to go into?

Our facility is privately owned. The International Centre is a multi-use facility that opened in 1972 and was designed to hold trade and consumer shows. A trade centre and a convention centre are different businesses. Conventions move around; trade shows stay quite fixed. Trade events draw from a larger area; consumer events are extremely localized. The turnover rate is very low. If they're successful, these shows repeat annually or biannually — whatever their market and their industry sector will support. So unless their whole industry goes belly-up, they just keep on repeating.

A convention usually comes once in a while, has a very strong meeting component and might have a trade show as part of it, as an add-on. But the real reason that people come together for a convention is to mix and mingle. It gives people an opportunity to increase their knowledge of their industry. One of the ways that they attract people to a convention is by being in a different city, perhaps a place that the attendees have not been before, so they can get some R and R, a little bit of golf, a little bit of change of scenery. That's basically what a convention is.

A pure trade show is something else. I talk about a trade show as something that stands alone, separate from a convention. Quite often there is some strong economic reason why that trade show is being held in that specific city or specific venue, a reason that does not change over time. Because it usually generates profit for the people who put on the convention, a trade show might be attached to a convention, in a big hall. The people who attend the convention might go to the trade show floor and look through the vendors' booths. That's the extent of the trade show part of the convention.

Clientele for a trade show is a little different from the clientele for a convention. For example, we have an annual furniture show. It has been held at the International Centre since 1972. We actually launched our business with the Toronto home furnishings industry show. The clientele is probably every Canadian furniture manufacturer, supplemented by furniture manufacturers from elsewhere. Attendees are primarily furniture retailers from across Canada and buyers from other communities or other countries looking for something unique. The primary audience — 75 to 95 percent of the attendees — is countrywide.

The furniture industry is focused in and around Ontario and Quebec. It's just not likely that the furniture industry would be supportive of that event picking up and moving somewhere out of its jurisdiction. Another example of a trade show is the oil-based industry trade show in Calgary. Well, that industry is centred around Calgary. It's not likely that the oil industry is going to pick up and move their trade show to Toronto. It's just not going to happen. Some trade shows have a more regional focus, with attendees from three or four provinces.

A consumer show, on the other hand, might be quite focused — a home show, for example. There's probably a home show going on in every province across Canada at one time or another, and the draw will be very localized. People will be coming from the immediate vicinity. On the other hand, the attendees for a convention can be worldwide, they can be countrywide or, rarely, province-wide. Sometimes it's a provincial, national or international association putting on that convention.

There's always the hope that if you build a facility you will attract all sorts of events, incremental new business from outside your trading area. That's wishful thinking on some people's parts. People will come from outside the area, it's true, but you have to know very specifically what industries you're talking about and know the business extremely well. First of all, the Canadian market is fairly saturated. Certainly Toronto is very, very saturated. Most industries already have a trade event or consumer event.

This is a business; it's not entertainment. People come to a trade show because they expect to do business. The focus is on the tools that will enable them to do business. The building itself usually is not the tool by which they can do business. The building is a box that the business is placed in for a short period of time, and what you have to provide are basic creature comforts. You have to provide a roof, you have to provide heat or air-conditioning, and you have to provide good floor loads and shipping and receiving services. But you don't have to provide an architectural monument.

As a matter of fact, any grandiose architectural monument winds up being a distraction from the event and is not perceived as adding value to the event. For example, rarely will you see windows and natural light in a trade centre, so that an exhibitor can light his display without fighting with the natural light. The building itself has to be very focused on the user and how the user wants that building to function. It can't really go off-track and become a monument to somebody's ego or to civic pride.

I worry about the process by which the National Trade Centre got built. I worry about the choices that are made by these governments when they decide to fund one project over another. I worry about governments that use a process without checks and balances, a process that has no accountability in the end — dollar-and-cents accountability. If I were to give them a report card, I'd give them a D-minus on the process. The process really needs to be done better because things are changing.

It's just good business to look at what you've done in the past and look at ways in which you can improve it.

The government starts out with the idea of the greater collective good of the community. I accept that. What I don't accept is their idea that if private enterprise won't do it because it's not economically feasible, then government will do it. When I look at the National Trade Centre, private enterprise wouldn't build it because it wouldn't financially support itself. The scale on which they did it, for civic pride and for communal spinoff benefit, was way beyond what needed to be done.

There was a committee whose mandate was to take input from the public and integrate their responses into the plans, as they were evolving, for the National Trade Centre. The committee was set up to hear comment from the public at large and interested parties. We asked to speak to the committee and the committee allowed us to speak to them, but I don't think they listened. I think they dismissed what we had to say as being of no consequence, as being biased and as being fearful that our business would be negatively affected by the National Trade Centre. Anything we had to say was rejected out of hand. As the general manager of the International Centre, I really was offended by that. We are experts in the field that they were endeavouring to get involved in, but they dismissed what we had to say as sour grapes.

I said at the hearing that I didn't expect my business would be negatively impacted, that I thought this would be good for my business. And that's exactly what happened. I picked up some major shows from the National Trade Centre, large shows that were so put off by what was happening down there. They didn't feel that they were treated well during the consultation process and in the pre-construction process.

There were people involved in the National Trade Centre who were self-proclaimed experts, who were doing things without consulting their customers. Their customers pointed out that people would not be able to get by the construction, or that there wouldn't be places to park. They were fearful that the disruption during the construction process would harm their business, so they came up here. They had no qualms whatsoever about leaving.

We never said, "Don't do it." We just said, "You are doing it for the wrong reasons and in the wrong way, and spending far more money than is necessary." I think the bureaucrats took at face value the information they were being given and the concepts they were fed. If you look at the words "export market," "new business," "international trade" — those are admirable goals. That's what they were being fed, over and over and over again.

I saw some of the reports that the consultants submitted with respect to international trade. The reports named no one they talked to, but they did give a pretty clear idea of how the questions were structured. I got the impression the questions were structured like this: "If a new, state-of-the-art trade centre was built of approximately this size, would you consider coming to Toronto?" I think a number of people — we're talking human nature — I think two dozen people might have said, "Yes, I would consider coming to Toronto."

That was in direct contradiction to what we knew about shows and how they don't move, how they're attached to an industry in a certain region. But this was the basis on which they built the National Trade Centre: human nature. People did not want to be rude, didn't want to be negative, didn't want to rain on anyone's parade by saying, "No, are you out of your mind? Toronto is cold in the winter and my show runs in January, February."

I don't believe that people lied to them outright. I do believe that the answers were misleading because they weren't structured by somebody who knew the business. I don't think the person who asked the question knew about the seasonality of shows. I don't think the interviewers or the market research company knew enough about the business to construct questions that would flush out correct answers.

I don't want to blame the bureaucrats. There was no source of unbiased analysis. We gave them some clues as to where they were wrong and they didn't check out the clues. They thought they had expert advice, but they didn't.

Everyone who was involved in that project stood to benefit from it in some way or another. All of the consultants benefit, just by consulting. I deal with consultants; anybody in business does. I've learned that on occasion the consultant is only as good as the direction you give. You set the tone and the direction. You instruct the consultant about how to ask the question and who they're going to ask. The consultant then comes out and does exactly what you tell him and gives you the answer that you already decided you want. As bizarre as that is, that's the process of using a consultant.

As experts in the trade and consumer show business, we thought they could refurbish the property. It was then called Exhibition Place. It could have been revitalized, but the price tag was not $200 million. The real price to do what we, as experts, thought our clients and customers needed was around $50 million.

We hired a consultant to help us to communicate with government. Like many consultants, he was an ex-bureaucrat and an ex–elected politician from a highly regarded political consulting firm. He knew the process, and he was advising us on how we should present our point of view. We said to him, "We want to tell the government that they can and should build this project because that property is old and rundown and needs to be revitalized. But we've done some analysis and we think it could be done for $50 million."

Our lobbyist said, "Please, don't make a fool out of yourself. Don't say that to the politicians. If you're going to say that, don't even refer to a figure less than $100 million. They'll laugh you out of the room. The minimum amount you should say they should spend is $100 million because a project of any less scope than that isn't even worth talking about." His experience was bigger is better.

That project could have been done, the building refurbished, for $50 million. Even if we're wrong and it was $75 million, it would have been more than enough for the business that it's really doing, which is local business or business that they already had. It still would have acted as a catalyst for new business. But it would not have been a burden on the taxpayer, with an operating deficit which no one talks about but which is going to continue for all eternity with that building.

The public should be mad. I don't know if they'll ever find out, and if they do, who are they going to blame? There's no accountability. There's no identifiable prime mover behind any of this to come back to and say, "That was a dumb thing, why did you do it and what are you going to do now to make up for doing it?" At least there isn't anyone that I've been able to find.

I see a huge difference between ourselves, as private enterprise, and accountability in government. I see no accountability whatsoever in government. There's reverse accountability. When you're in government, if you make a mistake, somebody pays you a lot of money to go away and gives you a golden handshake. You're put on the pension payroll earlier instead of later. When you're in private enterprise and you make a big mistake, you go away but nobody pays you anything. Governments should have the same systems of accountability that private enterprise has.

If you compare the International Centre to the National Trade Centre, there's no comparison. I don't think it'll ever be successful in terms of paying its own way, as we do in this facility. We pay our costs, we pay our debt service and we actually make money for our owners. So the lesson is that a trade and consumer centre can be built by private enterprise, can pay its own way and can create a return on investment.

ILA BOSSONS

Toronto City Councillor

Ila Bossons sits on several Toronto boards, agencies and corporations. As a city councillor she represented Toronto's Midtown ward, but did not seek re-election in 2000; she said that local politicians had too little power.

I'm a city councillor in Toronto. I represent Midtown, which is really the centre of the new 2.2 million-people city. Of all the cities in this country, Toronto is probably most capable of finding the money it desperately needs from property tax, which will become very high. But there are other cities that can't even do that. There are gaps in the system and it's regrettable that we have spent federal-provincial money on things like bocce courts or ice rinks, when we miss some of the true basics of life in this country.

The Canada Infrastructure Works Program money was offered to municipalities. The municipalities then presented the projects they wished to fund. While we were given money, we had very tight restrictions attached to it.

What goes on behind the scenes, I cannot answer. How were these decisions made? Why did councils decide on one project over another?

The minute you offer a city council "free money" from the province and from the federal government, a council may change its mind about what is essential in that particular city. Politicians like to have glory, to have "achieved something." They like to say, "And this is the recreation centre, or the trade centre, or the subway we've built for you."

I think Canadians pretend that they have a modern, up-to-date country. In reality it isn't. All you have to do is look at which cities have good sewage treatment. That's sort of the basis of civilization — what you do when you flush. It goes back to the Romans. We are a long way from cleaning up that part of our environment.

I know that there are many small towns that desperately need help with having better sewage treatment. We've got cities that don't even have a safe water supply. Occasionally they have to shut it down because they don't have filtration plants that are good enough. If you make your children sick or if you have to start boiling your water, that's a pretty basic issue. That's Third World. That is not what we say is a modern country.

If you want to be quite honest about Canada Infrastructure Works Program dollars, they're goodies given by the federal and the provincial government at times when they need to look good at the local level to win elections. It's really a disgraceful way of looking after your country. I've been in this country for 30 years or so and there's been a real decline in cohesion. You've got cities, you've got provinces and you've got the federal government. We have no overview. We have no federal involvement in public transit, for example. Yet in Toronto we are driving millions of cars. We're suffocating in our own pollution. The province used to subsidize Toronto's subways. They have now stopped. We are now totally on our own.

You're seeing the two senior governments throwing cities to the wolves, letting them rely on the property tax. It isn't going to make for livable cities. It isn't going to make for good public transit; it isn't going to make for good anti-pollution measures; and it isn't going to make for decent sewage treatment systems or water filtration plants across the whole country. That to me is not the sign of a progressive country.

Maybe I'm an environmentalist and care about this, but I think it's pretty basic that if there is federal and provincial money available, that's the kind of thing you should spend money on — helping cities catch up.

There's catching up to be done. A lot of money could have been spent on this but wasn't.

Toronto is somewhat different from other cities. We manage our sewers and water treatment completely outside the property tax system. The water bill pays for everything. If we know we have to build more sewers, we increase the water rate. We have a 10-year plan and a capital reserve, so sewers are not an issue.

Many Canadian cities haven't done it this way. They've done it partially out of tax money. They send water bills to their customers. And they have not made good management plans. They didn't have the nerve to tell their customers that there were big expenditures coming down the pike. So they find themselves with neglected or nonexistent systems. Really big expenditures are water production plants and sewage treatment plants. They cost hundreds of millions of dollars for a big city like this.

Metropolitan Toronto was a world-famous regional government. In 1953 it started making major expenditures, consciously putting really good infrastructure in place. Cities within Metro Toronto also put on the water bill the cost of fixing the local drain, fixing the local water supply. It's a very safe way of doing it because it's pure user fee.

In offering this infrastructure program money, the federal and provincial levels of government left it up to the cities to propose projects. That's a self-defeating process. If you've got a city that has managed itself badly and chosen to neglect its bridges or its sewage treatment, that city may well propose a fancy project that really is not infrastructure. If you're offered infrastructure money, you will have the roads commissioner, the parks commissioner and the commissioner of social services saying, "We have structures that are falling down or new ones that we would like to build. Here are our priority lists." Decisions are made by the city council, based on lists from staff.

If any mayor says, "I don't know why they built a bocce court" after all of this, he's being disingenuous. Infrastructure is sewage, water, roads, bridges, that kind of thing. In many other cities the councils simply decided what their particular glory project was, and that is what they proposed. Well, I can't tell you how each city decided which projects were needed. They know where they ought to have spent the money, but they also had projects that they wished to build out of civic pride. A council could deem a hockey arena as infrastructure. In Toronto we proposed a trade centre.

Metropolitan Toronto council decided that the bulk of the national infrastructure program money — about $180 million, one-third of which the city paid — would be spent on the construction of the National Trade Centre. I did not support that decision. I didn't think it was worth the risk. I was not convinced that the business plan would really justify spending $180 million on that one particular building. The National Trade Centre was a glory project. Toronto wants to be on the North American map. The word "national" should give you a hint just how obsessed this city was with getting a piece of the glory. It is true that the Canadian National Exhibition (CNE) buildings were antiquated, not attractive, and it was difficult to get shows in. My concern was that every major city on this continent is building a trade centre. The National Trade Centre is downtown. Usually these things are near airports because people fly in.

The question is, is your business plan actually a good one? Are you going to attract all the business that makes all this spending worthwhile? It will take several years to find out if we are attracting business.

The good thing to be said about the way the Trade Centre proposal came to council is that outside consultants evaluated the business opportunities. At least in theory that is better than having your own staff promoting it. In some instances staff will tell council what council likes to hear. What the consultants told us was rosy enough for council to vote for the project. Their projections were that we would attract enough business to make this project worthwhile. You know, you have to trust these people. That's their business, to evaluate the viability of all sorts of undertakings.

There are two ingredients in many decisions a councillor makes. One is facts. The other is pride, or what you want your city to look like. There are probably some councillors who didn't even read the reports, who only made their decisions based on the pride factor, if you will. That's how political decisions are made. Political decisions are not physics or mathematics, where one thing has to follow logically upon the other. There are emotions involved in decision making. So the facts don't always count. The more glorious the project is, the less the facts will be considered. That's the reality of decision making. I suspect that's true from the smallest village council up to Ottawa.

With the Trade Centre one of the factors in the decision was that the centre would get exemption from provincial taxes. That would of course help to make the business plan look wonderful. Other trade centres — for example, the International Centre, which happens to be not in Toronto but near the airport, in Mississauga — do not have the privilege of not paying taxes. It is a rather unfair way for one city to promote its trade centre over a trade centre that may be competing with it. But I'm sure that persuaded a few more people at Metro council to vote for it.

It was very seductive to take the $120-million "free" money from the federal and provincial governments. I decided that was the wrong way of spending the money, so I opposed it. Only three voted against it. It was not popular or fashionable to vote against it. There was political pressure from the trade unions and the construction companies who wanted us to create jobs. That project was built when the economy was pretty slow. We had a conference table full of people in hardhats occasionally shouting opponents down. They wanted those jobs. I didn't feel the pressure of the unions, but obviously others did.

There's always a left wing on any council, and it was in favour of building the Trade Centre, to create jobs. Now, that's all very well, and you can say this creates tens of thousands of man-years of work. But it is tax money. For the next 20 years, is this project going to drain money from those same people, in the form of taxes to maintain it? That's the issue. The city had to invest $60 million out of property tax money, out of the capital budget. You typically borrow that amount over a period of 10 years, so eventually you can sink double the $60 million into the project. The Trade Centre will crop up on this year's capital budget, on next year's capital budget. It's part of the dead maintenance.

When the $60 million was debated it was made clear what its impact on the next five and 10 years' capital budgets would be. But the Metro capital budget is very large, so it was easy to think, "Well, $60 million is just another item." It was not, in the general scheme of things, a large item. It didn't whack the capital budget one way or the other. On the property tax bill the project will affect taxpayers by, say, $10 a year for the individual residential property tax bill. For a large business it might be $100 or $200 a year.

This happens quite often when something big is proposed. Councils will say, "Well, it's only $5.47 a month on your bill, now do you really mind?" And people tend to think it's not very much. Except that of course everything is $5.47, and when you add them all up it can turn into a few hundred extra dollars. It's incredibly easy to fool the public by presenting large numbers in terms of small numbers, you know.

It's very easy to focus just on the short term and it's easy to get caught in a spiral of debt. Quite often the press concentrates on the short term. Taxpayers are easily swayed by what the local papers will say, and the National Trade Centre was promoted by both the left-wing and the right-wing local papers. There's lots of press attention on that type of project. It is much less sexy to say, "We have made sure that your water filtration plant works and we have built bridges." The minute there is "free" money, you go for something that is without political drawbacks for you. It's only human nature. You go for the glory projects.

The National Trade Centre would not have gone ahead without that "free" money. We were already hard up for money. We couldn't fix our roads. I will tell you precisely why the roads in Metro Toronto were so neglected over the last 10 years. Beginning in 1988 Metro used road money to spend on welfare. I was elected to Metro council in 1989. Since the late 1980s when we had a recession, we have had a welfare crisis. Metro had to pay 20 percent of every welfare cheque. It was obliged by Ontario to do so. Metro had to use anything it could find to fund the welfare cheques.

The province obviously has an interest in seeing its money go to the glory projects. On a small portion of the money, the province of Ontario said, "You do it our way, or you don't do it at all." We could have used all of the Trade Centre money on roads, over two years. There would have been no shortage of projects.

People complain when you build the bridges and roads because there's going to be an inconvenience. It took two years to fix the bridges over the Humber River. I was glad that some of the federal-provincial money went into the reconstruction of Yonge Street and Avenue Road, which are two major arteries leading to downtown Toronto. They had not been reconstructed since the 1920s. But I got extraordinary criticism from my voters and I lost a lot of votes — it happened to be municipal election time. I lost a lot of votes because I had supported the reconstruction of these roads, which was delaying everyone's trip downtown.

You can neglect roads for a long time before they get really bad, but you can't neglect the subway system for very long before it crashes. We had a longer list of roads that had reached the absolute bottom and needed repair. On the other hand, we didn't have the money to do it because we were obliged to spend on something else.

Metro Toronto decided to spend the second wave of that funding — the first one was essentially spent on the Trade Centre — on the deep-lake water-cooling project. Now that's true infrastructure, that's 21st century infrastructure. That money will bring almost ice-cold water from deep in Lake Ontario. It gets filtered to be drinking water, but before you drink it, it gets run through heat exchangers in office buildings, which will use it for cooling. This means they can get rid of their chiller plants, which run electrically or with natural gas. So that's a useful application of infrastructure money.

JACK LAYTON

Toronto City Councillor

Jack Layton has been a Toronto city councillor since the 1970s. He has also served as vice president of the Federation of Canadian Municipalities.

I have been a councillor in the City of Toronto for close to 20 years. There was certainly a lot of excitement when the Canada Infrastructure Works Program was announced. Municipalities had been pushing for an infrastructure program for quite a while.

I'm vice president of the Federation of Canadian Municipalities, which conceived the program initially, mostly because our cities' basic infrastructure needs were not being met with property tax as a funding base. It was suggested that we form a partnership with the federal and provincial governments and get some dollars flowing into our cities so that we didn't have crumbling infrastructure. It would also create jobs and help to meet the gap in our infrastructure capabilities. So there was a great deal of excitement when the project was announced.

It's good to have our federal level of government investing in the cities with a program like the Canada Infrastructure Works Program. After all, the cities only have one source of income — property tax — and some user charges like Toronto Transit Commission (TTC) fares and that sort of thing. But we don't have a tax regime that allows us to raise the funds that we need. In fact, if you go to the great cities of the world, most of them have either income taxes or sales taxes, or significant support from federal governments to keep their cities viable.

In the case of the City of Toronto, the city was one part of a two-tier administration at the time. The city was the smaller, "lower" tier. It chose to tackle the problem of pollution in the western beaches area, based on an approach that had been tried with some success in the eastern beaches area. Meanwhile the second tier of municipal government, the Metro tier, chose to invest in a large economic development project at the Canadian National Exhibition, known as the National Trade Centre. Other cities did many other different kinds of things, but in Toronto those two projects emerged as the largest consumers of the dollars.

The western beaches tunnel is not a stand-alone project. It was part of a vision by some engineers to clean the city's water system. By "cleaning the water system," what they really meant was intercepting it and delivering it to Ashbridges Bay. That's the giant treatment plant in the east end of Toronto. By expanding that plant dramatically, we could burn the sewage sludge and put the treated water out into the lake, with a big shot of chlorine on its way out.

Many environmental groups resisted that plan. Then came this concept of a storage tunnel, a "structural alternative." You're basically diverting the pollution from the beaches. It is a large structure and a very expensive engineering project. It's really just a giant pipe carved out of the rock 10 storeys or more below ground. The tunnel will store the water that comes in during a rainfall — water that has mixed with sewage from the combined sewer systems in older parts of the city — to prevent it flowing into the lake. The sewage sludge will settle in the tunnel and be pumped to the main treatment plant for processing and perhaps burning. The water that's been stored will be somewhat less turbid. Later, with a shot of radiation, it can be sent out to the lake, away from where people swim.

Many environmentalists argued that you should approach the issue of water in cities in a non-structural way. You should look upstream, as it were, to where the storm water first lands on the city, and come up with innovative ways of dealing with it there. The so-called non-structural alternatives came a bit late in the game, and the momentum was awfully strong for the big engineering solution. That's why the engineering project went ahead, essentially. An immediate injection of cash from the infrastructure program forced the council to make a decision to go forward with the structural solution, rather than to innovate.

No question, the infrastructure program had an impact on the kind of decisions that were made and on the way they were made. Suddenly you had a pot of cash that had to be spent within a tight time frame. That was a real carrot for city council to jump to the big structural solution. Had that cash infusion not been there — or had it been available over an extended period — council might have said, "Let's do a series of smaller projects over a longer time, which might actually be better for the environment, as well as solving the problem."

The environmentalists and neighbourhoods were split, but the engineers were united, and that created the political context for the project to be supported. Landscapers, ecologists, the environmental community — they tended to push for alternative approaches. It took the environmental community awhile to get organized. By then the horse was out of the barn. They were trying to catch up, in terms of getting city council to shift direction from the old-fashioned pipe-building solutions into the more ecological, holistic, more complex approaches to dealing with water in the city.

Councillors were split on the question on geographical lines. Those from the west end of the city were enthusiastic about this project because they wanted to deliver a swimmable beach to their constituents as part of their legacy. The westerners looked at the easterners and said, "You've already got water-detention tanks and you're swimming in your beaches. You've got to give us the right to do the same." In the east end of Toronto councillors didn't like the idea of sludge from the west end being pumped over to the east end and burned and processed. They have very high asthma rates there, as a result of such things as the burning of sewage sludge. At the end of it all an environmental assessment concluded that the city should develop a comprehensive plan for its water and develop non-structural solutions. But in the meantime the assessment said, fine, go ahead with the big pipe.

City engineers were delighted that the program was pushing council because the engineers wanted to build their pipe. The engineering firms, the construction unions, the big economic players of the city — they saw the tunnel approach as a quick way to create some good jobs and invest in a piece of city infrastructure.

The jury's out on whether this project will clean up even the western beaches, let alone the Toronto bays. We'll have to see. I'm a bit skeptical that this project will give us many more swimmable bays along the waterfront. I think it's a quick-fix mega-solution that doesn't recognize the original sources of pollution. I don't think Toronto Bay will be cleaned up by more large pipes. I think what you'll see is the Toronto Bay Initiative, which is a community initiative, bubbling up from the surface of the bay, in a sense, with lots of interesting, innovative, non-structural approaches, combined with some small engineering interjections. I think you'll find that that initiative is what will move forward now, if we're going to clean up the bay.

I would have preferred that we didn't put all the money in the big western beaches tunnel, but instead had invested in more localized solutions, such as rain barrels. I'm sure if we'd proposed to hire students to take rain barrels to people, though, somebody out there would have decided to ridicule that as a use of infrastructure dollars because they might not have understood how it was being used.

Livable cities are not made just from roads and sewers. Parks and recreation services are infrastructure. A playground set of swings, for example, that's rusting and falling apart is just as important a part of the city's infrastructure as the roads are. And a bocce court is a facility primarily for seniors from Eastern and Southern Europe to play sports. If we were talking about lawn bowling or golf courses or other more typically Anglo-Saxon, North American sports, I'm not sure you would have had the same reaction. Frankly I find this reaction around the bocce courts to be pretty close to racist.

I would say the downside of the infrastructure program was that it was a one-shot thing, with very tight timelines — primarily to match electoral objectives — rather than a long-term ongoing plan for financing urban infrastructure. It was sort of a taste of a good thing. Investment strategies can sometimes be a bit dangerous. They can tantalize people into making wrong decisions. I think that did happen in a few instances.

The rationale of the program changed to some degree from the original Federation of Canadian Municipalities' concept, and the definition of what constituted infrastructure became broader. In big Ontario cities, for example, the sewage treatment was already up to reasonably good standards, so people began to look at other interesting kinds of economic development projects. The National Trade Centre, for instance, certainly wasn't the kind of thing that the FCM had initially been talking about. Not at all.

We've been reducing the level of federal assistance to cities in Canada. We're starving our cities. Of course we'll pay the price for that in the end. If our cities start to fall apart and investment doesn't come here, then we're going to be in trouble. We're at risk there.

We used to have federal assistance in housing. That was probably one of the largest federal-provincial-municipal collaborations over 20 years. It provided a very large number of affordable housing units, resulting in a relatively low level of homelessness until recent years. Those programs amounted to a kind of social infrastructure, in the form of housing construction. But now those programs have been cancelled and we're seeing the consequences. We'll see similar consequences with our roads, our transit system, our sewer and water treatment processes if we don't get those partnerships with other levels. Any partnership that brings the federal government in to help improve the infrastructure of our cities is vitally important.

The National Trade Centre was a good example of using the infrastructure program to produce spinoff benefits. There's ongoing investment in the city as a result of that trade centre. It produces a sort of shadow, or echo, effect through the years. It's much like the Better Buildings Partnership, which was an innovative way that funds were used in Toronto to help retrofit some buildings for energy efficiency. And that money was saved, came back to us, and we're using that infrastructure money over and over again.

It was actually the NDP caucus at city hall that proposed, back in the mid-1980s, that we have a trade centre in Toronto. Frankly this is how it emerged: instead of putting public dollars into the SkyDome stadium, we said that we should put money into something that actually had job-creation potential, that could enhance the economic infrastructure of the city. The SkyDome consumed over $350 million of public resources, after it had promised to be self-financing on $30 million of public investment, which was to be recovered in taxes. I hope that moral indignation will extend to the real culprits, namely the private sector people who built that stadium. There is no accountability at all in that situation.

In the case of the National Trade Centre, there seemed to be a broad consensus, across a broad range of groups who normally don't come together. People like myself and social groups who normally oppose megaprojects like the SkyDome and railway land development and things like that came together. We saw it as potentially creating jobs for working people, regular jobs as opposed to the high-flier sorts of jobs. It had that sort of mystique about it. If it doesn't turn out that it accomplished that, that'll be quite sad.

When you pick one large project for an infrastructure program like this, that decision is going to skew some of your priorities. It acts as a magnet, sucking all the resources into one place. Ideally you'd want to invest in a variety of aspects of the city's infrastructure at the same pace, so that your environmental remediation, your new economic development structures and your transportation infrastructures were all moving along at the same pace.

The National Trade Centre required a large infusion from the city's capital budget. It drew away from other projects. Had we chosen to split the funding up among smaller initiatives, with some to roads, some to transit and some to environment, we wouldn't have had the National Trade Centre. At the time the entire tourism and trade sector in the city was urging us to spend this money. They were the most active proponents of it. Some private companies, in an earlier incarnation of this project, came forward in response to a proposal call. Those projects didn't end up coming to fruition, but there was certainly widespread public interest in building and operating a trade centre.

The Trade Centre is showing close to a $9-million shortfall every year. We had long discussions about this at council, and a lot of these questions were asked. And we ask a lot of tough questions before we give the CNE any financial support. Usually lots of people get raked over the coals. Lots of tough questions are asked by our budget committee about those matters. What do you do about a situation where you have a large facility that's losing some money? What do you do, close it? Everybody resign and say, "We made a mistake, we better all quit and let somebody else run the city"?

196

JACK LAYTON

I think council made the right decision. The Trade Centre is a piece of urban infrastructure. It is part of what allows a city to thrive. To me it's like investing in a university or investing in a port or investing in an airport. Over the long term it could be a real economic engine for Toronto. It can make us a centre for idea exchanges, which is what the great cities of the world are. They never are manufacturing centres for very long.

We'll have to judge the National Trade Centre at the end of another five years or so to see if it's begun to capture the sort of economic development activity that we've all been hoping for. It is possible that it was an error, but it's far too early to judge. My guess is that in the first few years after the CNE was built, considerable public money went into it and probably people said, "Gee, was it really worth it?" But then years later, over many years, the benefits became clearer.

Certainly it was in the headlines — that one percent of the average citizen's property tax rate is financing the Trade Centre debenture for the next 10 years. I think that those who have gone down and used it would say it makes sense. This is a 30- to 50-year project. It's going to be in existence for that length of time.

JOHN FILION

Toronto City Councillor

A former journalist and book editor, John Filion was a city councillor in North York from 1991 to 1997 before being elected to the new City of Toronto council in 1998.

When the Canada Infrastructure Works Program was announced, North York council knew it had several million dollars to spend, of which it only had to pay a third. Everybody was quite excited by that. The mood on council was, "This is great, we got some money. Let's figure out how to spend it."

There was sort of a mad scramble to identify projects to get done through this program. There was a very tight deadline for the municipality to figure out what the projects would be and to actually spend the money. You couldn't spend it on anything that was already in your five-year capital program. It had to be new projects, which affected the legitimacy of some projects because the projects with the biggest need had already been identified. I assumed the big rush was to get this done before the next federal election.

Was the program abused? Well, it depends what you mean by "abused." It was turned over to municipal politicians. Municipal politicians did what municipal politicians do, which is try to get facilities for their communities. I was never clear on what the main objective was. I think that by "infrastructure" the federal government was probably thinking of larger projects, ones that municipalities just can't do by themselves.

A good chunk of the money was spent on legitimate infrastructure projects. Certainly we did spend some money on sewers and rusty water problems. On some streets you get rusty water because the sewer pipes are old and they were built with the wrong material.

Generally speaking, North York was very well managed. We had Mayor Mel Lastman here for 25 years. He's always had a very good business approach, so the city was very well managed. We've had excellent services and we had a regular road maintenance program. I can't recall our ever having any serious infrastructure problems that we had no money to address.

A decision was made to set aside a portion of the infrastructure money for parks and recreation facilities because that's what helps get municipal politicians re-elected. The public doesn't get too excited about a new sewer, but they will get excited about a new community centre, a new bocce court, new playgrounds, different facilities like that. So it was really a political decision to include some projects in there that the public was going to be happy with.

It was mainly with the parks and recreation facilities that you had the big political scramble by councillors to see who could get their projects to the top of the list. It's not a story that anybody has been very interested in. There are two million stories like this in the naked city.

There were some meetings in North York to decide how to spend the infrastructure money. At one of the meetings I naively suggested that we come up with some sort of criteria, some rational way of determining which projects were most needed and how the money should be spent. I suggested that the staff review all projects and rank them according to need. There was absolutely zero support for that.

It was decided that a list of projects would go to the capital planning committee. The capital planning committee recommended to council which projects to approve. Because nobody wanted a big fight on the council floor, the capital planning committee was supposed to work something out. If you got frozen out by the capital planning committee, you had eight votes against your project at council.

Basically whoever yelled the loudest, manoeuvred the best, and stick-handled the thing through got their projects to the top of that list. If you happened to be on the capital planning committee, that gave you a huge advantage because whoever was manoeuvring needed your vote.

At that time I wasn't especially good at working that process. As a result, a project that I very much wanted — a community centre that I thought would have come at the top of any sort of objective needs assessment — didn't get funded. I represent the area right around Yonge Street and every month there's a new condo going up with 350 more people coming into the neighbourhood. My ward was the only ward in the city that didn't have a community centre. I thought the system would make some rational decision to include my community centre.

When it came to the capital planning committee, the project got cut out because other politicians who were on that committee wanted the money for their own projects. My first reaction was extreme anger. I remember being so angry I couldn't sleep. I was just furious that this project was pitched out and less worthy projects got the money. And some politicians were almost gloating about it: "See how we outmanoeuvred you."

Injustice tends to make me very angry. For a few days I was kind of plotting to correct this injustice. I was planning to make a big splash about the inappropriate use of the money and how it hadn't followed any kind of rational process. I tend to rely too much on some sort of legitimate process to produce the best results, but I'm not sure the result would have been any different. I might have been less disillusioned. When it was clear that the process was "let's make a deal," I belatedly made a deal too.

After talking to some members of council and some staff members, I thought the more prudent thing to do, since my objective was to try to get a badly needed community centre for my area, was to become part of the deal making. What I got was a promise that the community centre that had been cut out of the infrastructure project would be approved a year later, through the regular budget. The councillors lived by the deal; that community centre just opened last month.

Each councillor had a different way of identifying projects to take to council. We all represent wards, or geographic areas. Part of the local councillor's job is to try to meet the requests of constituents. I decided that we needed a community centre at least five years before the infrastructure program money became available. In fact, I wanted a different kind of community centre. I wanted one that was connected to the school and would be a real community centre, as opposed to just a parks and recreation centre. I'd had numerous community meetings about having a community centre and about what type of community centre it should be. So I guess I initiated the idea, but I had a whole big round of community consultation before I formally brought forward the request.

I'm guessing that with the bocce courts, an Italian seniors club got together a petition of several hundred names, or made a request to the councillor for a bocce court. Bocce ball is a sport that's very big with the Italian community. It's like Italian lawn bowling.

If your residents are screaming for a bocce court, you get them a bocce court. If you need a community centre, you get the community centre. There's nothing terrible about that. I'm not faulting any of the municipal councillors who managed to get bocce courts approved. They were responding to the wishes of their local residents, and that's what municipal politicians are supposed to do.

North York is probably the indoor bocce capital of the world. I guess the reason is that council figured if the federal government's doing this to buy some votes for the next election, we should do the same. Because of the infrastructure program, anything that anybody could possibly have wanted got done one way or another. Every councillor who bought into the package — which I think in the end was everybody — got looked after.

You can be mad at the federal government for lack of direction — or appropriate direction — about how to spend the money. You can get mad at the municipal politicians for building something that you didn't think needed to be built. There was some questioning of a couple of projects, about whether the city was properly spending taxpayers' money, regardless of whether it was federal, provincial or municipal money.

The Canada Infrastructure Works Program was a good concept, but everything was extremely rushed. I don't think there were any terrible projects approved. But if you had a rational process and not just a big political scramble, you would come up with a different list of projects, which would not only provide short-term construction jobs, but would also create some infrastructure. That would in turn improve the economy and create some permanent jobs.

I would have asked our parks and recreation staff to do a report on the relative merits of all of the proposed projects. If you're looking at creating permanent jobs, building bocce courts does very little of that. You create short-term jobs while you're constructing the bocce courts. After that there may be some marginal increase in parks and recreation staff to supervise, clean and maintain the bocce courts. But other than that, it really didn't create any long-term jobs. If the objective of the program was to improve infrastructure and create long-term jobs, then presumably you'd be looking at much larger infrastructure projects.

A lot of politicians are saying that getting the three levels of government together is probably the way to go in the future on more projects. Looking at this, I have to question if that is the best way to go. Three levels of government working together is essential to solving all kinds of problems. It makes perfect sense for them to co-operate on an infrastructure program, on projects that would otherwise not happen. It just has to be handled differently.

We need to establish what we're trying to achieve with this money. We're trying to not just stimulate the economy with construction jobs, but to put in facilities that benefit the economy in the long run. For example, with the New Deal (the United States Depression-era economic program) they built the Hoover Dam. If you were really doing this properly, you'd be looking at convention centres to bring in visitors and dollars, to boost the economy of the city. You might be looking at something like creating a link between the airport and downtown. You could build highways so that trucks can travel faster. You'd be looking at providing facilities that are going to have a long-term economic benefit, rather than ones that have a very limited payoff.

I don't think the federal government got much political credit for the infrastructure program. The ones who got the political credit were the local politicians. The local politicians were the ones who got to manage the projects and involve the community in the design. If you did a survey on who built these facilities or where the money came from, I'm sure most people would say the City of North York. They wouldn't say the municipality paid a third and the federal government paid a third. They would probably not even know the province was involved because the province didn't seem to be in the picture anywhere.

JOE PANTALONE

Toronto City Councillor

Now a councillor in Toronto, Joe Pantalone was the chair of the National Trade Centre Building Committee and spearheaded the approval and construction of the building. He is the current chair of the city's Planning and Transportation Committee.

I'm a City of Toronto councillor as well as chair of the board of governors at Exhibition Place, which is an agency owned by the City of Toronto. It's within the National Trade Centre. And I was the chair of the National Trade Centre Building Committee, which oversaw its construction on behalf of the then Metro Toronto council.

Well, the National Trade Centre had its genesis about 1987. There was a future-use study done of Exhibition Place. The Blue Jays and the Argonauts sports teams were moving away from the Exhibition Place because the SkyDome was being built. And there were some studies done at that time which indicated that the way to go was to trade and consumer show facilities on the grounds, which would give it a shot in the arm.

The Exhibition Place grounds, in which the National Trade Centre sits, are a strategic piece of Toronto real estate. It's where the Canadian National Exhibition, which has been around 120 years, is. Where the Royal Agricultural Winter Fair, which has been around 76 years, is. Where the Molson Indy is, where the CHIN Picnic is, and where the highest collection of heritage buildings anywhere in the City of Toronto are — some of them nationally designated. So these grounds are very precious, and once the sports things left the grounds, the financial viability that supported all these programs was in question.

The question for Metro council became, what should occur in order to revitalize those grounds and allow these events to continue, in the life not only of Toronto, but also the province and the country? It was deemed that a trade and consumer show was essential, and a trade centre fit perfectly within that. So it began back then.

Exhibition Place was under the auspices of the Metro Toronto council, which asked for expressions of interest at that time. Council wanted to build this private sector–public sector partnership because we knew that we weren't experts in the field. A number of consortiums replied. And the one which won, if you will, the ability to get to the next stage was the Metrex group, which engaged with us in terms of estimating what the total cost of the project was going to be. At that time I think it was deemed to be something like $450 million. It was perceived that we would get $360 million of government funding, split evenly between the municipality of Metro Toronto, the province and the federal government, and approximately up to $100 million in private sector money.

Metro was ready to roll. The Metrex group said that they were interested in doing it, and the province was thinking about it. We contacted the federal government, the Brian Mulroney government, at the time. We had a meeting with Finance Minister Michael Wilson and with the municipality of Toronto. We also contacted the provincial government of Bob Rae. I think it was in September of 1993. Mr. Doug Lewis was the federal culture minister. He made a statement just as the federal election was called, to the effect that the Trade Centre made perfect sense, but the federal government was not going to fund it.

We've been investing in this city. Toronto had the road building under control. We have our recreational centres and arenas under control. We've been investing in that for many years. We had our transit system sort of under control. We're not dumping raw sewage into the lake, like some other cities. People in Toronto pay taxes like everybody else.

Toronto felt, and still feels now, that the federal and provincial governments were not really paying enough attention to the city, in the sense of investing in it, even though it's essential to the economic well-being of the country. Don't forget, we were in the middle of a recession. We still have an unemployment rate in Toronto that is greater than in the Greater Toronto Area (GTA) and greater than the provincial rate.

There had been an organization to which I belonged called the Toronto Job Start Coalition. It was composed of government and representatives from the private sector, the construction industry and the labour movement. We argued that the federal and provincial governments needed to invest in this city to get the economy moving in Toronto. The Job Start Coalition argued for things like the federal government investing in another runway at Pearson International Airport. It was pretty well the only airport in the country that made money for the federal government, and yet they have terminals there that resemble a Third World country's terminals, thanks to the feds.

The provincial government has always been our partner. TTC (Toronto Transit Commission) construction, capital works, for example, would always be funded 75 percent provincially, 25 percent ourselves.

The Federation of Canadian Municipalities had long argued that the federal government has a role in the infrastructure of this country. Historically they built the railways, they built the Trans-Canada Highway, and I guess they were managing the airports. But in the last 20 or 30 years the federal government seems to have withdrawn from that. They've withdrawn from building housing. They sold the Canadian National Railway. The Trans-Canada Highway, it's now a two-lane road in places. They haven't put any infrastructure money into it.

We were arguing also that a convention centre was needed because the tourism industry — which has been a pillar of strength in Toronto, with something like 21 million visits a year to the city — was suffering. We were losing conventions because our convention centre was not large enough. The Trade Centre was deemed by everybody to be one of those pieces of economic infrastructure that was essential if this city were to compete in a world-regional basis. The whole community was convinced that we needed something like that. Mr. Art Eggleton and Mr.

Jean Chrétien during that election said that if they were elected, they would fund the building of a national trade centre in Toronto.

After the election the Canada–Ontario Infrastructure Works Program was presented for Ontario. They pledged $2 billion across the country, over three years initially, on the condition that the provinces and the municipalities would equally match that amount. So actually they were leveraging $6 billion worth of investment in the country, with a $2-billion investment over three years. A proposal would come from municipalities, school boards or in some cases the private sector, rather than from the province and the feds. They would say yea or nay to each other's projects.

It became feasible to fund the National Trade Centre under the infrastructure program because otherwise the federal government would appear that they were being "too nice" to Toronto. People across the country think that this is a rich province, even though there are more poor people here within defined poverty limits than some provinces have residents. It probably would not have been politically sustainable for them to say, "Here, Toronto, here's $60 million." They're always building museums in the hundreds of millions of dollars in Montreal or Quebec City, but somehow the country is unified in hating Toronto, so you can't give anything to Toronto. And they didn't give anything to Toronto. All they did is give us our fair share.

The municipality of Metropolitan Toronto was entitled to $244 million worth of this expenditure: one-third to come from Metro, one-third from the province, one-third from the federal government. The municipality of Metropolitan Toronto decided that $180 million out of that $244 million would be used for the National Trade Centre.

There was tremendous pressure, primarily from the Metro Convention Centre itself and the rest of the tourism industry, for the Trade Centre. There was a study done by the consulting firm Ernst and Young before the municipality put in that application. The federal and provincial governments agreed that they would co-sponsor a study, and that both of them would be bound by the position of the study. At the time the provincial government of Bob Rae wasn't sure whether they wanted to expand the Convention Centre, and wasn't sure whether they should consent to the National Trade Centre under Infrastructure Works Program.

Also, there was some misunderstanding that a convention centre and a trade centre may be similar things. They were wondering whether you could do with building one, as opposed to both. Trade centres are primarily for showing goods and services and they are almost industrial-looking — concrete floors, high ceilings, no paintings on the wall. A Convention Centre has a hotel-like finish, with carpets, relatively low ceilings, chandeliers and things on the wall. A Convention Centre is primarily for people conventions, as opposed to trade shows and consumer shows.

The question posed to Ernst and Young was basically, "Here's the business plan for the National Trade Centre. Does it make sense? And secondly, do you need both the convention centre and the Trade Centre in Toronto, yes or no?" Their answer was yes, you needed the convention centre; yes, you needed the Trade Centre; and yes, you needed both.

As a result Metrex, which was to have been the private sector contributor to the Trade Centre complex, was dropped and another plan was revised. Instead of a $360-million brand-new exhibit hall, the project was scaled down to a brand-new area of approximately 750,000 square feet, attached to a somewhat renovated older space, which is the Coliseum complex. That came to $180 million. That's why the application was for $180 million, and why it was a completely government application, rather than the private sector–public sector partnership as originally envisioned. At a duly held council meeting that was properly discussed and that was the decision, overwhelmingly.

We required approximately a million square feet. Around 700,000 square feet is new, and the other 400,000 square feet is old space, which is attached to the new. We never contemplated building anything over a million square feet of space.

The reality is that the major trade centres are pieces of economic infrastructure, if they are big enough to fulfill a truly original, competitive role with other regions across the world. The private sector simply cannot do it. We were following the example of the Americans and the Europeans. We looked at other major trade centres across North America and Europe with whom we are competing. In Chicago the government approved a billion-dollar expansion, with tax dollars, of the McCormick Place centre, which is three times the size of the Trade Centre and is one of our prime competitors. There was no private-public funds to do the McCormick centre in Chicago. Atlanta and other competitors also have trade centres. So again, there are public funds. In Europe it's the same thing, and in Taipei, Taiwan.

Our competition is not the International Centre in Mississauga. It's not Hamilton, it's not Montreal. Rather it's New York, Chicago, Atlanta and so forth. The world economy is what makes a difference now. Why is it OK for the Americans to build a big trade centre all with tax money and we Canadians cannot do the same? Don't we want to compete?

In Europe, for example, the trade centres are all state-run. It could be that they're the equivalent of our province, but they're all state-run centres. I think it makes sense because so many people across the world have looked at how you build these things, and so many people can't be so wrong. Even if they're wrong, if they're introducing an element into the marketplace, a subsidized trade centre facility in Chicago, Atlanta or New York, then we in Toronto would be stupid not to introduce an equally subsidized facility. Because that's what allows us to compete.

Private sector–public sector interest did not completely fall off the agenda, but we don't want the tail to be wagging the dog. If there's a $450-million investment, and $350 million or $360 million comes from the public sector — your tax dollars and mine — and $90 million comes from the private sector, we don't want the $90 million to be controlling the full $450 million. We did not wish to have this huge investment of the taxpayer being held to ransom by any private owner.

So we had structured the deal in such a way that the exhibit hall, where the exhibits and the auxiliary uses are, would stay in the public sector. You make money indirectly from sales tax, income taxes and the economic multiplier effects. That's why there was a division. The private sector is not completely out of it. We made a request for a proposal call, for who will manage this centre. Olympia & York/SMG, which is the largest manager of trade, consumer and sport facilities in the States, applied. We chose O&Y/SMG as our private sector manager, if you will, of this public asset.

Metro Toronto council at that time did not give a tax increase because of the Trade Centre. We debentured the money. When you factor in the debenture and the interest on that debenture, the true cost to Toronto for the Trade Centre is higher than $180 million, of course. When you buy a house for $150,000, by the time you finish paying for it, it probably cost you $300,000. Does that mean you don't buy the house? That's not how our decisions are made. If you use that form of calculation, of course it's more than what you pay because of interest and all that, but that's how calculations are made.

All the business plans and analysis that we saw indicated that the federal and provincial governments would get their money back within five years. When you build something, first of all, people work and pay income taxes. The material that you buy, you pay sales taxes on that. There's an increase in employment, and these new workers also pay income taxes and sales taxes.

The National Trade Centre is running an operating profit. In other words, this year the revenue is greater than the expenses. It's an economic generator. That original $60-million investment on the part of the municipality was never expected to be paid back. That was part of the business plan which Ernst and Young and three or four other consulting companies looked at and said it still makes sense.

The government doesn't tax itself. Therefore there is a subsidy, yes. A lot of the trade and consumer shows that helped build this city and the province were always at Exhibition Place, in the old Coliseum, the old Automotive Building. And they didn't pay any property taxes there, either.

You've got to look at what you get indirectly, in the economy. If you don't use that argument, then shut down all the schools because they don't give us any money directly. Shut down all the libraries, they don't give us any money. Shut down all the subways and transit because they don't give us any money.

The International Centre would never have been built new, as a trade facility. I think we have an obligation, the public sector, to make sure we rehabilitate and rejuvenate grounds. You take your asset, which is trade and consumer shows, and it doesn't matter whether it's federal money, provincial money, municipal money — you rehabilitate your asset. You don't let it decay.

Nobody questions building subways or sewers or arenas. This building makes economic sense and adds real value to our community. To tell you the truth, we were despairing of Metro Toronto. We were in the middle of a recession. We knew that the municipality was limited in terms of what it could invest in economic development. We couldn't find $180 million; without federal and provincial money it could not happen. It helped us out tremendously to achieve that goal at that time.

In my view this project was analyzed to death, almost. That's why it took so long to build. Thank God the federal and provincial governments did something right at the end. The decision making was very appropriate. It was infrastructure. Infrastructure. You have to feed the economy, as well as make sure you have running water and proper sewage.

Let's not blow it out of proportion. It is not really that much money. The program was extended to five years, eventually. If you divide the $2-billion federal contribution over five years, for the whole country it's $400 million a year. That's less than building the SkyDome. The former Metro Toronto spent more than that every year for its own capital works program, in terms of scale.

That $180 million included a few other things, like relocating the streetcar loop, you know. The actual building itself was $148 million. We built a new road, kind of a boulevard. I think we've got excellent value for money. It was ahead of schedule, it was on budget, so I think we did very well. Actually it was a great public relations exercise for Mr. Chrétien and the Liberal government, and I'm glad he was there. All sorts of nice things happened across the province.

Wasn't it Winston Churchill who said, "Democracy's a lousy system — except for the alternatives"? We have a democracy in which elected people, federally, provincially and municipally, conduct business in public — municipally more than anywhere else. And that is the accountability that the citizen has. If you don't like the bums, throw them out. That's the ultimate accountability.

RUTH GRIER

Former NDP Provincial Cabinet Minister

Ruth Grier was an alderman in the former City of Etobicoke before being elected to Ontario's legislature as a New Democrat MPP in 1985. During her time in the legislature she held the positions of minister of environment and minister of health.

The Canada Infrastructure Works Program didn't just arrive. There had certainly been pressure on the federal government to do something to create jobs, from our provincial premier, Bob Rae, as well as from the premiers of the Maritimes. We found ourselves in the worst recession since the Depression. Ontario and the Maritimes were particularly badly hit. So at federal-provincial meetings Ontario had been one of those urging the federal government to do something about jobs. The Canada Infrastructure Works Program was a response to that.

We welcomed it. We were delighted when this was finally announced. The Canada–Ontario Infrastructure Works Program, known in Ontario as COI, was an opportunity that our government eagerly embraced. I'm prepared to give the federal government the benefit of the doubt that they too wanted to create jobs. I don't know what led to the decision that it would be an infrastructure program. I suspect it was the idea that that would get things going more quickly.

There was no doubt that the need to restore infrastructure was a high priority. Our government had begun to question whether we could continue to spend as much on infrastructure as had been spent in the past, so the federal cost-sharing program provided an opportunity to continue or even enhance what was happening.

The Federation of Canadian Municipalities had been singing for decades about the need to improve infrastructure across this country. There was certainly a case to be made in the early 1990s that both federal and provincial governments had been spending less on infrastructure than they had previously. Dollars got tight and the cost of doing a mile of road was much more than it had been 10 years previously.

Certainly the program required less provincial funding than a joint cost-sharing with the municipalities. At a time when we had less money to spend on infrastructure, we saw the program as an opportunity to maintain the same level of expenditures, with 33¢ of every dollar coming from the province, as opposed to 50¢ of every dollar. It's leveraging your dollar. It's the clout that senior levels of government have when they want lower levels of government to do something. With these kinds of federal-provincial programs, if the federal government comes up with money, a province isn't going to say, "Sorry, I can't afford to be part of that." They will have the municipalities saying, "Hey, we want to be in, and this is going to cost you less than just doing a bilateral project at some future stage."

The rationale for the infrastructure program was clearly jobs. That was what the people of Ontario desperately needed in 1992, 1993, 1994. Our government saw it as an opportunity to get some federal money at a time when the federal government was also beginning to retrench with respect to spending. The program could create jobs and allow projects to proceed.

Because jobs were our big priority, we wanted to administer this program in such a way that the money was spent quickly and those jobs got out there quickly. We made a conscious decision to try to administer it in the least bureaucratic way possible, to cut the red tape. A key to doing that was our decision to allow the municipalities to set the priorities. We established a small team out of the Cabinet office which worked with the Ministry of Municipal Affairs.

I don't think there was a huge amount of debate around how to implement the infrastructure program when it was announced. This was fairly routine. We set up a committee to administer the program. It had two federal representatives, two provincial representatives and a representative from the Association of Municipalities of Ontario. Projects were vetted by that committee and that was really where the responsibility lay.

The province assumed the responsibility of making sure that the applications were legitimate and the financing figures added up. The federal government didn't wish to exercise any of that control. Their attitude to Ontario was, "As long as it's a three-way sharing of the costs, you can manage this and administer it as you wish."

The only slight hiccup came when some of my colleagues got over-enthusiastic and announced projects as soon as they were approved, without asking the federal member of Parliament to be there for the photo opportunity. At that point the federal government certainly made it plain to us that while they didn't want to nickel-and-dime us, their members had to be there to have their picture taken at the same time. It's entirely legitimate that both levels of government wanted to get the credit for what was going on. I certainly never turn down an opportunity to be on camera. In my constituency there were a number of waterfront projects.

We developed a formula and told the municipalities, "Here's the pot of money that will be available to you. You submit projects that would qualify for that funding. If you can't spend it all, tell us, and we will reallocate to other municipalities or to boards of education," which also have a pot of money. But once the municipalities had submitted their projects, we didn't get into the nitty-gritty of saying, "That's a good project; that's a bad project." We let them make those decisions.

It was also a question of, did we want to absorb the costs of setting up a bureaucracy and second-guessing the municipalities? Given that we knew that every municipality had a list of projects they would like to do, we laid down some fairly simple criteria.

The criteria included projects for which a lot of the planning had been done — environmental approvals and permits and all of that — projects that had already gone through the public consultation phase. It was to be a project that would not, in the regular course of their own budgetary decisions, have been done in 1993–94. They had to take something off the shelf that they wouldn't have been prepared to pay for themselves and accelerate it. They had to be projects that met the criteria that the federal government had laid down for cost-sharing. The municipality had to be prepared to put in a third of the cost. But aside from that we didn't impose very many constraints on the municipalities.

One person's checks and balances are another person's red tape. I happen to believe checks and balances overall are beneficial. There was a sincere desire on our part not to impose a lot of red tape on this program. I mean, three levels of government is perhaps a bit much. Having said that, the federal government opted out of taking responsibility. One could also say that they recognized that the provinces were big enough and mature enough to exercise that responsibility.

One of the things we did require was that the availability of the infrastructure money not be used as an excuse to short-circuit a normal approval process, which would have involved consultation. As an environmentalist I asked that municipalities not be allowed to avoid environmental assessment. The availability of the money was being used by proponents of the western beaches tunnel project as an excuse for getting on with the decision making.

The western beaches tunnel was a project that the City of Toronto had first talked about in 1989. The tunnel is a huge storage tank that is going to take this storm water and sewage, allow the solids to settle, and then put the water out into Lake Ontario near Ontario Place. At that time the price for doing a whole master sewer plan for Toronto was huge, and so they began to break it down into components. There was a lot of opposition about the nature of the project and about whether the cost was justified. It's a good example of where the Infrastructure Works Program enabled the city to move ahead with something that they might not otherwise have been able to do.

The tunnel is also a good example of where the province's hands-off attitude created some difficulties for the province. As minister of the environment and as an environmentalist, I certainly had concerns as to whether a huge tunnel that contained storm and sewage water and then discharged the liquid out into Lake Ontario was the best way to go. I shared the views of many of the opponents of the project. If you'd moved back up the watershed and looked at how to prevent storm water from getting into sanitary sewers, and to prevent industries from dumping some of their discharge into the sewers, you might have done a better job environmentally.

The western beaches tunnel had become a lightning rod for a whole lot of opponents of what the city and Metro Toronto were doing about dealing with sewage and storm water. So there are probably more opponents of COI out there, around the nature of that project. COI was just one element that allowed the proponents to succeed.

It wasn't only the environmental issue of prevention that was part of the western beaches tunnel, it was what happens to the sludge that is left in the tunnel and how does that get disposed of? And that led to another whole huge debate around the sewage treatment plant and whether that sludge should be incinerated in the sewage treatment plant or whether it should be spread on farmland.

The western beaches tunnel became the focus of an ongoing and broader debate about how to deal with these things. Environmentalists don't often prevail in those debates. Otherwise the world wouldn't be in the state that it is. We wouldn't be breathing polluted air and drinking water that is at risk of becoming contaminated. I like to think that during the five years of our government we addressed that balance somewhat. But those gains have all been lost under the current government, which has cut back on environmental funding to a level that it was in the 1970s.

There's a tendency to look for technical solutions, as opposed to trying to prevent the problem from occurring in the first place. Environmentalists call for trying to clean the water and the discharges before they enter the ground or the creeks or the rivers. Some huge technical fix at the end of the river or at the end of the pipe is prone to failure, as well as being much more capital intensive. We could separate the storm water from the sanitary sewers at the time when the water enters the pipes, and with every building in the future and with every building that exists now, look at what happens to their storm water and their sewage.

There were others who argued that if you had taken that approach, you might have created more jobs because the project would have been on a larger scale: more jobs and less machinery and technology. The kinds of jobs that you create by insulating everybody's home and putting in water conservation measures in a community are quite different from the jobs that are created by building a new generating station.

The existence of the infrastructure funding provided the proponents of the tunnel with a cogent argument: "Look, this money is here, and if we spend three years more arguing over the merits of the project, that money will be gone. We'll never have a chance to do it, even if we should ultimately determine that it is the best thing to do."

Now, there are a lot of environmental and green consultants who consult on prevention and energy conservation. Citizens groups' access to expertise, to lawyers and to lobbyists to assist them in making their arguments is always much less than that of the proponents of solutions where there's probably more money to be made. Consultants, mostly engineering firms, are far more influential with municipal works departments than are citizens and environmentalists. As a citizen my only opportunity to get involved would be to try to get the municipality to put a project on the list, or to take off a project that I didn't want them to do.

Another pressure that the tunnel proponents were able to exert was the infrastructure funding timelines. We needed this environmental approval to happen quickly. Our government had referred the whole project to the environmental assessment advisory committee for public hearings and discussions. We imposed a very short time frame on that process, in order not to preclude the opportunity for the city to submit the project for the COI funding. So the existence of COI certainly benefited the proponents of that particular project.

Another big factor in letting the tunnel go ahead was the change of government in 1995. The requirement for a full environmental assessment was lifted by the Conservative government in Ontario. Our government was not satisfied that the city had looked at all the alternatives and options and was requiring them to go through some more environmental planning. I suspect that the existence of the COI funding, which had been approved for the project while we were still the government, was an argument that was used to persuade the Mike Harris government to lift the requirements for that environmental assessment.

There were other options that weren't pursued and that weren't evaluated in terms of job creation. There's been years of argument about the western beaches tunnel: whether it was appropriate financially, whether it was good environmentally. Nobody really looked at whether you could create more jobs by doing the tunnel or by doing more preventive measures in a broader approach to sewage treatment. That was not a requirement that was imposed when COI came along. It was sufficient to say, "We can qualify for this infrastructure funding and here's the number of jobs we will create."

The western beaches tunnel had been in various stages of approval for three or four years. Environmentalists and other opponents were asking the provincial government to intervene and to require a full environmental assessment for the project. We asked the environmental assessment advisory committee to evaluate the project and hold public hearings, and to make a recommendation to the minister of the environment as to whether a full environmental assessment was required. Those discussions occurred in June of 1994. It was at that point that the proponents of the project, the City of Toronto, were saying, "We have this infrastructure money, we need to do this quickly, you need to make up your minds quickly."

The chair of those hearings says that he did not feel under pressure because of the availability of the infrastructure funding, but he did feel under pressure to make a quick decision because the timelines were tight if this project was to get the funding. This environmental assessment advisory committee recommended to go ahead, with a certain number of conditions.

They did not recommend a full environmental assessment. The opponents were very unhappy about that. They went to the minister of the day and said, "Even though this committee has not recommended a full environmental assessment, we believe you ought to put it under a full environmental assessment." And so our government did that, early in 1995. The city was furious — not only because they thought it was unjustified, but also because they felt that it put at risk the infrastructure funding.

In early 1995 the city's works commissioner was arguing that the city should ignore the recommendation of the minister and refuse to do a full environmental assessment. But the city was able to continue to argue with the provincial government about this environmental assessment because there was an extension given to the infrastructure funding. Because there was going to be a second phase, the city could grandfather the project. The proponents won their case when the government changed. When the Harris government came in it lifted the requirement for a full environmental assessment and gave the city an exemption.

I think the jury is still out as to whether, from an environmental point of view, it is the best way to treat combined sewage and storm water in Toronto, and whether it will clean up the western beaches. Boston in the same period, 1994, was looking at doing this kind of a megaproject and decided not to. For much less money Boston is doing a much more effective job of moving into the watershed and looking at how to clean up and prevent pollution in the first place. The watershed is all of the rivers and streams and sewers that flow into the lake in a certain area or flow into Boston Harbor.

All of the infighting and argument speaks to the issue of whether the infrastructure program did what it was designed to do, which was to create jobs at the depths of the recession. It took until well into 1996 before the city was in a position to call tenders on the tunnel. The first allocation of funding for the western beaches tunnel was the biggest project in the city's infrastructure program funding, but it was still only enough to do phase one of the tunnel, let alone the other four phases of a total cleanup and separation of storm and sanitary sewers.

There are five phases to the project to clean up the Toronto Bay. The plan calls for the tunnel to start back at High Park. All that is under construction now with this $10.7 million they got from the infrastructure program is the section of tunnel from the Exhibition grounds to Ontario Place. Who knows where the money's going to come from for phase two, but having got the approval and the money for phase one predisposes the decision makers to approve phase two.

Anybody who's been in government has been part of arguments that say, "Look, we can't afford to do it all, but let's just get a start on it and then worry in another day as to how to complete it." When the Toronto beaches tunnel was first proposed as part of a huge master plan to clean up the Toronto waterfront, city council of the day, back in 1989, rejected the huge plan as being far too expensive. And so the works department regrouped and began to propose pieces of that overall plan. One of the arguments around the tunnel was, "Wait till you have a master plan. You shouldn't just do the tunnel."

But the engineers were able to make the case that they should proceed with the tunnel when the infrastructure funding was only going to be sufficient to do half the tunnel. They managed to describe that portion of the tunnel as a self-contained project and developed an argument that by merely having this huge underground tunnel as a containment tank, they would improve the quality of the discharge to the bay and make a contribution to cleaning up the waterfront.

I would be prepared to bet everything I have that when they come back for approval of phase two at some future time, the fact that they've already expended all of this investment in phase one will be very much part of the argument to proceed with phase two. And I don't think that's unique to this project.

You have to make a distinction between the process of deciding whether a project ought to occur and the process of deciding how to finance the project. The controversy around the National Trade Centre was whether this was something that Toronto needed. There were members of city council who felt passionately yes, and some who felt passionately no. There were certainly approaches made to us to put 50¢ dollars into the Trade Centre before the infrastructure project came along. At that time we were having a discussion about whether the Trade Centre made more sense than expanding the Convention Centre, which was in fact a provincial project, and would require more provincial money.

In terms of allowing infrastructure to be built that might not otherwise have been built in recessionary times, I think the program got a good grade. Give it an eight or nine out of 10. From the point of view of doing environmental good works, with the exclusion of some of the larger ones like the western beaches tunnel, I think there were some sewage treatment plants that were expanded and some new pipe laid. I would think that probably the infrastructure projects contributed to improving the environment, by and large. So let me give it a six out of 10 on that.

In terms of job creation I would have to say that a capital project of that nature is less effective than some federal-provincial programs that we saw 20 or 25 years ago. Municipalities were given money and could only hire people who were currently receiving employment insurance. In terms of actually creating jobs for those people who needed them in the depths of the recession in 1993, I don't think that an infrastructure program is the best way of doing that. From the point of view of actually meeting the need for jobs that Ontario had to put people back to work, I think I'd have to rate this project at about a four or five.

A criticism that can be made of COI is that the nature of the jobs was never part of the criteria. The Infrastructure Works Program was brought in to create employment at a time of recession. I don't think there was any analysis of the workforce: who was unemployed, what skills did those people have and what kinds of projects would best meet the needs of those people.

The opponents of the tunnel will tell you today that the only people who've been employed so far are engineers. I've heard that as the project has incurred overruns they've had to hire more consultants to co-ordinate the consultants. Now, whether consultants were out of work in the recession of 1993–1994, I don't know, but they certainly have been the ones who have benefited most from this kind of huge megaproject which was done with the infrastructure funding.

As a capital program, which COI very deliberately was, it takes a long time sometimes to actually put money in the pockets of the unemployed. If you're going to build a bridge or a tunnel or a road, there's a fair amount of professional planning that goes on before you let the tender and put the average person back to work. And certainly in the very complicated western beaches tunnel megaproject, I don't know how many people who were actually unemployed in 1993 got a job in 1996 or 1997.

It would be interesting to look at the number of projects that got approval in the first phase of COI that then needed an extension. That to me begs the question whether the program in fact met the need for which it was designed, which was to provide employment in the time of recession, in 1993 and 1994. It may well be that many of the projects in fact were only going as boom times began to come back. I wonder how much cost escalation occurred as a result of the fact that tenders were being let at a time when the economy was on the upswing, as opposed to when things were really bad.

The Canada Infrastructure Works Program was certainly a quick fix. One can talk about some problems that that created, but if I go back to my years on municipal councils, we certainly had 10-year road plans and sewer plans, and work for the federal government on grade separations. Those were on a priority list and would be done when the money became available. So I'm not sure that it's fair to say that municipal politicians have a three-year or two-year timetable. Yes, as a municipal politician you certainly want to try to accelerate those projects that you would like to see done, but often merely getting a project — a recreation centre or a road or a bridge — on the list of capital works is an achievement.

One of the issues around whether a capital works project is the best way to stimulate the economy is the acceptance of a trickle-down effect — that the engineers and professionals who do the consulting and the planning will ultimately create jobs for less skilled people. For me the need was to get those less skilled people back to work, not the consultants and the engineers.

The other downside for an infrastructure program that is based on capital projects like the western beaches tunnel is that they set the stage for a slippery slope. I suspect that if a municipality gets the infrastructure funding for phase one of a project, it's going to be very hard for a municipal council to deny funding for phase two. Somebody can say, "You built half the road, you've got to complete it." Or, "You built one span of a bridge, you've got to do the second span."

You may just be creating pressure on provinces and municipalities to spend money in a certain way in the future because you've allowed the project to begin by funding phase one. Particularly in a case where the project may be controversial, you have created the preconditions for continuing the project to completion in the absence of an overall evaluation of whether the project meets the environmental objectives that it was alleged to meet.

If a citizen believes that a project ought not to have happened, once the tenders are let and the decision is made, for that citizen it's hard luck. The fight is lost. I've lost many of them, and I've won a few. I'm not sure that there was a great deal of consultation at the municipal level about which projects would apply for COI and which ones wouldn't. I don't think you'd find very many people who opposed that use of the money on bridges, on expansion of libraries, on recreation centres that were also done in Toronto.

I suspect that the vast majority of municipalities had been wanting to put a new roof on the library, or to pave a certain section of road for a long time, but hadn't the money to do it. They wouldn't see the need for broader consultation and would decide as a council which projects to put forward. Political competition would occur to get something for somebody's particular bailiwick, as opposed to somebody else's.

I don't think the average citizen knows where the money's coming from. The citizen wants to see the library built, wants to see the park improved, but it's not a vote-determining issue for many people. Citizens are far more sophisticated than politicians give them credit for.

It enables the federal government when criticized to say, "We have a works program, we have done something about employment"; frequently the media don't press any further than that, to say, "Well, what did it actually do?"

I haven't seen an evaluation of an infrastructure project. I suspect that it hasn't been done from a job-creation point of view. Given that it took much longer to roll out the money than had been envisaged when the program came in, it would be interesting to see if, for example, $10 million was allocated to a project, how much of that went into the planning and pre-tendering stage, how much went to labour-intensive areas and how much was spent on machinery? There just isn't time to evaluate those factors if you're looking for a quick fix, and for a quick political fix, and you perhaps were elected saying, "jobs, jobs, jobs" and you haven't created them. This kind of capital program allows them to say they've done it, without a real analysis.

We tend to analyze our expenditures based on which level of government actually made them, as opposed to whether it was the best use of the total pool of taxpayer dollars — whether it's sales tax, income tax or business tax. In the complexities of a country like Canada, with the various jurisdictions, I don't know whether there is a better way. If you waited until somebody had the vision to look at the entire country, to set priorities and determine the best use of all the federal dollars, we'd never do anything.

There was no project-by-project analysis of projects that municipalities put on the infrastructure list. I don't know at what point the city put the Trade Centre on that list, but once they decided that it would be on that list we would not have second-guessed it. The debate and discussion about whether to build the Trade Centre would have occurred before the decision to put it on the list. On the western beaches tunnel it was more complicated because the two were happening at the same time. Proponents used the infrastructure program as an argument to get on with it, and the opponents resented the infrastructure program because it appeared to be facilitating the decision to move ahead. There may well have been the same kind of debate on the Trade Centre.

I don't know how much the existence of the infrastructure program accelerated the decision to put the Trade Centre up-front and to get on with it. I suspect that, as in many other major projects, it was a factor in the timelines, but I think the decision to do the Trade Centre was certainly at the city and the Metro level. For the province, once they had decided that it was necessary, there was support there.

A subsidy from a level of government that would not normally be subsidizing a project skews the decision-making process. Municipalities have always been dependent on shared-cost funding, but seldom from the federal level. Grade separations are, I think, the only things where you were trying to get federal money at the municipal level. It has usually been the province and the municipality. In the last decade the province has been pulling back from that funding and has created new agencies to try to manage that funding and to consider private sector partnerships in funding, which is where the whole issue of privatization comes in.

There is some benefit in the provincial government's broader vision and strategic plan, one hopes, about the funding of these projects. An example is the servicing of new lands for development. Under our government we were trying to diminish urban sprawl and used the fact that we cost-shared the funding of sewers and roads as a way of stopping municipalities from just paving over good agricultural land.

By being a partner in the cost-sharing you have an opportunity to influence the decisions. He who pays the piper calls the tune. What's interesting about the infrastructure project is that the federal government chose to not call the tune in Ontario. They left that to the provincial and municipal levels. Our government chose to leave the determination of priorities to the municipal level, and I think, in retrospect, missed the opportunity to be strategic in the use of that funding. With time and with hindsight and with the wisdom that comes therein, we might have used that money to meet our strategic objectives — whether to constrain urban sprawl or to improve the environment or to accelerate public transit — more effectively than we did in 1993–94.

Every program is different, every time is different. I suspect the jury is still out as to whether this huge expenditure of taxpayers' money was wise and whether it achieved its objective of stimulating the economy. The jury will probably always be out because it's very hard to do that kind of evaluation. We each bring our own bias to it. One person may not like megaprojects and say it was a bad program, but somebody who really wanted to see this construction done would say it was a great opportunity. Unfortunately nobody sits down, other than Ph.D. students,

10 years from the inspiration of a project like that to say, "What was the final result?"

How you evaluate whether things would have been even worse without the infrastructure program, I don't know. Obviously it did create some jobs. I've argued about whether it created the jobs for those who most needed them. I don't think anybody knows. But it certainly generated some employment and generated some economic activity. That presumably had some trickle effect outwards and downwards to those people who needed it.

SHEKHAR PRASAD

Director of Budget Services, Toronto

Shekhar Prasad is a former director of budget analysis control for Metropolitan Toronto and was director of budget services for the amalgamated megacity of Toronto.

I'm director of budget services for the new City of Toronto. I was director of budget analysis and control for Metropolitan Toronto, prior to the amalgamation.

In 1991 council had been looking at the possible future uses of Exhibition Place and one particular aspect was having a trade centre facility at the east end of the grounds. The budget was going to be about $380 million. And the only way we could afford that is if the province and the federal government kicked in a share of it. And when it went up to the feds and the province, their response back to us was, "It's too rich, it's too high, we're not prepared to pay that level, scale it down."

In 1993 we had brought in a level of around $180 million for that particular project. That's when the national infrastructure program was introduced.

When we're looking at financing capital expenditures such as the National Trade Centre, then we have a portion of that capital expenditure that we finance through what we call "capital from current." That's something that we've built up over the years and it's already in the operating budget base. It's like a down payment on your house. Let's say we have $60 million available every year. We put that down, the balance of that, and let's say $40 million more. We would then go out to the bond market and debenture. We'd borrow it, basically. And we'd borrow it over 10 years or 20 years. The city has been borrowing for most of these capital projects over a 10-year time frame. We don't want to extend the debt too long.

We borrow that money and we pay for it through our operating budget in the form of debt charges. That's the servicing cost. A person is paying principal and interest on a loan until it's retired, and that's what we do with our debentures. A $60-million capital expenditure would be debentured. We needed to pay back on an annual basis, every year for 10 years, $12 million a year. So we needed to find $12 million in our operating budget to pay the debt-servicing cost for this infrastructure project.

At the end of 10 years, if you added every year, you'd end up paying $120 million for this. If we had the money in the bank, it would have cost us $60 million. But because we didn't and we borrowed the money, it's cost us $120 million over a 10-year time frame. That's the basic financing of that project.

The cost of the National Trade Centre was $180 million, but had three sources of funding, in the city, the province and the federal government. If we had to pay the full $180 million ourselves and we borrowed it, then over a 10-year time frame $360 million would be the approximate cost. I think the province paid its share all in one year. I'm not sure what the feds did on that. So it's hard for me to say exactly what the total would have been.

The question is whether they would have gone with $180 million for the Trade Centre if the infrastructure program was not there. In most likelihood they probably would not have at that point. They probably would have chosen to spend money on rapid transit. But because it was leveraged, and that $60 million really bought you a lot more, it was a good deal.

CHAPTER 7

BRITISH COLUMBIA

Sometimes we get projects we never asked for.

The interviews conducted in British Columbia illustrate the political tussles that took place among the different levels of government. Some of them suggest that the system was manipulated to meet the objectives of one particular level of government.

When we started talking to people in British Columbia, we stumbled into an ongoing fight that had erupted among the NDP provincial government of Glen Clark, the federal government and many of the province's mayors. Many felt that the province was trying to pull a sleight of hand and use the infrastructure program money to pay for services that were the province's sole responsibility.

The B.C. interviews raised some questions about how spending power is divided and negotiated among the three levels of government. Are the municipalities really mere "creatures of the provinces," or should they have had more say in how the CIWP money was spent? Greg Halsey-Brandt, mayor of Vancouver's next-door neighbour, Richmond, and Doug McCallum, mayor of suburban Surrey, were puzzled that projects they had listed as priorities were often completely ignored by the province.

David Anderson, who at the time was federal fisheries minister and the minister responsible for the program in British Columbia, was interviewed about the federal government's intervention and intentions with respect to the infrastructure program in B.C. In most provinces, if the proposals met the CIWP criteria, the provincial and the federal governments generally approved them. But municipal leaders we talked to in B.C. said they had been alienated from the decision-making process. The mayors seemed to have little idea as to who was actually making CIWP decisions or why they were being made.

This underscored a nationwide dilemma for municipalities, which have no recognition in the Constitution and therefore no authority under which to negotiate spending programs directly with the federal government. The Union of British Columbia Municipalities (UBCM) and the Federation of Canadian Municipalities (FCM) are lobbying for such recognition.

As in other provinces, in B.C. politicians debated about how much infrastructure money would be committed to "soft" or non-traditional infrastructure. The agreement that was eventually signed by the federal and provincial representatives called for 15 percent dedicated to soft projects, which included theatres and recreational facilities. The Stanley Theatre project brought together such disparate players as Hedy Fry — the newly elected MP for Vancouver Centre, who was named minister responsible for multiculturalism — and the NDP member of the provincial legislature for Vancouver–Little Mountain, Tom Perry. An active arts-community member who was involved in a successful CIWP application spoke to us about how having supporters in high places helped to secure CIWP funding for the Stanley Theatre restoration.

Our researcher in British Columbia was Leanne Hazon, a graduate of the Carleton University journalism program. This assignment was Leanne's first up-close look at the management of government finances. "I had an idea going in that I was going to find inefficiency and bureaucracy," she said. "I just didn't expect to come up against some of the obstacles that I found in British Columbia. When I wanted to find out why the decisions were made, who was deciding what and what was the basis for these decisions, I found a wall of suspicious bureaucrats who didn't want to talk." She said she found no one in government who accepted complete responsibility for any controversial CIWP decisions: "Sometimes I'd speak to my friends about the research that I was doing. I would be worked up, ranting, raving and complaining about the provincial and federal governments and how they're wasting my money and their money. They'd say, 'Leanne, what do you expect? It's government. You shouldn't be surprised.' A lot of people in my generation just don't think that they have any control. I was cynical before this experience, but now there's no hope for me. I'm beyond cynical."

GREG HALSEY-BRANDT

Mayor of Richmond

Greg Halsey-Brandt served as mayor of Richmond for 11 years, sat on the Richmond city council for 20 years and has been active in municipal government lobby groups.

The Canada Infrastructure Works Program has been quite successful. It creates many person-years of employment. We recapture most of the money that is spent, provincially and federally, through sales and income tax, and the government makes some money back. It has enabled us to get a head start on a lot of projects that we might have done only eventually. They weren't just something that we dreamed up. This program has just enabled us to accelerate them.

The program was supposed to be a partnership between the municipal, provincial and federal governments. But it really only operates between the provincial and federal governments. The municipalities are not party to any of the discussions of what the guidelines and criteria are, or of how much is going to be spent on hard services or cultural items. We're not involved in picking the projects.

All we get is a request to submit a list of projects. We get a phone call or a letter, giving us anywhere from a week and a half to three weeks to get $20 million worth of project priorities to the provincial government in Victoria. So we meet with our engineers, parks people and anybody else involved in our capital projects, and we come up with a list of priorities. We take that to city council and debate it to decide if these are the right priorities and to make any changes. Then we send that off to Victoria.

We don't hear anything for a while. Sometimes it takes a few months. We usually get announcements from Victoria. But sometimes a federal or provincial minister will announce projects in different parts of the province. I also get phone calls from Victoria and Ottawa saying, "There's some money left. Do you have any priorities?" And they have to know by 5:00 p.m. So then we scramble around. We pull out our old list and say, "Yes, some of these are still doable. These would be our priorities as of today." And then we wait to hear.

You need between eight months and a year, by the time you conceive something, design it, go to tender and build it. To be given six hours' notice, or even two weeks' notice, puts us at a real disadvantage in terms of what's doable within these time periods. It depends very much on who's calling, whether they're provincial or federal, as to how they see those particular projects. We give them the information, it disappears into a black hole and we wait for the press release to come out to see who were the winners and losers. Sometimes we get a good announcement, a project that we want. Sometimes we don't get any projects in our city. Sometimes we get projects that we never asked for.

It's run politically, that's why it happens that way. I believe that there's too much political interference in the selection. There's almost a randomness, from our point of view. The projects chosen could be anywhere in our priority list. For example, if there's a list of 20 projects from our city, we'll get number 19, with no rationale. We have to have an open process of decision making or this infrastructure program will not be continued.

I don't know why the municipalities were shut out of the process in British Columbia. The thought may have never occurred to the federal and provincial governments to include us. The municipalities do have a say, in the sense that we send the list. I'm happy that any of them get done, but I think that we have to have a role in deciding which projects are going where. David Anderson, as senior minister for British Columbia, has said that he's going to make a spot for us in those negotiations if they come up with an infrastructure program in the future.

The municipalities having a role at the table and deciding the criteria of project decisions could be accommodated if the federal and provincial governments wished to do so. But constitutional recognition for the municipalities would be necessary so that we couldn't just be dismissed by the provinces at their whim. If it were part of the Constitution, the provinces would have to negotiate. We have to get the municipalities in the process to get some confidence back. We want to be there as partners.

Sometimes the province has different priorities than the federal government has. The second round of the infrastructure program was a very good example of that. In Phase II of the program the only money we got was for some bicycle routes. We didn't even ask for the money for those bicycle routes. They weren't on the list.

It was part of this problem between the federal and provincial governments. The province had a cycling program, 50 percent municipally funded and 50 percent provincially funded. So they gave us some of these bicycle lanes. If you're the province, you think that this is great because federal money is funding some of our bicycle lanes. We're not complaining. Presumably it was either the bicycle lanes or nothing. But it just shows you that the rules are — well, we don't know quite what the rules are. We'd like them tightened up so that there are some firm criteria for how this whole system operates.

Transit is a provincial responsibility here. They pay 100 percent of it. But the province was using one-third federal dollars and two-thirds provincial dollars to fund buses. The province was essentially hijacking the program. When the federal government found out what was going on, David Anderson put a stop to the program and we negotiated with Premier Glen Clark.

I think that the tension between the province and the federal government was almost a necessary evil. We said, "We're not going to be part of this anymore unless the municipalities are at the table," and the federal government agreed with us. A whole batch of projects were announced which had more of the traditional types of infrastructure, like water and sewers, though we had some fairly significant cultural grants in Burnaby and Vancouver.

When the Federation of Canadian Municipalities was first dis-cussing the infrastructure program in the 1980s, Mike Harcourt worked very hard on it. He was the mayor of Vancouver before he became the premier of British Columbia, and it was something that he was pushing for.

It was about hard infrastructure — bridges, roads, sewers and water lines for the municipalities. Infrastructure was getting older in the cities across Canada. Some of it really needed help. Here in the City of Richmond we needed more diking. We needed money put into infra-structure to keep our cities functioning well.

It's not a glitzy sort of program, but nevertheless, we thought that with the three levels of government working together we could upgrade those facilities and at the same time put a lot of people to work. Through taxation, the federal and provincial governments at least would recover most of the money that they put into the program. That's the way it was originally designed, so we were quite surprised with the cultural component.

In British Columbia nearly 15 percent of the money could be spent on the cultural component of a program. The problem is that once you intro-duce a cultural component, the whole program starts to fly apart. Drainage projects and things like that aren't glamorous. They're always competing with projects like new theatres, where there's a lot more public support. If you introduce something like an ice arena, a theatre or any of those sorts of things, there's a whole crowd that wants that particular project to be number one on the priority list. There's a lot of public demand for those sorts of easily visible and usable facilities. There are some political rewards for those projects. But they weren't the original intent.

For our part the City of Richmond put up a real selection of proj-ects for consideration — sewer lines, drainage, roads, intersection improvements, park improvements and cultural improvements. We tried to cover off most aspects of the gamut so that we could get some infrastructure money for the city. We didn't include much in the way of a cultural component. The bulk of the first infrastructure program went into secondary sewage treatment in the greater Vancouver area (Annacis secondary sewage treatment plant). We had some money for one park here, but the rest of it was for hard infrastructure projects.

Within the provincial government — and I assume that the same is true in the federal government — there is a small group of people who make the recommendations to their respective ministers. The final decisions, I would assume, are made by the ministers. Provincial or federal politicians seem to view capital projects as a re-election issue. They want to be seen to be doing things in their constituencies, as opposed to sitting in Ottawa and Victoria, debating things that are often very hard to nail down for the electorate. If they can say that they actually did something in their municipalities, then they can stand up at election time and say that they delivered. So they wanted just to work amongst themselves to decide what they were going to deliver in the communities around British Columbia.

Local politics doesn't work that way to nearly that extent. We're identified with everything that we do in the community. Accountability and transparency are the ways that cities work. Most of us don't work in political parties, where there's caucus solidarity — everything is secret and everyone has to vote the same way. City councils are much more inclusive in our decision making. Also, we can only deal with four or five things in camera (not in public), usually labour negotiations, personnel problems and land purchases. Everything else is there for everyone to look at in our clerk's department.

In my city any constituent can walk into my city hall, ask anybody a question about what the city is doing, and get an answer. But if I go to Ottawa or Victoria and go to the civil service, I can't do that. I have to go through channels starting at the top and try to get answers that way, and the answers have to be cleared by the government of the day.

The civil service shouldn't be seen to be working for the government only. Members of the opposition or any political party have to be able to go to any civil servant and ask for information. Right now they can't. They won't get the information. They usually have to go through the minister or deputy ministers to get information.

That's a terrible corruption of our civil service, which is meant to provide an objective service to the community. As mayor I've made a few calls provincially and federally to get clarification of projects, decision timelines and how much money is available. And I'll get answers to certain questions, like roughly when they're going make the next announcement or how much money is left. But I can't get any answers as to why they chose this project over that project.

DOUG MCCALLUM

Mayor of Surrey

Doug McCallum entered politics in 1993 when he was elected city council-lor in Surrey, B.C. He served as chairman of the finance committee before successfully running for mayor in 1996.

Canada's at the stage now in its history that it needs to look at its infrastructure and provide money for fixing up and putting in new infrastructure across the country. The infrastructure program is excellent, and I have encouraged the federal government to put more infrastructure programs into place in the future.

The intent was good, but the way they proceeded was flawed. They went with provincial governments across Canada as a source to distribute the infrastructure money. When you go with provincial governments, then you bring politics into it. When you start to bring politics into the distribution of infrastructure money, then the programs start falling apart. They'll distribute for political reasons rather than for infrastructure reasons.

That's exactly what happened in British Columbia. The B.C. government had political reasons for where and how they wanted to spend the money. That's why a lot of the money that came to B.C. wasn't disbursed to the infrastructure projects that were needed in the province. If they had included the cities and the municipalities at the table, and included the UBCM (Union of British Columbia Municipalities), which is an organization of all cities and municipalities in B.C., we could have had proper distribution. Instead it was manipulated by the provincial government to satisfy their political needs rather than for the main purpose of the program, which was to provide money for infrastructure that's badly needed.

We have a theme in Surrey: "Working together to create a great city with a heart." Part of that is being an active city, encouraging residents to get out and enjoy this great region.

In Surrey our top infrastructure priority is what we call the south perimeter road, which is a road that we want to build. It will move truck traffic and get our economy and goods and everything moving within our region — not just in Surrey but within the greater Vancouver area. That was our top priority and we received nothing, as far as that project was concerned. In fact, our six priorities that we applied for didn't get any of the money. About three years ago we did receive a little money for some road work, but none last time. All of our priorities were discarded.

I think there was an unfair distribution of the money within British Columbia. Surrey's population is about 330,000, according to the 1996 census. With that kind of growth we certainly need to have money to provide for infrastructure, and we accept that willingly. That huge growth also provides a lot of extra dollars to the federal government in taxes. So given those taxes, given our size, we should have received more cash in a program like this.

I understand that most of the money went out to smaller communities in the province. They need it too. We certainly respect that. It's not fair for us to sit down in the Lower Mainland and make a comment on what was spent in Prince George or Kamloops or Kelowna. With the bigger population in Ontario, they should get more money. The same goes for Quebec and B.C.

I think that the interference by the provincial NDP government was in areas where they wanted to either increase or reinforce their support. That's where we see the lack of accountability for the program — in the ability of the provincial government to just about dictate how the money was going to be spent. It ended up being to their benefit, rather than to the real benefit of the residents.

Our residents have a lot of frustration over the lack of accountability in the infrastructure program. It's disgusting from a taxpayer's point of view, and I'm a taxpayer. I'm disgusted with not being able to know how the process works, or how the money's distributed or who's making the decision on my tax dollars. We have no idea who is making the decisions about the program. No one seems to have an idea of how the money was disbursed.

The federal government tried to provide accountability. They actually delayed the program and ended up in a number of fights with the provincial government over the disbursement of money. But the federal government needs to have some share in the blame. I can't say at this time whether there was any political motivation at the federal level, but I can say the three federal MPs in Surrey are all Reform.

The sense was that the federal and provincial governments were fighting over the distribution of the infrastructure money and that caused a very long delay in B.C. Part of the criteria was that the money be spent within a certain period of time. The federal government asked all the cities in B.C. what their priorities were and we set out our priorities. This created a tension between the province and the federal officials. The provincial government certainly had other ideas where they wanted to put it.

It doesn't matter where the money comes from — federally, provincially or city — it's the same taxpayer. Our residents are saying that they pay federal tax and, being the fastest-growing city in Canada, we're also probably generating the most new federal tax dollars for the federal government. Our residents want their share and they didn't get it. There are too many layers of government right now, and the taxpayer is forgotten.

Most of the highways that go through Surrey are owned by the provincial government, and they're not spending any money in Surrey. Just to give you an example, we spend $35 million a year on our city roads. The provincial government, which has more miles of roads and highways than city roads through Surrey, spent $3 million. They hardly spend any money on their roads and, as you can see, their roads are falling apart. There are huge bottlenecks. We're trying to get our economy going in British Columbia but businesses can't get their goods in or out because their trucks are all jammed in gridlock. Transportation will be one of the top priorities in the next five to 10 years and will create jobs when our unemployment rate is starting to climb. We need to create those jobs in our country.

There was some money for cultural buildings and some arts buildings in Vancouver, and very little in the way of transportation infrastructure. Transportation infrastructure in the Greater Vancouver Region is absolutely essential to get our economy going, to create jobs, encourage businesses to come, and also encourage movement within our region among our people. We have to start to get our transportation systems back in line.

I think the 15 percent funding for arts and cultural projects would be OK if the other 85 percent was given out in a fair way. It wasn't. It appears that the priorities of the infrastructure program, at least in our region, were all wrong.

In Surrey we got some money for bike paths, which we didn't even ask for. That shocked all of us because it's not a priority with us. The province had its own program a couple of years ago. They would match their money with city money to provide bike paths. It appears the provincial government decided to put the bike path — its own program — into the federal program. That way they only have to put out a third of the money, not half. They saved themselves money and then gave it back to us. Then they are able to say that we did get some money. It certainly wasn't a very fair way to do it. To include it with the federal program was just not fair.

We're at the point that Surrey may not even participate in the next infrastructure program. We spent a lot of staff time on setting out our priorities, and sending reports in and following up, and we feel that we haven't received any money to speak of.

Maybe we should start forcing the issue with the federal government. We have a number of very large federal buildings here and they're not paying their fair share of taxes. If provincial and federal governments want to have their buildings in Surrey, if they want to do business in Surrey, they will have to pay all the current taxes, the same as everybody else.

The provincial government in B.C. talks about image and what they want to do in the future. What is needed is raw spending of money on infrastructure programs right away — within a six- or seven-month period — not to look two and three years down the road. There have been far too many discussions and reports. The infrastructure program as it was first announced was good. You got your money and you had to spend it within a very short period of time. That's what people throughout Canada want, including in our region. They want to see that money come in one day and construction on something start the next day.

Hopefully they'll continue to provide the program each year to improve the infrastructure. They must bring accountability into the process. They need to be sure the decision-making process is well known and that all the players are at the table.

DAVID ANDERSON

Liberal MP, Victoria; Federal Cabinet Minister

David Anderson has represented the federal riding of Victoria since 1993. He has filled a variety of roles as a member of Cabinet. He served as minister of national revenue, and later held the portfolios of transportation, fisheries and oceans, and environment.

The municipalities were very interested in the prime minister's federal infrastructure program. We were very enthusiastic, too. The province was somewhat reluctant. We had difficulty in British Columbia determining the mix of projects for the infrastructure program. As a result of those discussions, B.C. was the last province to sign on to the national infrastructure program.

We agreed that about 15 percent of the projects could be what we called "soft infrastructure" — arts centres or some other cultural facility, like a theatre or museum. The other 85 percent would be so-called "hard infrastructure," which are things like sewers or waterworks or roads. The municipal governments argued for more soft infrastructure, 30 percent. The province argued for five percent. We compromised on

15 percent. That was the debate that we had with British Columbia at the beginning of the infrastructure program.

We tried for rough equivalency across the province. We tried to make sure that each of the 10 regions of British Columbia had appropriate amounts of money spent in accordance with population.

We wanted projects to come from the municipalities. There were six or eight times as many projects proposed as we had money to fund. So six out of seven were unhappy because they didn't get their projects funded. They were put on a provincial priority list. We then approved what came forward. So the decision making really was municipal, provincial and federal.

There was some bargaining back and forth. We were on the phone to the mayors involved to determine the best way of spending the money. Then they had to fit in with the overall provincial priorities and be reviewed by the provincial government, in terms of the budget. We then looked at it a third time with federal-provincial discussions, and occasionally haggled over which would be chosen.

Municipal politicians look to the boundaries of their constituencies, and if it's not being spent in their constituencies, they're not getting anything. Wrong. We didn't say, "Because the boundary is here between the City of Vancouver and the City of Richmond, we're going to split it up that way." We said, "What are the needs of the area?"

Vancouver argued that they got far less than another community next door to them. Why? Because we took $220 million — the largest single infrastructure project in the country — to put into sewage treatment plants on the Fraser River, in another constituency. That was definitely a benefit to the entire Greater Vancouver Region. We took the greater Vancouver area and looked at, for example, a historic theatre, a cinema which needed refurbishing. We looked at the need for a new earthquake-proof police facility for 911 calls, which we funded.

When you look at importance, don't forget history. Let me take two communities in British Columbia of much the same size. I will describe one as the "industrious ants." They carefully programmed all their waterworks, their sewer and road projects over many years. They've been very careful. They do not have a lot of urgent hard infrastructure requirements because they have been so careful and they also taxed people quite heavily. We have another community of much the same size which has not bothered to look to the future. They have critical hard infrastructure requirements. It would not have been fair to say, "We'll ignore the first community because their priorities are not as important and critical as the priorities of the second community." The second community had bought its own trouble, created its own problems. The first community, which wanted soft infrastructure, got it for arts-related activity.

In the second round (Phase II) the province was trying to divert the entire infrastructure program into transit. When I say transit, that included everything down to bike paths. We tried to protect the municipal priorities as best we could because the federal government didn't have any great priority objective. We wanted to make sure we had the best municipal projects approved. We compromised and said, "OK, half of it will go into transit."

When it came to value for money, we were pretty confident that because provincial money was being spent, their auditors would look at the expenditure of provincial money. We knew in the federal case the auditor general would be looking at the expenditure of federal money. We knew that the municipalities had pretty good oversight of the expenditures they made, politically as well as technically, through audit processes. So in fact there was probably a great deal of overseeing.

All three governments are accountable for the process. The process was reasonably straightforward. It didn't create enormous bureaucracies and vast mountains of paper and innumerable meetings of bureaucrats to determine issues of priorities and rankings.

I made a speech to the Union of British Columbia Municipalities a little over a year ago. I made a commitment to the municipalities that if we ever sign another infrastructure program, it will not be with the province's ability to skew municipal priorities toward provincial priorities. That's not to say the money wasn't well spent. It simply wasn't spent in accordance with what was understood by the municipalities at the beginning of the program, in terms of their priorities. We had other criteria in the province of British Columbia. That was where the diversity of Canada and the diversity of local concern were important.

The program overall was, I think, a very good one, even with the difficulties we had in British Columbia.

BILL MILLERD

*Artistic and Managing Director,
Arts Club Theatre, Vancouver*

*Bill Millerd was a prime mover in the renovation of the Stanley Theatre in
Vancouver as a result of his involvement in the Stanley Theatre Society and
other performance-related organizations.*

The Stanley is a heritage movie theatre built in 1930 and is much
beloved in Vancouver. Vancouver is fairly young, so there are not a lot
of heritage buildings. When it closed in 1991 a "Save the Stanley" committee formed. The Vancouver TheatreSports League came up with the
idea of transforming the Stanley into a live theatre. The Arts Club Theatre
got involved with the project. It started in 1994 and it's quite exciting.

I heard about the infrastructure program and I knew that the
province was going to participate with the federal government. I heard
that 15 percent of whatever money was going to be available would go
toward cultural or similar projects, that it wasn't all just going to be
roads and sewers. Without the infrastructure involvement, I don't
think the Stanley Theatre would have been restored at all. We started
talking to the local politicians about who we should talk to, to

advance the project. We knew that there would be some political decisions in how all of this would be awarded because ours was a fairly major application.

There were quite a few newspaper articles written about the Stanley. Restoring it and adapting it to use as a live theatre made a lot of sense. A historical building wouldn't be lost and there would be a cultural group energizing it and bringing it to life. The Save the Stanley campaign had gathered about 30,000 signatures from people who were interested in it not being lost and turned into a retail store.

There was a lot of sympathy and help from Ian Waddell (former NDP MP), who was on our board. Our local MLA, Tom Perry, got the application and with a great deal of help from the member of Parliament, Hedy Fry, put in the application. Hedy Fry had been newly elected, so it was important to involve her. Tom Perry was a very keen supporter of the project, right from the beginning.

Hedy Fry felt this project could lead off a number of infrastructure grants for other culture projects in Vancouver Centre. I think that was very important in us getting a sense of what to do and who to talk to and how many letters to write, that kind of thing. We didn't know how these grants would be awarded, whether there'd be a whole bunch of small ones or whether there'd only be one large one. We were told there was a limited amount of money, of course, and there were a lot of other applications: museums, other arts projects, cultural projects, not just theatres.

The original budget was $6.9 million, which included the purchase of the building and the renovation of the building as a theatre. The cost of buying the building never changed, but the budget increased to over $9 million. So where has the budget gone? Basically the delay in getting the whole project done certainly raised the cost of it. Originally the project was for two theatres. Restoring it as one, more glorious theatre cost some of that extra money. It went into the effort to really make it a very special theatre.

After we became part of the infrastructure program, one-third had to be raised locally. So we went to city council and we were awarded a grant. City council knew that they probably should do something and it was not that difficult to convince them that this was a worthy project. We had $1.3 million from the province, $1.3 million from the feds, and $1.3 million we had to raise locally.

When the announcement was made by then premier Mike Harcourt, the federal minister responsible, David Anderson, came to the Stanley to announce a whole series of cultural infrastructure grants. They chose the Stanley to make the announcement because they knew it had such a public profile.

CHAPTER 8

OTTAWA

Trust us, we know best.

All of the interviews we did seemed to lead us right back to Ottawa. With the information and background material gleaned from dozens of interviews, our Ottawa researcher and overseer of the project, Jay Innes, had a full quiver of pointed questions to direct at a few of Ottawa's most knowledgeable people in the field of government accountability.

Jay felt that the Canada Infrastructure Works Program — despite all good intentions — had come off the rails. He simply wondered why. "I originally wanted to follow a dollar through a spending program, but my efforts turned into more of an examination of Canada's political system," Jay said. "Despite all of the flaws in the infrastructure program, the real problem goes far beyond things like poor project selection and incompetent management. The problems are fundamental to our system of government."

Some sources in Ottawa bring a more national perspective than others interviewed by our team. We spoke to people who deal directly with the issues of accountability, transparency and secrecy in government. We wanted to find out more about why the federal government seemed to lack control over CIWP spending, and whether it had filled its role in administering the program adequately.

McGill economist Reuven Brenner criticized the CIWP from the perspective of job creation. His complaints were directed toward the entire concept of government job creation. Brenner examined the inherent problems governments run into when they attempt to intervene in the marketplace and create jobs. He argued that governments can indeed create jobs, but the cost associated with this job creation ultimately destroys more jobs than it creates. Moreover, the taxes that have to be raised to create these jobs cripple the private sector's ability to invest in new endeavours that lead to real market-based job creation.

We talked to John Williams, chair of the Public Accounts Committee, who offered his perspective on the question of accountability in government and the obstacles that make his committee's job more difficult. He also spoke from the viewpoint of an MP in the House of Commons. Williams emphasized that MPs have lost their traditional role as holders of the purse strings and no longer adequately scrutinize the spending decisions of the prime minister, the Cabinet and their central agencies, like the Prime Minister's Office (PMO) and the Privy Council Office (PCO). He spoke to us about a few measures that he is spearheading to get these powers back.

Former information commissioner John Grace gave us his opinion on what he called a "culture of secrecy" that exists in government. He argued that bureaucrats ultimately believe that government information is *their* information, when in fact it belongs to the public. Grace noted that bureaucrats are very reluctant to let information get into the public domain for fear of embarrassing their political masters. Being helpful and giving journalists or the general public information is not a great way to endear yourself to your bosses.

Grace also pointed to the generous exemptions given to the government under the Access to Information law. These exemptions allow the government to withhold or censor documents for any number of reasons.

REUVEN BRENNER

Professor of Economics, McGill University

Professor Brenner lectures on finance in the Faculty of Management at McGill University in Montreal. He has held the chair in Management since 1989 and is the author of several books, including Gambling and Speculation *(1990) and* Labyrinths of Prosperity *(1994).*

The whole job-creation approach is wrong because the issue for a country is never how many jobs governments create. Governments can always create jobs. Think about communism. There was absolutely no unemployment there — everybody was employed. You can just legislate that everybody who is unemployed gets a salary from the government and — presto — they are employed. The unemployment rate was zero point something. How did they do it? Well, everybody had to go to work. If you didn't work, you were defined as a hooligan and you entered into the criminal statistics or jail, and you were not counted at all. There are other ways in which governments can create employment. If they make a country very poor they can, let's say, not import snow-removal equipment, and then the people have to shovel or clean snow with teaspoons. You will have plenty of employment. You will also have a lot of poverty.

Yes, they can always create jobs. They can also enlist people in the army and the unemployment rate will go down. That's not the issue. The issue is what type of jobs the country is creating, not just whether somebody is employed or not. So first of all the whole departure point is wrong. Canadians want to prosper. The question is, are these jobs creating wealth or not?

It's meaningless to look at job-creation numbers, even if they are accurate. If you look carefully at the Infrastructure Works Program reports of the government, the job-creation figures are exactly proportional to the percentage of the population in the provinces. Now, what are the chances that the government creates jobs within a province which are exactly proportional to the fraction of that province's population in Canada? It's zero. So you can see very easily, both from the numbers and from the approach, that this is a sham and a mythology.

The numbers are wrong and if somebody just bothered to look carefully at the government's own statistics they would discover that very quickly. The number of jobs created through this program is proportional to the fraction of the population of the provinces within Canada. So let's say if Quebec has 25 percent of the population, then it received 25 percent of the jobs created. If Newfoundland has two percent of the population, then two percent of the jobs are created there. If these jobs had any relationship to wealth creation or any serious consideration other than just a political decision, then there is absolutely no chance that this fraction would be equal.

Let's say you have the cities of Montreal and Toronto. The taxation of Quebec is different than in Ontario, and the regulations are different. So very different numbers of jobs will be created in Montreal and Toronto, if it is based on any type of calculation. If the demography in a place is different, if the skills in a place are different, you would expect different rates of job creation. It doesn't matter in which country you look — the job creation in Los Angeles is not the same as in New York. Sometimes in one place it's higher, and sometimes in another place.

The idea that somehow job creation every year is proportional to the population in a city or in a village or in a wider area is simply false. So you have to ask yourself how to explain this very strange correlation, that everything that is created through this infrastructure program is so perfectly correlated with population, rather than looking at the details like taxation. You may ask yourself, "Well, why isn't the number of jobs created in France the same as in the United States or in Canada? Why aren't those somehow proportional to the population?" It's a political calculation, an arrangement between the federal and the provincial governments, and that's it. Does it imply that there is no job-creation formula? I would say yes. The facts imply that there is no job-creation formula.

The government farms out scientific research to some academics or to some consulting firm who provide the veil of science to suggest that there is science behind it. Then people say, "Oh, this or that company or this or that academic checked these numbers, so this should be OK." They want to sell you the illusion that there is some scientific work behind it. Whatever that secret formula is, it's just pseudoscience and jargon, that's it.

Statistics Canada doesn't release the job-creation formula, so what type of accountability is that? Nobody has the slightest idea what it is going on. Statistics Canada is fed some numbers, they plug in the numbers and that's it. Then you have some consulting companies outside who again keep both the numbers and all their complicated formulas secret.

I would not say it's a conspiracy. This is how governments work when they can get away with murder. For various reasons, and in every country the story is a bit different, governments don't have those internal institutions of accountability in place. Then you get, today we call it "lack of transparency." Every age invents its own jargon. Previously, or in other countries, it's still called corruption. We don't like to call it corruption; we call it a lack of transparency and we promise that the situation will be better. Meanwhile we are hiring the current priesthood called economists to justify our calculations and our language. That's exactly what most of the economists are today. Many of them just serve their political masters and I would not call it science.

Let me illustrate from Statistics Canada's own work, so that they cannot blame me for putting words in their mouth. So here is just what they are saying. "TIM is a sophisticated simultaneous model with extensive current-period and dynamic linkages between and within each segment of the model structure. TIM incorporates 112 sector input/output model to consistently represent the simultaneous relationships between detailed final demand categories and the 112 industry output measures."[1]

It means nothing.

Let me just end the paragraph: "The unique level of detail allows a more straightforward introduction and evaluation of judgmental and other non-model information such as product-specific information from Canadian Capital Projects, an inventory of major investment plans, maintained by Informetrica Ltd." It's absolutely meaningless. First they are talking as if Canada had 112 very well-defined sectors. Well, if you think about our economy today, when the borders between industries are blurred, telephone and Internet, postal services and Internet, and entertainment and games and telephone services, are those 112 sectors so well defined? I don't have a clue and they don't provide it.

Then, to take themselves off the hook from such criticism, they say at the end, "The unique level of detail allows a more straightforward introduction and evaluation of judgmental and other non-model information." In other words, to escape this, whatever they defined as the model, if it doesn't come out the way they wanted, they could introduce a judgment. Now, what is that subjective judgment that they introduced?

Of course the numbers are always political. I don't think that anybody is under the illusion that they are not. By the way, the numbers are political also, in a kind of narrower sense, in a private company too. Pick up any annual report. From the annual report you cannot find out if you should buy that stock or not. Think about it. What does Wall Street do? What do all the financial analysts do? They in fact pick up that annual report, they destructure it, take off the layers of cosmetics, and then they make their own recommendations. They do detective work. Now, why would both private companies and governments want to manipulate numbers? For a very simple reason: because both of them want to have access to credit, to financial markets at the lowest rate. The difference is that for private companies you have an army of financial detectives and you have a lot of rules and regulations, as well as the SEC (Security and Exchange Commission) and the GAAP (Generally Accepted Accounting Principles), which limit to some extent what you can do with your accounting. With the government you don't have these rules and you don't have access to information. That's another reason why they can get away with murder, for the moment.

251

But it depends on what type of political institutions you have. Unfortunately, in Canada many institutions that held politicians in check and government institutions in check were destroyed. In the U.S. you have more of those checks and balances than in Canada or almost anywhere else, and that's why they correct their mistakes more quickly.

Let's say we look at the infrastructure program, which cost about $8.3 billion. That comes from taxes. What is never taken into account is how many jobs were lost because the $8.3 billion must come either from taxes or from increased borrowing. So the governments always can point out they are employing 10,000 people on building this road. What is not visible is that maybe 10,000 jobs were lost in other parts of the economy.

Second, the fact that you are building a road or you are building a bridge doesn't mean that it creates wealth. The road can lead nowhere. If there is no business that the road is used for, if there is no commerce on it, then it's just a mistake and a cost for the economy. The road is just empty. The fact that we are building buildings or bridges or roads or anything doesn't mean that we are creating wealth. Take a very simple example. The value of any real estate comes only from the rents that either businesses or people will pay. If the building stays empty, then it is a cost. The same applies to roads or bridges that are not being used.

So this whole idea that the building of infrastructure makes a country richer is completely false. Our politicians can build roads to their constituencies, or to the places they want to retire, but that wouldn't create much wealth. It may create jobs for the moment, but again the invisible loss of jobs and the increased taxes are just out of sight and mind. Those are losses for the economy.

Let's say that the government picks up some project that really is good. Then it depends on the execution. If we don't have institutions in place that follow up on how that job is carried out, who is held accountable? What happens if there is a mistake? Do I have the right to fire the management? None of this is done within government.

Sometimes this contrast between the private sector and the government is put in the wrong light. I don't want to argue that the private sector doesn't make a lot of mistakes. It does make a lot of mistakes. And it makes a lot of miscalculations, there is no doubt about that. The big difference is that if you own a company and you make mistakes, then at one point you will not be able to have access to the financial markets and borrow more money to spend on that idea. The government faces this problem to a far lesser extent because the government has the right to tax.

When I speak about the private sector, it must truly be private and not count on government subsidies one way or another. If I have a company and I want to pursue an idea, what can I do? I can use my internal savings in the company or go to the financial markets and try to convince them that this is a good idea and they should advance me the money under certain conditions. Let's say that they believe in my idea. Let's say they believe that I have a good idea on some Internet commerce and they advance me $100 million. So I start spending the money. And let's say that I make some mistakes and I run out of money.

I have to go back to the financial markets and ask again, "Please, get me some more money." Then they may or they may not give it to me. Consider, now, the government. Suppose that the government decided to build some road, and then they noticed that in fact very few trucks, very few people used that road. What do you do now? What does the government do? Well, the government doesn't have to go back, necessarily, to the financial markets, but it can tax you to maintain that road. The big difference is that the government, because of the ability to tax, can persist much longer with a lot of mistakes than a private company can. Now, for the country this is very important because every mistake is a cost, and it is a cost you must pay for. So after a while the taxes accumulate, or the amount that you borrow accumulates, at compounding interest rates. At some point, and you can see it in many countries around the world and in Canada a little bit, the financial markets look very closely at the government books and will not advance credit to that particular government.

We come to the big difference between government and the private sector. In the private sector there are a lot of complex institutions internally, and externally, financial markets, to stop the mistake from lasting too long. We don't have that within the government.

We don't have that because, I would say, since Pierre Trudeau many institutions that kept governments in check and kept internal institutions within the government accountable were destroyed.

When you have a private company, just consider all the wide range of institutions that are exactly there for checks and balances. First, you have a lot of institutions within the company. How do you decide to spend the money — to consider all of the alternatives and so forth? You have a board of governors who consider if the CEO or the CFO is OK. Is he prudent? If the board fails, then you have all those leverage buyout firms and takeovers and acquisitions to keep both the board and the top management accountable. Now, within the government you don't have any of that — nothing.

When the government announces that it invests, we are speaking here about jargon and vocabulary again. But what does the term "investing" mean for a private company? What do you have to go through? I have to prepare a very precise business plan. I have to approach a venture capitalist or an angel investor or a bank, or try to issue bonds or do an IPO (initial public offering). I have to go through that process. To get any money, the bank, the investors will ask you hundreds and thousands of questions. Who is the management? Who will be responsible? Who will be accountable? What happens if the one responsible for this business becomes sick? What types of management are there? How do you solve all these problems? This is what is called investment.

Now, the government doesn't go through this process at all. More than that: let's say you are within a company and in the company there are a couple of different departments that would like to expand. All of them then go through this process that I just mentioned and then they are compared one with the other. Well, in the government we don't see that at all. The government just approved this infrastructure program — how many, 17,000 projects? Now try to imagine who is going through a careful calculation of these 17,000 projects? We don't know. We don't know who is accountable. We don't know anything. This is not investment, this is just fiction. It's pieces of paper and jargon.

The issue is not the words that we use, whether it is "spending" or "investment." Of course the government will say that it is investment. But what does it mean to invest? We don't know today if all this Internet commerce will succeed. Maybe only part of it will succeed. The private companies call it investment. They invest $100 million in it. We don't know if this will be an investment or a mistake. What we do know is that in the private companies you do have those institutions to prevent mistakes from persisting. In the government we don't have that. That's the big difference.

The $8.3 billion, I would say, and all that we know about how it is spent is really symbolic of how the rest of the government's budget is spent. If the government made only a mistake of $8.3 billion from that one budget, Canada would be the richest country in the world. As I said before, the private sector also makes mistakes. Everywhere you have waste and mistakes because nobody's perfect and we don't know all the answers. The question should be, "Is this infrastructure program symbolic of the way the government manages all its business?" I would say this is where the danger is and I would say, unfortunately, from what we know about how the other money is spent, it's not spent much better.

Is this really symbolic of the way the federal or the provincial governments behave? Obviously it's just a guess. But from what we know already about the way the money in our education and health systems — and the way, now, the money on infrastructure is being spent — I would say that it is a good hunch. Now, is it self-perpetuating? The answer is yes, for a while. The ones who will correct this mistake are the same institutions who would correct it for a private company eventually: the financial markets.

What makes a country prosper? I would say the ability to finance risk-taking people. So it has two aspects: the risk taking — the willingness to take risks — and financing it. It's not enough that you have wonderful, brilliant ideas. They must be brought to life. Once you put in the word "financing," that implies two things: one is that you have relatively open, democratized financial markets, and the second is that you have the proper regulatory, fiscal and taxation systems so that people have the incentive to invest in that particular country.

Think about what it means to become an entrepreneur and to finance a project. Let's say 80 percent of these projects fail. The tax system must be such that if I put money on various people, the return on that one success must compensate me for all the losses. If the tax system is such that it doesn't provide me with these expectations, I shall not put my money in that country. I shall put it elsewhere. That's how the tax system is killing the financing of entrepreneurs. The entrepreneurs have two choices. Either they lower their aspirations and stay here and accept a government job or a much lower-level job, or they move to the United States.

A few years ago there was a huge migration from Hong Kong to Vancouver because people were afraid of what would happen in Hong Kong after the Chinese takeover. They came here and they stayed for about two or three years. They took a look at our 55 percent marginal tax rate and they all went back to Hong Kong. So they preferred the Chinese risk to the 55 percent marginal, but very safe, Canadian tax rate.

I would say the issue is even less the taxes than having a much more responsive government or those institutions to correct the mistakes more quickly. This is the issue. The tax issue is really a symptom. A much more important thing to fix is the issue of the institutions and correcting mistakes.

Politicians are not stupid and they see what is going on in the rest of the world. So it would be hard for me to believe that some of them at least don't understand what is really going on. But they have to play the political game and that's it — it's political power. I also have no doubt that some of them are sincere, but then remember that delusions can be very powerful when they serve people's interests. So I'm not saying that all these politicians are insincere. Some of them may sincerely believe in the wrong theories.

You have to always remember that the country can perform well, not because it does very good things, but because all the other countries are doing much stupider things. I would say that these mistakes of the rest of the world helped the prosperity of Canada and the U.S. even though our governments were making a lot of mistakes. Today many countries, at least in principle, try to correct their ways. We saw what happened in Asia — the whole issue of corruption and transparency — and this is what is happening in Brazil and in Mexico and all over the place.

These countries have been democracies for seven or more decades. How come 95 percent of their people are still very poor and it is the same two percent who stay on the top? Because democracy is not the answer. It's what the government does with the money — what the internal institutions of government are — and whether you open financial markets. If you don't allow your people to have access to raise money and try to struggle and bring their ideas to life, these countries will stay poor, even if on paper they are democracies.

Look how many countries have governments that don't want to give up power, don't want to lower taxes and don't want to privatize. At one point they will default on their loans. What does it mean to default on their loans? In fact they are bankrupt and are unable to raise money. Now, the moment the government is unable to raise money, it is not able to maintain all those bureaucracies and press tools and everything to sustain them in power. You can look way back in history, or you look at more recent history, to the French Revolution or to the Magna Carta. Why did kings give up that power in the French Revolution? It was not that suddenly they saw the light. They were bankrupt, and when they were bankrupt they couldn't maintain the army. Today Reagan is still considered to be controversial in some areas, but many people will realize that his Star Wars program and his defence spending forced the Russians into bankruptcy, and this led to a much earlier demise of communism than otherwise would have happened.

Government is a matter of power. A lot of people and institutions now depend on handouts. So there is this myopic, very short-term calculation made by politicians. Take the example of Newfoundland and the fishermen. It's an excellent example of how governments destroy skills which are then very difficult to repair in the long term. In fact, before the government decided that the unemployment benefits apply also to so-called seasonal workers, the Newfoundland fishermen had a variety of jobs. For about three months they fished and for the rest of the time they either worked in agriculture or manufacturing. Then for political reasons a huge mistake was made, and government decided that even somebody who is only working three months a year has the right to get unemployment benefits for the whole year. So what happened? The fishermen accepted it. Why not work for just three months and relax for all the rest of the nine months? What happened? They relaxed.

They lost that complicated network of other jobs, all those skills and all the people who knew and trusted them. Now we are 30 years on, and these people don't have any skills other than being fishermen, whereas previously they had a wide variety of skills. So guess what? If the government says, "OK, we are not paying you anymore, we want to reduce benefits," of course the fishermen will not like it because this payment destroyed their skills. So whom will they vote for? They will vote for the politician who promises to maintain that standard. This is just a small example, but you have that all over the economy.

Unfortunately many governments believe that somehow to redistribute poverty is better than to create wealth. It seems to be for the moment the ideology here.

JOHN WILLIAMS

Alliance MP, St. Albert (Alberta);
Chair, Public Accounts Committee

John Williams chairs the federal Public Accounts Committee. He was first elected to the House of Commons in 1993 as a Reform member representing St. Albert. One of his regular Waste Report *newsletters — bulletins that outline government spending — was devoted to the CIWP.*

The Public Accounts Committee is the committee that holds government to account. Unlike the other committees that deal with policy, Public Accounts focuses strictly on government from a retrospective basis of what went wrong, why did it go wrong, and what are we going to do to fix it to ensure that the taxpayer doesn't end up being taken to the cleaners. So the Public Accounts Committee focuses on all areas of government.

We work very closely with the auditor general, Mr. Denis Desautels, who publishes a report about three times a year and tables it in the House of Commons. By looking at the auditor general's report we see the full analysis of the issue: the pros, the cons, the facts, the losses, the waste and the mismanagement. From there we're able to understand the issue in depth.

The Public Accounts Committee asks the deputy minister, assistant deputy ministers and those in the senior management positions to come to the committee of parliamentarians to explain why. Of course no bureaucrat really enjoys receiving an invitation to explain why to Public Accounts, and just knowing that they can be asked to explain why is in itself some measure of accountability for the civil service, to think that we must act properly and prudently on behalf of Canadians.

We start off with an opening statement by the auditor general outlining his synopsis of his chapter, followed by a presentation by the appropriate committee or deputy minister giving his rebuttal and explanation as to why things have gone off the rails. From there it's opened up to questions where all members of the committee, both government members and opposition members, have the opportunity to ask the questions that they think are important.

We then table a report in the House of Commons, and from there the government is required to respond within 150 days to the recommendations that the committee has tabled. So there's a full circle. If the committee doesn't like the response, we can call them all back and start the process again so that there is accountability.

The report that we prepare goes to the department, and our report gives a synopsis of our perception of the issue, with clear recommendations to the government. They then come back and say, "Yes, we agree, we are taking action." Or they may disagree and say, "We feel the situation's quite appropriate as it is today." That's when the committee can take exception. But we want to ensure that action is taken. We don't want this to be just another exercise in futility where people talk, talk, talk and nothing happens.

We don't have the powers to fine and sanction and fire and so on. But we have derailed careers in the civil service by virtue of the fact that testimony in front of the committee obviously demonstrated that some people were incompetent. The fact that you are asked to appear before the committee is not really something that people relish. I for one believe that it's an excellent method of accountability. We're not here to hold hands and say to the deputy minister, "I know that you meant well and I know you're going to go back and do a better job." No, we want to ask the hard-hitting questions, to really put them on the spot.

These are senior executive officers of large departments in charge of billions of dollars of taxpayers' money. If they're not competent and if they cannot run their departments well and properly, then let us show that to be the case. At the same time, if it's not a major issue, then they can explain it and we can carry on. But usually there is a systemic problem that needs to be addressed. We want the deputy ministers, assistant deputy ministers to really know that things better change.

In the Westminster model of government, which we have taken from the United Kingdom, the chair is from the Opposition because we want to ensure the transparency and want to ensure that there's no manipulation of the committee. We never have it from the government side. It's the only committee of substance that is this way. All the rest are policy committees, where the government wants to look at policies, like of agriculture, defence or foreign affairs. These are proactive, forward-looking issues where the government would want to develop a report along the same general lines and thinking as the government itself. So if you have a Liberal government, you have a Liberal chair. If you have a government of a different persuasion, you would have a chair of the same persuasion. That way you're going to get a report that they can live with as far as policy implementation is concerned. But we're not into policy. We're here for accountability, and therein lies the big difference.

I think of a recent issue involving social insurance numbers, where hundreds of millions of dollars were being wasted and people had dozens of social insurance cards, that was uncovered by the auditor general. For 35 years the system had been going on, issuing social insurance numbers. Nobody had checked to see if we had updated our security.

Hundreds of millions of taxpayers' dollars had been ripped off. Remember, when social insurance was set up in 1965, it was set up as a file number for your income tax return. Back in 1965, in the days before computers and social programs, tax returns were basically, "I have to pay the government." Who wanted more than one social insurance number? They'd have to pay the government more than once. But now we're into all kinds of social programs administered through the tax system. So a social insurance number is now a key to cheques in the mail from the government, rather than having to pay taxes. That's why it became beneficial to have a whole bunch of them, if you're going to act fraudulently. The government never twigged to the whole change in concept of why people have social insurance numbers, and for that they had to get their fingers roundly slapped. Now they're addressing the issue, but why didn't they do it 10 or 15 years ago?

If you don't have timeliness in your accountability, it's not worth anything at all. I've talked to other countries where the auditor general's report comes down five years after the end of the fiscal year. It's meaningless by that time. Who is going to go back and investigate the facts in 1999 for 1994? We're far more concerned about the future than five years in the past. So timeliness is crucial in accountability. Being proactive is crucial in accountability.

Accountability is a very difficult but fundamental thing to grasp. I give the example in the private sector. The private sector has what I call systemic accountability. These are forces out of its own control, yet it must respond to them. The easiest one is called competition. If you run a grocery store in Ottawa, for example — and there are many grocery stores in Ottawa — unless your prices are reasonable, unless your product quality is up there, unless you run a clean store, unless your service is up to par, you're going to find that your clientele is going to drift off somewhere else. Therefore you're forced to ensure that your prices are in line, you're forced to ensure that your service is up there, you're forced to ensure that your quality is up there and that your cleanliness and presentation is up there. Not because you want to. But your competitor is doing the same thing and perhaps better. Therefore you have a force over which you have no control. That causes you to do the best that you can.

Government doesn't have competition pushing it around. Therefore we have to create accountability. We, as a federal committee, can't hold the provinces to account. Program evaluation is another part of it. Lobbyists pushing in all directions is another part of it. Having to balance the budget is another part of it. Taxpayers pushing and demanding results are another part of it. But we're always trying to create this real systemic accountability which is a force that managers have to respond to, and over which they have no control. I use competition as an example. Not to say that we want competition in government, but we want a systemic force like the private sector has to operate with. If we could institute that kind of thing in government, we would have a better-managed government, a more efficient government, a more productive government and a more responsive government than we have today.

There's not enough accountability in government today because we haven't been able to design these forces outside government that are beyond the scope of government. Remember, government, in the final analysis, holds all the power. It can legislate any force out of existence if it so desires. It can change the public policy of a program. It can widen the public policy, or it can lower the standards. There's no force that government has to respond to unless it imposes it upon itself. Access to Information is one force on government that they have imposed upon themselves. Now when you want to investigate an issue in government, they have to deliver the documentation.

Transparency is one of the fundamental ways of holding governments to account. We must have access to the process of decision making and the facts that they have to arrive at their decisions. When we find that decisions are made on a whim, on the back of a cigarette package or on no written basis whatsoever, then we have to suspect, what kind of motivation was there to approve that? Was there influence? I'm not saying that there was, but you can't prove that there wasn't. Were there other influences other than straightforward economic play? We don't know, but we can infer that perhaps there could have been. Otherwise, why isn't it documented? Then we ask the next question. If you are a manager approving these applications based on no evidence whatsoever, how good a manager are you?

We tolerate all these things in the public service because it's very, very difficult to change the system and make sure that managerial results are the best that they could be. Now it comes back to accountability. Transparency — knowing that your decision making and your paperwork is going to be out there in the public domain — will in some way push you to do the job better and do the job properly. If you feel that only one percent of your work will see the light of day, you may want to take the risk. In the private sector that wouldn't be tolerated on an ongoing basis, but it seems to be tolerated quite well in the public sector.

With respect to the Infrastructure Works Program, there's no question that there's not enough debate about the wisdom of spending. But remember also that when a government, especially the federal government, spends a dollar, somebody earns a dollar. And when they earn a dollar they pay taxes back. Think of the Infrastructure Works Program that was announced in 1993 at the election. Remember "jobs, jobs, jobs" was a Liberal slogan. Underpinning that was, how are you going to create all these jobs? Well, we've got this wonderful infrastructure program that's going to create all these jobs. We're going to spend $6 billion — $2 billion from the federal government, $2 billion from the provinces and $2 billion from the municipalities. Everybody thought this was great.

Now, the federal government spent its $2 billion, and so did the other two levels of government. But then when that expenditure became profits and wages and income for other people, or people were no longer receiving employment insurance, which is an expenditure of government, but paying employment insurance premiums, which is revenue to government, the net cost to the federal government was not that significant. The biggest cost was passed on to the municipalities, who had virtually no recovery at all. The provinces got a little bit, but the federal government was the biggest beneficiary of the infrastructure program because they got the other levels of government to kick in equal shares. Now, that does not get them off the hook for being accountable for the quality of spending.

Are we going to get some real return on the money spent? Are we going to get a road from here to there that's going to cause new development, new factories and new houses to be built? That was the intent and that was the promise, but unfortunately, as the auditor general pointed out in one chapter that he wrote, we got a lot more, or let's say, a lot less for our money than we had anticipated.

One town in Ontario put an elevator in a brand-new building. It was a building about two years old, two storeys. Obviously the building code did not require an elevator. However, somebody said, "We want an elevator in this building." OK, we've got some infrastructure money, so we put an elevator in a two-storey building, with the taxpayers' money, where the code did not require it.

You can always get a number on the jobs created by the infrastructure program, but is that the right number or a real number, or just somebody's number that's politically correct to make the whole program look like it's going to work? It's absolutely impossible to go and count the number of heads that actually got a job out of the infrastructure program. Then you've got the spinoffs. If you happen to be building a new road, for example, you can say, "OK, there were

50 people working on the crew paving that road," but what about the people back in the gravel pit who got a job to dig the gravel? What about the people back in the tar sands? What about the people who got the extra contract for the extra fuel that was consumed? It keeps going on and on and on.

So you never can get an actual figure. It has to be all based on statistical models, and if you take a look at the auditor general's interim report, you'll find that his numbers and the government numbers are miles apart. Of course his numbers are lower.

Remember, maybe it sounds quite cynical, but it was an election platform of "jobs, jobs, jobs" that was underpinned by, "How are you going to do that?" "Well, we're going to have infrastructure." They won the election. The motivation for ensuring that everything went well from that point on was gone. The concept of infrastructure had accomplished what it set out to do on the 26th or 25th of October, 1993. They got the election — end of story.

As a member of the Opposition I say, "Wait a minute, that was $6 billion of taxpayers' money, $2 billion out of the federal coffers." Did we throw the money at the wall hoping some would stick or did we get value for our money? Now we're into the actual business of infrastructure and then we find out it didn't work. But from the government's point of view they didn't care because it had done its job before it started.

We would never think of running our household budget the way the government does. The reason for that is that even today we are still operating on a simple cash basis. The money I collect is the money that I can spend. Everybody else, every other business, from the little corner grocery store up to the big banks, works on accrual, sophisticated accounting systems to know what their capital is, what their investments are, what their return on investments is and what their expenditures are. But the government says, "Money in, money out, we've got a surplus or we've got a deficit."

The infrastructure program may or may not be repeated in the future, but what we want to try and do is ensure that we are getting good business management of the program from the federal point of view. We can't hold the provinces accountable. If they decide that they're just a flow-through mechanism by adding their one-third share, that is their responsibility.

We, as a federal committee, can't hold them to account. They have their own public accounts committees, which hopefully will be doing their job too. And for the municipalities, they don't have a public accounts committee, but they have the local taxpayers who can say, "Well, it's my road that's getting paved or it's my bridge that's being built." They can have the fights there too. So with the Infrastructure Works Program it is not so easy to put on an accountability lesson and project it into the future.

I'll give you an example of why accountability should be a fundamental part of the process. The Atlantic Region Freight Transition Assistance Program started in 1921 to subsidize a railroad that we built from the Maritimes into Quebec and Ontario, to help subsidize the movement of goods. A laudable objective in 1921, I'm not going to dispute that. But then the railroad fell by the wayside, so the subsidy moved over to the roads. By then it was no longer a subsidization of stuff moving from Atlantic Canada into Quebec and Ontario. In 1991 when they finally did a program evaluation, they found that at that time the $108-million-per-year program was providing *zero* economic benefit. The program was killed. But it cost us billions of dollars before somebody said, 70 years after it started, "Are we doing any good here?"

The solution does not lie in more people and more overseers and more inspectors or more members of Parliament. The key lies in systemic outside forces that promote good management. We have to create external forces for accountability in government. Unfortunately the culture of accountability is not there.

Government privatized NAV CANADA (NAV CAN), the air navigation system, a few years back. Privatization sounds good. We're moving into the capitalistic environment. But look at it. It was granted a perpetual monopoly. It was given power to tax the public. The public has no representation on the board of directors. Because it's a non-profit organization on a cost-plus basis, whatever it costs to run, that's what you charge to cover your costs. The auditor general has no authority to look at NAV CAN. Information is denied. This organization is in a cocoon that is totally and absolutely without accountability. Even Parliament can't look at it because it's in the "private sector." NAV CAN is a bureaucratic nightmare, and it will cause serious safety problems down the road because it has no accountability to anybody. I'm not saying today that they're incompetent, but they will become totally moribund in managerial style 10 or 20 years from now through a lack of accountability. That bothers me a great deal.

Government would run better as a business, more efficiently and with more accountability. Unfortunately, in my mind, party discipline is far too tight. The backbenchers rally around the government regardless of the issue and regardless of how they feel. Remember, in the concept of Parliament the parties do not exist. We talk about parliamentarians, those who support the government and those who oppose the government. But the concept of Parliament is not broken down into clear party divisions — these MPs support the government and these MPs are in the opposition. It talks about parliamentarians supporting the government's initiatives, and if the government can carry the day in the House of Commons, then it has the confidence to govern. But this has evolved into this tight party discipline that says if you are a member of the government, you will vote their way regardless of whether you like it or not. That allows them to stay in power, even though perhaps they really do not enjoy the confidence of Parliament; but by the vote it appears that they do.

Do we need a better calibre of MP? We certainly need MPs who are prepared to stand up for their beliefs. When they run for election they say, "When I get down to Ottawa I will stand for this and I will stand for that and I will vote for this and I will support these policies." But when something controversial comes along and they capitulate to the leadership rather than saying to leadership, "Let us do the right thing," that's when Parliament fails.

On a clear, simple issue they could call the government to account. If they did it once, the emperor — the prime minister — would find his clothes were wearing very thin, and he would start to recognize that he has to deal with parliamentarians of all parties and not just assume that certain of them will vote for whatever he wants.

It's difficult to step out of line where people have toed the line for so long. But we have to break this circle. Mind you, confidence is a difficult thing to put your finger on. I remember talking to one member of Parliament. He said, "I voted that way because I wanted to. It wasn't confidence — I didn't have to vote that way. I did it because I wanted to." It's hard to defeat that logic. But you do know confidence applies. When the prime minister stands up and says, "It's confidence, you toe the line," and they toe the line, that has to be broken down. If that can be broken down, you're going to see Parliament exercising real authority over government, and that is a huge measure of accountability.

There's no question that Parliament has allowed, over the last 50 years, or even more, for the power to flow from Parliament right into the Cabinet and into the PMO. Confidence has a very large part to play in that. In 1998 there was the vote on hepatitis C, where many government backbenchers said it was despicable not to compensate people who were infected with hepatitis C through tainted blood. Yet when the prime minister said, "This is a matter of confidence," they fell in line.

It's the Cabinet and the prime minister and those who wield power — deputy ministers. The last thing they want is more accountability. They're the ones with the finger on it. They will squash it and that's the end of that.

Parliament is best when it represents all of society. We'd never ever want Parliament to be a Parliament of accountants. Heaven forbid! Or lawyers or anybody else for that matter. We need a cross-section of society. Everybody has their own issues, their own perspective on life and their own feel as to the way that Canada should go. And of course these have coalesced into political parties in the House. But we need some people who are focused on accountability, and we need people who are focused on social programs. And we need these people who are focused on balanced budgets, and those people who are focused on productivity on the economic side.

It's only right that we have Parliament reflect all of society. So it doesn't bother me that there are only a few accountants on Parliament Hill. Frustrating at times, when you want to try and elevate an issue, but I know that other MPs have just as difficult a time elevating their particular issues as I have had raising the level of accountability. But that doesn't make my work any less important. That's just how it is on Parliament Hill.

The Public Accounts Committee is the one committee where you do have to do your homework in anticipation of the meetings being held so that you are up to speed, you have read the auditor general's report, and you do understand the issues. We provide briefings for the members ahead of time where the auditor general's staff will come in, in camera, and answer the questions and bring them up to speed so that they can hold these people accountable as much as they can.

If MPs don't discharge their duties well on the committee, they're certainly not discharging their responsibilities to their constituents very well. Then it is their responsibility to go back and explain to their constituents why they come to a committee and haven't prepared themselves ahead of time.

The vast majority of MPs on the policy committees — health care, defence or foreign affairs — are looking at their issues from a prospective point of view. What should we be doing today for tomorrow? They're not looking back. Every department, if it were to look back, would find as many horror stories in their areas as we would just looking at infrastructure programs.

The system breakdown, as far as the role of the Public Accounts Committee is concerned, is part and parcel of this erosion of power of Parliament. The subcommittee report on the business of supply is my work to try and get the tide to change. It calls for the estimates committee to be more proactive in anticipation of expenditures. Look at the Estimates. Every committee is supposed to look at the Estimates of $150 billion in spending. They spend a minuscule amount of time, if any, examining how the money is spent because the MP says, "I don't understand all these numbers, they're too complex." So we have done quite a bit of work as far as trying to improve the presentation of numbers, and Parliament has made some efforts to cause the government and the civil service to improve the presentation.

The business of supply report, if I can get it adopted, will account for program review where we start evaluating programs prospectively based on four questions. First of all, what is a public policy program designed to do? Today most programs don't have a statement of public policy or a mission statement of what it is they're trying to achieve. The second question: once we know what it's supposed to do, how well is it doing it? Third, how efficiently is it doing it? And the fourth question: can we achieve the same results in a different or better way?

We asked these four fundamental questions. They have never been asked before, on large programs or on small programs. And it's not just the Public Accounts. All members of Parliament have allowed that power to leave the House of Commons, and government is not responsive to Parliament. But if we could have Parliament asking these four questions on all programs on a regular basis, we would see government change.

This is light-years ahead of where the government is today. It gets back to accountability and people. The government can control everything by legislation, and they can legislate accountability out of the way. If you've got accountability out of the way, why would you want to bring it back? Because it causes you to sit up and take notice of something that's pushing you.

The subcommittee on the business of supply that I worked on, chaired under Marlene Catterall's direction, has the real potential to make change. That report was tabled in the last Parliament, retabled back in December of 1998, and now we're waiting for the government to respond. It calls for an estimates committee. We only vote on one-third of total spending, approximately $50 billion, so there's about $100 billion of program spending that's never brought before the House at all. Now, this estimates committee would have the authority to look at that.

It would look at loan guarantees that show up as $1 items but may have hundreds of millions of dollars of liability behind them. It looks at Crown corporations that nobody looks at today, which cost hundreds of millions of dollars a year. The estimates committee would also look at tax expenditures that are not deferred or forgiven tax revenues, which is a cost to government. A good example of that is retirement savings plans. When you make an RSP contribution you can deduct your taxes from your income. So that's what we call a tax deferral or tax expenditure. We don't collect that money that we otherwise would have because public policy says we want to motivate people to save for their retirement.

The estimates committee would look at these areas in a prospective, sustained way to ensure that the lessons we learn from the Public Accounts Committee are projected in the future.

I enjoy talking about accountability. I enjoy trying to create and understand the forces that motivate people and motivate governments in how they've been able to legislate accountability out of the way. I bring out the *Waste Report*, which tends to focus on small, stupid or irrational types of expenditures. Small things that people can just gasp at and say, "My goodness, how on earth would anybody in their sane mind do that?" In the Public Accounts we deal with the large issues, the $10-million, the $100-million and the $500-million issues, which are far too large and complex to encapsulate down into a small statement for the general public to grasp in their busy lives.

So to me the *Waste Report* fits that bill of pointing out to the population at large the small things so that they can realize the lack of accountability and the lack of managerial focus on ensuring value for money here in Ottawa. That complements my role as chairman of the Public Accounts, where we're dealing with the same concepts but on a much larger, more complex basis. The *Waste Report* gets a significant amount of attention. I bring them out periodically. It gets a quick blast of publicity when it comes out, and it lasts for about three days. No department really wants to have to suffer the ridicule of the *Waste Report*, but they do. It's one small piece of pressure that augments the accountability.

There are two things that we have to do. One, we have to change the culture of society and the fact that they think that governments cannot make a mistake. I use the example of crime. Nobody suggests that if we will spend enough money, there will be no more crime in this country. We have a tolerance for crime. When crime gets too high, there's an outcry by the public, and we'll allocate more resources to try and bring it down. But nobody ever advocates there'll be no crime in this country. We tolerate a certain amount of crime. We have to start recognizing that no one is perfect in this society, or any society, and that governments, which are run by people, will make some mistakes. Provided they're within the range of tolerance, that's OK.

But our system has become so adversarial, and because party discipline is so tight, the slightest mistake is blown up into the greatest of proportions. Therefore the government will expend all efforts, regardless of the cost and benefits, to try to bring mistakes down to the barest minimum or none at all. That's why they're not interested in public policy being too well defined. Programs don't always achieve what they're designed to achieve. If you don't set out and say, "This is what I really want to do," if you don't articulate that, then obviously the program is a success because you spent the money. That's the thing: governments don't want to be held accountable because we set the benchmark so high that the slightest mistake is a huge embarrassment.

Setting standards of measurement is crucial for accountability. The Government of Alberta has done a really good job of introducing benchmarks for the different programs that they produce and that they manage. Right across the board, they have set out benchmarks and each department has to publish quarterly how well they have achieved these.

They are introducing this concept that if we didn't make 100 percent, it's not the end of the world. If we got the 90 percent, which is better than the 80 percent we had before, then that's progress and we're getting there. But let's not hang them because they didn't get the last 10 percent. Good management says you will make some mistakes because you're creative and things don't always work out. Ask Coca-Cola about when they introduced that new Coke.

Accountability is rather esoteric and difficult to grasp. The public goes about their live. They've got busy lives, jobs to do and families to raise, and they expect the members of Parliament and their elected people to carry out that responsibility on their behalf. That's what they sent us down here to do, and I hope in my small way that I'm making that contribution.

JOHN GRACE

Former Information Commissioner of Canada

Before he retired in 1998, John Grace served as privacy commissioner and then information commissioner of Canada.

The Access to Information Act starts with the assumption that a democratic government is an accountable government, and it should be an open government. Access to information and democratic values are complementary.

In an ideal democracy you should not need an Access to Information law. The whole concept of democracy is that the people are the governors. We have tended to look up to our governors, as if there was still an era of princes and kings who knew best. But in a working, healthy democracy the resort to a formal request for information from your governors is a contradiction. In a working democracy you want the public to be as informed as possible, to make informed decisions: about whom to vote for at the next election, about spending priorities, about the whole vast array of issues that arise. The Access to Information Act recognizes that.

The Access law passed Parliament in 1982 and came into effect July 1, 1983. It sets out in general terms the proposition that government-held information should be available to the public as a matter of right, not as a matter of grace and favour, i.e., if you know somebody, somebody likes you, you get it. For the first time it's a right. If you ask for information, you have a right to get it unless the government can point specifically to a particular exemption under the law that enables it to withhold that information. For example, the Access law cannot be used to obtain personal information about other citizens.

The whole concept of open government is a novelty in this country. We inherited a lot of good things from the British. We inherited representative government, democratic government. But we did not inherit open government. We inherited a notion that your governors know best. That's a vestige from an earlier era when the public was not as educated and perhaps there was some justification for it.

The public wants now to know what the government — whether it be a federal, provincial or municipal government — is up to. That's what Access to Information comes down to. It's a very simple concept: what is the government of the day doing? Advocates of Access to Information believe that it's a right. I don't think it should necessarily be in the Charter of Rights and Freedoms, but it should be a right.

The Access to Information law was the child of, not the government of the day, but of a back-bench member of Parliament from northern Alberta, Jed Baldwin. Governments don't like Access. They don't produce Access legislation; opposition parties do. What usually happens, though, is that the opposition party becomes the government and they have to live under this regime. That's what happened in Canada. The Mulroney government was the first government to work under Access.

Our Access to Information law is based essentially on the American Freedom of Information law. The Americans have a first-rate law. I like "freedom" of information; it's a good American word, and the Americans are much more open than we are here. It's their tradition. The Americans say, "We're the government that broke away from the king." They weren't going to be governed by kings and bureaucrats; they were going to govern themselves.

But the Americans don't have my former office. They don't have an Access office and information commissioner. In the United States the individual who is frustrated must go to court and pay his own court costs. In Canada Parliament said, "We'll put this independent ombudsman — who's appointed by Parliament and who reports directly to Parliament — in place to represent the citizen who is seeking justice under the act. He should be the spokesperson for the act, the advocate for openness in government, for transparency."

I'm reminded of an episode of *Yes, Minister*. Sir Humphrey was asked to bring forward a freedom of information law for Britain, of all places. Sir Humphrey said, "Minister, you could have good government, you could have open government, but you can't have both." That philosophy still permeates. That's why people run into brick walls.

This might be the story of how an Access request is processed. You have made a request for information about an infrastructure program to the department that is implementing the program. That request would go to a co-ordinator. They send requests to what's called the Office of Primary Interest in the department, which would know how much money was being spent, or why this particular program is going ahead. That person would be asked to forward any relevant documents to the co-ordinator, who in turn would release them to the requester.

Now the timorous public servant would say, "Well, I'm not going to take it upon myself to release this information because someone may be embarrassed by it." So it would go right up the line to directors, supervisors, etc. Ultimately, if the issue was big enough, or if a department was so timorous, it would go to the deputy minister. The deputy minister should have more important things to do than worry about routine Access to Information requests, by the way. But some of them did get involved. The deputy minister might say, "Well, I think it's OK, but look, I've got to worry about the minister." He may send that request to the minister's office. It's going to sit there for a while. This is how, by the way, delays mount up.

The minister perhaps decides, "We can't hold it back." He will want to know when it's going out; he'll want to be prepared to answer press inquiries. It might go out. But it might not go out, and then the information commissioner will get a complaint, and he goes through the whole process again.

We had about 20 investigators. They have a tough job, going to a department day after day with a complaint in hand, saying, "Look, what's the problem with this request, why is this complaint here?" They are not received with open arms. Perhaps it's too much to expect they should be, but I would hope that as a new generation of senior public servants moves into place, public servants who have known nothing else but Access to Information, this attitude will change.

We had a case several years ago that involved a request from a reporter in Moncton, N.B., who wanted documentation to support a claim made by the Atlantic Canada Opportunities Agency, known by the acronym ACOA, that some 40,000 jobs were created under its program. "We have a breakdown of the statistics here, how did this figure of 40,000 come about? Where were the jobs created, in what businesses? Just give us the breakdown."

I saw that as a sensible and important request to make. One of the good uses of the Access to Information law is to allow the public to check up on the veracity of government statistics. It should have been easy to respond to the request. But the department argued that it had told the consulting firm that did the survey for it that the department would keep that information confidential. The agency was in effect contracting out of the Access to Information law. They couldn't do that.

Despite our strong recommendation that the information could not be held back, the department said, "Nay, nay." Indeed, some four or five years after, the reporter still does not know how the 40,000 figure came about. The reporter is still waiting. It's a long, tortured story. The case is now under appeal in the Federal Court of Canada and it'll be months before an answer is finally given as to whether that information will ever see the light of day. I have no doubt that the Federal Court will rule that that information should be released. A great amount of public money went into those subsidies. Was the money well spent? We don't know. We don't know how many jobs were created. Forty thousand looks like a suspiciously round figure to me, but I can't reveal what I saw.

The Access to Information law says all information, in general, should be open to public scrutiny, but subject to some important exemptions. There are many legitimate reasons why information should be withheld. Issues of national security and personal information about people should be protected. I have no quarrel with that. But the onus is on the government to say why information shouldn't be released. The department has to say, "The release of this information will damage national security; it will damage the reputation of an innocent person; it will damage the legitimate proprietary interest of a company that has had to give us information." The exemptions should represent only a small percentage of the vast information holdings of the Government of Canada.

I've recommended some changes to narrow the exemptions. But tinkering with the exemptions, narrowing them down or making a few legitimate changes, that's only tinkering at the edges. The real problem with the law is not the exemptions as they are now written; it's with the application of those exemptions, and the philosophy that is behind the person who is going to be dispensing the material. I think the great majority of the public servants who exempt information have good motives. They're perhaps a little timorous but they are not evil people. It's because they've been raised in a bureaucratic culture that puts a greater value on secrecy than on openness.

Bureaucrats are excessively zealous in imposing exemptions on Access to Information releases. There is an instinct to apply exemptions almost wildly. They tend to give the exemptions of the act the benefit of all doubts: "When in doubt, hold back." It could be a kind of a motto.

First of all, they want to err on the side of protecting bureaucratic values. Perhaps again it's an example of the bureaucrat protecting his own little turf, a turf that he enjoys to play on by himself. Public servants — good people, most of them — are not highly paid. They want job satisfaction, psychic satisfaction, and there's some satisfaction to be taken, some exclusivity from saying, "We know this, you don't know." Public servants take a proprietary interest in the information. But not the public servants' information; it's the people's information. The people pay for the collection; the people gave the information. Suddenly these public servants say, "It's ours, trust us."

Users of Access to Information laws are running into what I've called a culture of secrecy, and that's the culture that's been handed down to our rulers. Instead of a culture of openness — which I think the times demand and an educated public demands — we are really insulted by this notion of, "Trust us, we know best. This information might damage the national interest, you aren't able to handle it." It's a paternalistic notion. I think it's a notion based perhaps on preservation of power.

There are mixed loyalties. The public servants are loyal to the government and loyal to public service. I would want them to be loyal to the law. There has been an examination of public service ethics and standards. The big thing that's being pushed is loyalty. Loyalty is a big buzzword in Ottawa. I think that's a bit insidious in some ways because the implication is that you're loyal to your job. That's fine, but does the public interest come ahead of the departmental interest, the government interest? Sometimes there's a conflict. Loyalty is a many splendoured thing.

There's a fear of embarrassment. You don't want to embarrass the minister, the government or your boss. Unfortunately, in the federal system at least, being known as a person who believes in the concept of transparency and open government, it's not a job-enhancing position to take. It becomes, "Well, whose side are you on? Are you on the side of these people who want this information or are you on the side of your department who knows best?" and "We'll decide what goes out. We'll decide the spin." To say you're in favour of releasing that information easily is not a way to enhance yourself with your bosses.

In my naive youth in this job I wrote a letter to a relatively junior public servant, to thank her for her devotion to Access to Information and how helpful she had been in a difficult case. I thought that would be good for the office and good for her. She showed that letter to her boss, and he said, "Who are you working for? Grace, or this department?"

Access to Information is a request really not for information, though that term is in the title of the act. When you apply under Access to Information, you're applying for records — primary documents, really. It's not press releases or the spin that the government public relations or information people are putting on a particular topic. You want the basic documents upon which judgments are being made or will be made.

The answer to excessive exemptions is to complain to an information commissioner, a provincial or federal commissioner. That commissioner will examine the document, the document full of whitened-out materials. He'll see the original document and he'll make a decision as to whether those exemptions are legitimate and can be applied under the law. If he agrees with the complainant, he will recommend that the suppressed information be released. Of course then the fight starts — more delays.

The act says anybody can use the act, for a $5 fee. For that $5, the individual should expect to receive an answer from the government department to the request within 30 days. There are legitimate reasons why a response cannot be made in 30 days and the act provides for an extension of that period. If the requester feels this is an unnecessary delay, the requester can complain about the extension, and the Office of the Information Commissioner will make a report to the requester about whether the delay is justified.

In 30 days the individual should have a response. The requester should either receive the information, or the response is, "No, this information is held back in whole or in part." When the information is withheld, the individual is told, "If you are unhappy with this, you may complain to the Access to Information commissioner. Here's his name, here's his address."

The information commissioner's office receives about 12,000 complaints every year. On average, one out of 10 requests ends up in a complaint. Delay is the single biggest problem. We get more delay complaints than any other kind. I think something like 60 percent of all the complaints made to the information commissioner are complaints of delay. And of course, delay is information denied. Timing is important for many of these requests.

I think this chronic, insidious delay really goes to the heart of the act. It's one way of avoiding the impact of the act. In some departments — National Defence was one in my time — delays were endemic, just endemic. An extraordinarily high percentage of requests ended in complaints. The Privy Council Office — the prime minister's own department — had a very bad record on delays. Fisheries has another bad record. Each annual report sets out my "roll of honour" of the departments who sin most in this regard. Delays are a sign that there's something wrong in the department.

Delay discourages people. We're not talking just about journalists. The company that wants some information about what the government might be doing or has done, information upon which it will base a decision, needs that information soon. There is disillusionment about the act — some merited, much not. I'm going to argue that it's a good act and it's working. Not perfectly, but it's a hell of a lot better than what we had before. But there is disillusionment over the time it takes to get an answer, and that's the first thing that should be cleaned up by leadership.

I always felt that the information office is doing the work of the departmental Access offices in getting involved in this delay thing.

Requests made to the Privy Council Office should go to the Privy Council Office. Requests made to Fisheries, to Foreign Affairs, to other departments should not go, in my view, to the Privy Council Office.

Checking with PCO is too common, I think. Information requests should rarely go to the political level. I have always advocated that public servants should handle the requests. If they start routinely taking their orders from the politicians, that's going to slow things down and result in more exemptions and less openness. It takes a strong deputy minister not to tell his boss what's going out. One minister told me at one time, "I don't want to know about information that you are releasing. I want to know what you're holding back." That was a very wise minister. So often the bad stories come because information is delayed and is not released. People end up in court and the department gets a bad name.

If only politicians would realize that there are very few big secrets, and that openness in the long term is something to their benefit, certainly to the public's benefit. If only they would relax about Access and not fear it as "an instrument in the hands of the enemy." I've seen some of the big secrets of government. Let me tell you, most of them are disappointing. Anyone who's seen the big secrets will say that. And you wonder, why the hell was there a fight over this?

You know what one of the big secrets was when I was the commissioner? This ended up in court. The Mulroney government refused to release polling information that it had gathered using taxpayers' money, polling information about an important question, national unity. The Mulroney government took the view that Canadians should not be told what Canadians were thinking, even though Canadians were paying for this polling information. That was a monumental mistake, I felt. We took Mr. Mulroney to court. He was the head of the department, the Privy Council Office, and it was the Privy Council Office that was refusing to release the polling information.

The court agreed with us that the information should go out. But delay served the government's purpose. It took the judge a year before he made his decision. By that time the government didn't worry about any damage that knowing about Canadian attitudes toward, say, Quebec, would cause. So delay can sometimes be a very effective weapon for thwarting Access to Information.

The famous *Red Book* of the Liberals did speak of open government, but what do we have? The same old thing. Someone asked the Access to

Information office to investigate the denial of the request for the ethical guidelines governing the prime minister and his Cabinet. We of course accepted that complaint, and were told that the ethical guidelines were Cabinet documents and therefore secret. To this day Canadians don't know what these guidelines are. The whole business of the prime minister's ethical guidelines is a mystery to me.

I commented on this in my annual report. When the signal comes out that the prime minister himself is denying the public information about the guidelines under which he operates, what kind of a signal is that? It makes every public servant and every deputy minister pretty happy, that's what it does. How can they be criticized if the prime minister himself refuses to abide by the spirit, or even the letter, of the act?

There has never been a public message from any prime minister that this government wants Access to work better than it has worked. I don't understand the politics of it. I mean, this could be good politics for the governments, to do that. A clear sign from the prime minister and from the minister of justice would help. They should be the persons most anxious to show not just the appearance but the reality of openness. The word should go down the line to senior public servants that this government believes in the act. If that kind of message was sent out, I think attitudes would change. What the Access act needs, above all, is a signal from the top that information will be released, not only formally but informally.

Because of what I would call the failure of leadership in Access, junior public servants have felt freer to play fast and loose with the Access to Information law. Certainly they are not sanctioned within their departments for delays in getting a response ready. Junior public servants can show contempt for the act with some impunity. You know, eventually much of the information gets out in any event. The fact that you have to chase after it is not doing government any good. So many of the stories that give Access a bad name are simply process stories.

The big embarrassments that governments have experienced because of Access were not so much from the information that they were forced to release, but the story of the hunt for that information. For example, Michael McAuliffe from the CBC and their hunt to get information about the Somali scandal. That's basically a story about attempts to hide information and to alter records. That's where so much of the scandal is. The blood scandal was terrible in itself, but part of the story is the fact — which makes the story worse, which makes people's motives seem bad — that individuals destroyed records to avoid giving them out under an Access to Information request.

The Access to Information Act does not provide sanctions or penalties against persons who are found to have contravened the act. The last thing in the minds of the members of Parliament and the bureaucracy that drafted the act was that good, faithful public servants would contravene the act — by dragging out the answers, by chronic long delays and more — really almost viciously, or contravene the act by destroying and by altering records. I don't think it happens too often, but we know that on several occasions public servants did destroy records to avoid their release, to avoid embarrassment.

I have recommended that the act be revised to provide for penalties for willful destruction of records. It's up to Parliament to decide, but a penalty would show how seriously Parliament takes the act and takes any defiance of the act. I think a fine of $5,000 — or even imprisonment — would be in order.

I never felt that I was a toothless commissioner, even though I could not order anyone to release information. The commissioner, under the federal law, is an ombudsman. He's got to persuade. Even though I couldn't order the release of records, even though I couldn't recommend penalties, there's still pride and sensitivity in department heads. Deputy ministers in particular do not want to be singled out by a commissioner, reported to Parliament as being anti-openness, conspiring to withhold information that should be released. I've always thought of my annual report as an instrument for buying some kind of compliance with the act.

Maybe I'm being naive, but I hope that public servants and public service managers are still embarrassed by being fingered by, say, the auditor general for having blown money on a dubious project, or simply wasting money. I am convinced that the very fact that the Access to Information law exists makes politicians and public servants think twice before they spend extra money — renovating offices, running up big hotel and restaurant bills or other examples of egregious spending — spending that has been revealed only as a result of an Access request. I think the Access law, toothless as some may argue it is, is still a powerful deterrent against excessive spending and perhaps even a deterrent against stupidity.

You can't overestimate the impact the Access to Information Act had at the beginning. Here are people working their whole professional life writing things down, collecting information, compiling files, with no thought that this information would ever see the light of day. Suddenly this new law comes along and says this information must be released, possibly must all be released. No longer is it a matter of saying, "I'll get this information to you because you're a nice guy. I like your project. You're not going to embarrass me with it or embarrass the government." Suddenly that information must be released not by grace and favour, but under the law.

Before the Access to Information Act a journalist worked sources and his friends; he tried to have a network. I was an editorial writer. It was important for me, if I were to write intelligent editorials and to understand both sides of an issue, to call up a public servant and say, "Look, what's going on here, what's your side of the story?" You had to develop your own sources. You had to be trusted. The public servant would have to feel that "This reporter is going to write something sensible, so I'll give it to him." Now the Access to Information law is changing that, but not that much because not enough journalists are using the act.

Access to Information requires patience. Making an Access request is a long-term investment for a journalist who is interested in large public policy issues. I tell journalists to make a whole series of requests — one or two a week, for five weeks, or for as long as you want. In due time the answers, the records, just start coming out. Not enough journalists use the act well. The Access to Information Act was not written just for journalism, and it certainly wasn't written for tomorrow's or this week's or next week's story. Journalists sometimes are lazy and impatient.

Some journalists have used the act in a way that sometimes trivialized the act. Some people are making requests to find out how much was spent on a trip to Paris, or how much money was spent on lunches; small stuff. Perhaps even the writers of the act didn't have that kind of request in mind. I think the writers of the act felt that the act should be used to obtain primary information that would inform the public on the great issues of the day. Public servants expected that. They were perhaps disillusioned when they received requests for "Who'd you have lunch with yesterday?" I think, as a matter of fact, that's important too. I don't diminish that. But I think that bottom-feeding, so to speak, has made it more difficult for some more serious requesters.

This act is not intended to replace informal release of information. This act is for hard cases where there might be a dispute over whether information should go out. That's the spirit of the act. This is the paradox: Access to Information is not the best way to get information. The act starts by saying that this act is to be a supplement to the general principle that government should be open. Access to Information should be the method of last resort. It's cumbersome and it's slow. But I would also argue that the only chance of getting information that the government clearly wants to withhold is to go formal and to assert your rights under that act.

That doesn't mean that newspaper people shouldn't cultivate sources. They should. It doesn't mean that members of the public shouldn't go to the employment insurance department or go to any department and say, "What about this information? I'd like it." In the spirit of the act that information should be given out. But I would be very unhappy if a prevailing morbid cynicism about the act would deter people. If that happens, the enemies of the act would have won.

When I was in office, on days when I was discouraged I would pick up the paper and see stories, very important stories, based on documents released under the Access to Information Act. These were stories that would never have been released without that law and stories that were released without the intervention of the Access commissioner. The departments simply realized that they couldn't hold it back. So there are good signs too.

I think there is a downside to the Access law as far as the availability of information is concerned. It's a downside that should not have occurred. Minutes have been pared down to bare minimum because minutes by themselves should be releasable. But perhaps the worst example is not that the minutes are bare bones, but that people don't write things down at all. Too many senior public servants come up to me and say, "You know, John, what this law's doing — we don't write things down anymore. We wink, we nod, we speak; we don't write it down." This is an unfortunate byproduct of the law. It goes completely against the spirit of the law, but there's nothing in the law that says you must write things down. I've recommended that the law be changed to provide for that kind of evasive tactic.

I think public servants really must write the important things down. It should be a concern to our historians, by the way, and a concern to the archivist who's responsible for preserving the collective national memory that information is not being recorded because of fear that it may be released under the Access to Information law. I'm not sure what the solution is other than a change of attitude.

There are understandable frustrations that people experience under the Access to Information Act when they continually meet a stone wall. I can understand that frustration. But don't blame that on the act or on how it's written. We have to change long-held beliefs that governments know best and the changes will not happen overnight. There have been many cases of real abuse of the act, but the act has had some superb successes. You have to balance the two. The disappointments are real, but on the other hand, the fact that governments are going to court to avoid releasing information, the fact that they're stewing over a request, indicates that some of these requests are hitting home. Eventually they have to answer, most of the time. I encourage people to persist, to complain, to push the commissioner to go to court.

There's great support in Parliament for Access to Information. Members of Parliament are on the side of openness, at least when they're still backbenchers — and in opposition, in particular. I regarded members of Parliament as allies when I was in office. When I went before the justice committee each year, the members would say, "Do you have enough money? What's wrong?" It's not only opposition members.

The MPs are way ahead of the senior bureaucrats. I would suggest that if you were having a problem under the act, not only should you go to a commissioner for redress, but think of your member of Parliament because members of Parliament are now in the forefront of reforming the act.

The act has not been changed since 1983. There hasn't been one amendment related to the act. Government is reluctant to open the whole thing up for an amendment because it would, I think, be vulnerable to serious, sustained criticism of its performance under the act. A private member just last year had a private member's bill through the Commons that would provide for penalties for evading the act, for destroying records. Another Liberal backbencher, John Bryden, has crafted a whole new act, based on the existing act but with significant reforms. I think we should remember that the impetus for Access to Information came from Parliament, not from the bureaucrats. The act was forced on them. The impetus for reform, for narrowing some of the exemptions, for widening the application of the act, for applying sanctions is coming not from the government, but from members of Parliament.

I reject completely the idea that Access is costing the taxpayers money. I think that on balance it saves money by imposing prudence — the fear of discovery, the fear of exposure of waste. I think people fear the Access act more than they fear the auditor general. The information laws have also the good effect of forcing the government to manage its records better because they're going to have to find information that is being sought. So it has a profound impact there.

When human or financial resources are devoted to thwarting a legitimate search for information, it should result in a roused citizenry, in a populace that should rise up and say, "Enough!" I would hope that Canadians would galvanize to force the government of the day, at all levels, to respond to the fact that tax dollars are being wasted in a dead-end effort to withhold information. Make it an election issue. The previous government, for goodness' sake, said they were going to be *more* open.

Because of the delays, because of the nitpicking of some public servants, and of the unhappy experiences of some requesters, the act has a bad name in some places. Don't give up on the Access to Information law, despite some egregious actions by people who should know better. The law has been in place for some 16 years now. I've seen improvements, I've seen changes, but the changes and improvements are coming too slowly. The resentments are building.

NOTES

1. The quotations Professor Brenner refers to are taken from Richard M. Soberman, "Appendix A: Overview of Models," *Taking Stock: A Review of the Canada Infrastructure Works Program*, Vol. 2 (Ottawa: Canada Infrastructure Works Office, Treasury Board Secretariat, August 1996).

EPILOGUE

As we said in the introduction of this book, the essays from each province tell a story about how one government spending program functioned in that province. Whether the results were positive or negative, our task was to provide a forum for thorough and individual examination of the Canada Infrastructure Works Program and create a portrait of the process. Perhaps the best summary of this assignment may be presented here, in the words of those researchers who doggedly traversed the money trail and found a less-than-flattering portrait of how Canada is governed.

"It was difficult to be treated with such suspicion. I'd never encountered people being so suspicious of my motives. I've had to justify my existence and defend myself, when in fact I was asking them the questions. I'm getting so paranoid that I think there's a CSIS file on me because I dared to ask questions about the government."

— Lydia Miljan, Calgary, Alberta

"There are a few findings about the Quebec political scene that one may reach after three months' research of one particular program. One of those conclusions is that the political glitterati are closely related and, to my understanding, this is a little more obvious in the province of Quebec than in the rest of Canada. I don't know why, though. Maybe the language, maybe the French culture, maybe the religious, historical or legal frame. It's harder to pierce the veil, if you will — to get secrets, to get behind the door."

— Brigitte Pellerin, Montreal, Quebec

"If I can't get straight answers to my questions, how can I understand government spending decisions? If I don't know how government decisions are being made, who does know? If no one knows, the political establishment can just continue working in a haze."

— Anette Mueller, Winnipeg, Manitoba

"After studying political science as my undergraduate degree and working for a Crown corporation I had a grasp of how government works. I had an appreciation for the system, but then actually seeing it in action is a different story. What started as a study of infrastructure turned into an exercise to understand what goes behind the thought processes of three levels of government."

— Geoff Scales, Toronto, Ontario

"Sometimes I'd speak to my friends about the research that I was doing. They'd laugh because I'd be all worked up, ranting, raving and complaining about the provincial and federal governments and how they're wasting my money and their money.

They'd say, 'Leanne, what do you expect? It's government. You shouldn't be surprised.' It's not that they're apathetic, but they've just given in to the fact that we're stuck paying the bills of our parents' generation. A lot of people in my generation just don't think that they have any control over it."

— Leanne Hazon, Vancouver, British Columbia

"It's important to continue to ask questions and care about what the government is doing at all levels. And we have the right and the obligation to always hold it accountable, not just at election time."

— Jennifer Nunn, Charlottetown, Prince Edward Island

"Obviously the purpose of this project is not to intensify or accentuate apathy. On the contrary, the purpose is to get people interested in government processes. Because if a lot of people ask questions, then eventually the barriers will have to come down."

— Philippe Forest, Montreal, Quebec

INDEX